9720

286.062

...ne, E.A.

Baptist

...nion

D1587314

Please renew/return this _____ ____ ~~~~ dal date shown.

So that your telephone call is charged at local rate, please call the numbers as set out below:

	From Area codes 01923 or 0208:	From the rest of Herts:
Renewals:	01923 471373	01438 737373
Enquiries:	01923 471333	01438 737333
Minicom:	01923 471599	01438 737599

L32b

7/12

Hertfordshire
COUNTY COUNCIL
Community Information

1 1 JUN 2004

L32a

COUNTY HALL, HERTFORD.

L.32

THE BAPTIST UNION

A SHORT HISTORY

THE FIRST PAGE OF THE FIRST MINUTE BOOK OF THE GENERAL UNION
FORMED IN 1812

THE FIRST SIGNATURES ON THE FIRST ATTENDANCE SHEET

THE BAPTIST UNION
A SHORT HISTORY

by
ERNEST A. PAYNE, M.A., D.D.

LONDON:

THE CAREY KINGSGATE PRESS LIMITED

The Carey Kingsgate Press Limited
6, Southampton Row,
London, W.C.1.

First published 1959

PRINTED IN GREAT BRITAIN BY
EBENEZER BAYLIS AND SON, LTD., THE
TRINITY PRESS, WORCESTER, AND LONDON

CONTENTS

Appendices

ILLUSTRATIONS

PREFACE

THIS history of the Baptist Union of Great Britain and Ireland has been written as part of the preparations for the projected celebration in 1962–3 of its ter-jubilee. In a somewhat lengthy introduction I have tried to provide an outline of the story that follows, indicating some of the main issues that have emerged during the past century and a half as local churches based on the congregational principle have been drawn into ever closer association with one another. Some readers may find it more congenial to read this introduction at the end rather than the beginning. There may also be some who, at a first reading, prefer to skip Chapter 2, which deals with earlier attempts at union; some knowledge of these attempts is essential, however, if more recent history is to be understood. The final chapter is inevitably incomplete, for it will be some time before the developments since 1951 can be seen in proper perspective.

Part of the material here presented was given at Manchester Baptist College in June 1958, and at the Baptist Church House the following spring, under the auspices of the W. T. Whitley Lectureship. I am grateful to the trustees for these opportunities and to Principal K. C. Dykes and the Rev. W. Charles Johnson for the arrangements made in Manchester and London.

This study could not have been completed at the present time without the generous and efficient secretarial help which I have received from Miss Joyce A. Booth, of Regent's Park College, and Miss Enid M. Hobbs, of the Baptist Union staff. The Revs. B. Grey Griffith, Dr. F. Townley Lord and J. O. Barrett, and Mr. Gordon G. Fairbairn, kindly read the typescript, saved me from a number of errors and made valuable suggestions. I am the one responsible for the views expressed, the selection of material and the errors and omissions that remain. The Rev. A. S. Clement has taken much trouble in seeing the book through the press.

ERNEST A. PAYNE

Baptist Church House
4 Southampton Row
London, W.C.1

INTRODUCTION

THE Baptist Union of Great Britain and Ireland had its origin in a "Society" which, at its formation in 1813, was described as a "General Union", consisting of Baptist ministers and churches maintaining Calvinistic doctrines and the church-polity known as congregational. Two years later, the annual gathering agreed that it should be called "The General Meeting of the Particular (or Calvinistic) Baptist Denomination". The present title was not adopted until 1873, though by then the usual designation had long been the Baptist Union. The terms first used are of interest and importance for an understanding of the slow but steady growth of the Union during the past century and a half.

Since it was a voluntary association based on certain common interests and formed for certain specific purposes, it was natural at the time of its origin to describe it as a society. Scores of societies were started during the eighteenth and early nineteenth centuries in support of a variety of political, philanthropic and religious causes. This particular society was to be a union of certain of the ministers and churches belonging to what was known as the Baptist denomination. The word "denomination" had already a long and honourable history. For at least a hundred years Presbyterians, Independents and Baptists had been described as "The Three Denominations", to distinguish them on the one hand from the Church of England and on the other from a few smaller religious groups, of which the Quakers were the most important. The ministers of these three bodies in and around London and Westminster acted together on a number of matters, chiefly concerned with their position under the Toleration Act of 1689. They had established their right to joint access to the Throne. There was nothing necessarily derogatory about the term "denomination", though it was sometimes used in a derogatory sense. In his *Meditations*, written in 1746, the evangelical clergyman, James Hervey, spoke of our Lord opening the Kingdom of Heaven "to all generations and to every denomination of the faithful". On the other hand, a century later Gladstone wrote that he had "no fear for the Church of England in her competition with the denominational bodies around her".

The founders of the Baptist Union aimed at a nation-wide society, but one that was to be confined to only a section of the Baptist denomination, namely, that which was Calvinistic in theology. It was described as a "general" union because its purposes were to be of a more comprehensive character than those of several already existing Baptist societies.

These societies linked together individuals ready to support particular causes, foreign or home missions, education, Sunday Schools and so on. The notable thing about the General Union was that it was a union of ministers and churches. Since the churches were Baptist churches, they were regarded as autonomous Christian fellowships. "All manner of superiority and superintendence over the churches; or any authority or power to impose anything upon their faith and practice" was explicitly disclaimed—an echo of language which had been used by a General Assembly of Baptists at the close of the seventeenth century. The present Constitution of the Baptist Union recognizes that "each Church has liberty, under the guidance of the Holy Spirit, to interpret and administer" the laws of Christ.[1] The history of the Union shows both the necessity and the difficulty of uniting churches of this character. Tensions and anomalies are inevitable. For a century and a half—indeed, for three hundred years—successive generations of Baptists have wrestled with the problems involved in the effective co-operation of local churches which claim to be autonomous. What should be the basis of association or union? What its functions? How should it be related to other societies within the denomination? What should be the relationship of the Union to other Denominations and

---

[1] The article on Baptists in the *Encyclopaedia Britannica* is in error in saying "its (*sic*) laws".

Churches whose polity is of a different kind? These questions have become more complicated and pressing of recent decades. They do not admit of easy answers or ones simply in terms of what is practical or expedient. Inevitably they raise theological issues concerning the nature of the Church and the purpose of God.

The life of the Church and the organizations it creates cannot be divorced from their historical setting and their general social context. It was not purely accidental that the Baptist Union came into existence in 1813. There had been earlier attempts to bring Baptist churches together on a national scale, but they had been shortlived and ineffective. Regional and county Associations had, however, always been a feature of Baptist life and have so remained. In the Union as now constituted such Associations have their own recognized place. The oldest have had a continuous existence since the seventeenth century. The important Confessions of Faith which they then prepared are worthy of attention as answers are sought to modern theological questionings. But the story of the Baptist Union, if it is to be understood, must also be seen against the background of the religious life of this country as a whole during the last one hundred and fifty years. It must be compared with the closely parallel story of the Congregational Union[2] and with the development of Baptist life in other lands. The influence upon it of the changing climate of religious opinion and of various "non-theological" factors must be recognized, as well as the inevitable effect of internal denominational tensions.

When the Union was formed in 1813 it was, as has been said, a union of Calvinist ministers and churches. The founders affirmed their loyalty to the main doctrines of Calvinism as these were customarily defined by the Baptist Associations of the late eighteenth century and by a number of other non-Baptist churches. In 1832 the Union was re-organized and its objects were re-defined. It was then felt sufficient to describe it as a union of Baptist ministers and churches "who agree in the sentiments

[2] See E. A. Payne, "Baptist-Congregationalist Relationships," *Congregational Quarterly*, July, 1955.

usually denominated evangelical". Though at the time many felt
this to be too vague, it had the advantage of opening the door to
closer association with the churches of the New Connexion of
General Baptists, whose theology was traditionally Arminian,
though of an emphatically evangelical type. These churches had
broken away from the main body of General Baptists who, influenced by the rationalism of the eighteenth century, had moved
towards Socinianism and Unitarianism. By the middle decades
of the nineteenth century, the older conflict between Calvinism
and Arminianism had declined in importance. The defenders of
both traditions felt themselves at one in an understanding of the
Christian faith which was "evangelical". This they sharply distinguished from the "catholic" attitude, which found its main
contemporary expression in the Tractarian movement within the
Church of England, but equally from the rationalistic or "liberal"
view, which had given birth to Unitarianism. Within Baptist
circles there was, moreover, a general reaction against credal and
doctrinal statements. To speak of "evangelical sentiments" was
felt to be sufficient and enabled the Union to gather the support
of an increasing number of Baptist churches.

Forty years later, in 1873, when the basis of the Union was again
discussed, there was hesitation about the word "evangelical".
New trends of thought were making themselves felt. The main
emphasis in many quarters was on intellectual freedom. The autonomy and independence of the churches were more emphatically
insisted upon, as well as the right of the individual to his own
private judgment.[3] It was decided that all that the Union needed
was a Declaration of Principle that "in this Union it is fully
recognized that every separate church has liberty to interpret and
administer the laws of Christ, and that the immersion of believers
is the only Christian baptism". A number of Baptists felt troubled
about this change. The most famous Baptist preacher of the day,
C. H. Spurgeon, thought that the Union should have adopted a

[3] Note the specific assertion of "the right and duty of individual judgment" in the interpretation of the Bible, contained in the Declaratory Statement adopted by the Union in
April 1888.

doctrinal declaration similar to that of the Evangelical Alliance, which had been formed in 1846 by a number of Anglicans and Nonconformists. Spurgeon urged this at the time of the unfortunate Down Grade Controversy of 1887–8. Almost all those associated with the Baptist Union rejected his plea, which would have been in their view a putting-back of the clock and a denial of the theological freedom for which Baptists stood. But at the Assembly of 1888, when a serious split in the Union was with difficulty avoided, a declaration was adopted which was intended to make clear that the Baptist churches as a whole had not departed from the evangelical faith, even though certain doctrines would be by many less rigidly defined than had been customary two or three generations earlier.

In 1891 the New Connexion and the Baptist Union merged their organizations. No substantial changes in the basis of the Union were then found necessary. Thirteen years later, however, in 1904, after protracted discussions, the attenuated Declaration of 1873 was enlarged into a more elaborate statement. The Basis of the Union was declared to be:

"1. That the Lord Jesus Christ is the sole and absolute authority in all matters pertaining to faith and practice, as revealed in the Holy Scriptures, and that each Church has liberty to interpret and administer His laws.

2. That Christian Baptism is the immersion in water into the Name of the Father, the Son and the Holy Ghost, of those who have professed repentance towards God and faith in our Lord Jesus Christ who 'died for our sins according to the Scriptures; was buried, and rose again the third day'.

3. That it is the duty of every disciple to bear personal witness to the Gospel of Jesus Christ, and to take part in the evangelization of the world."

Two years later, in 1906, the phrase "our God and Saviour" was added to the first clause to exclude any possibility of a Unitarian interpretation of the Person of Christ. This Declaration has remained unchanged for more than fifty years, save that in 1938 the phrase "our God and Saviour" was altered to the more theologically satisfactory phrase "God manifest in the flesh", and the words "under the guidance of the Holy Spirit" were added after the word "liberty". Though skilfully drawn, the Declaration is not a comprehensive Christian creed. Notable and definite as are its affirmations, there are obvious omissions, when it is compared with earlier Baptist Confessions or with the ancient and traditional formulations of the Christian faith. Both the advantages and the limitations of the Declaration can only be appreciated in the light of the Union's history and purpose.

The changes in the basis came largely as a result of changes in theological interest and emphasis and through the drawing together of the Baptists of the New Connexion and the majority—though not all—of those formerly designated Particular Baptists. By the end of the nineteenth century this process was virtually complete. There remained outside the Union only a relatively small group of churches—known often as Strict and Particular Baptist churches. Their membership, and usually also the Communion Table, were closed to all save baptized believers and they clung to a strictly Calvinistic theology. Many of them were old churches which had resisted the more evangelical Calvinism preached by Andrew Fuller at the close of the eighteenth century.

The working out and extension of the original functions of the Union have come in the main through a changing relationship to certain other Baptist societies. When the Baptist Union was formed in 1812–13, the two larger societies already in existence were the Baptist Missionary Society (1792) and the Baptist Home Missionary Society (1797). The objects of the Union were said to be "to excite brotherly love" between ministers and churches and "to furnish a stimulus for a zealous co-operation in our own denomination, and especially to encourage and support our Missions". The work of the two societies already mentioned was specifically commended, also that of the theological colleges, the Particular Baptist Fund and the Widows' Fund.[4] In the fashion of the day, the Colleges—then called Academies—were independent "societies". Each served mainly its own area—Bristol the west of England and South Wales, Stepney the metropolis,

[4] This was the fund disbursed by the Society for the Relief of Necessitous Widows and Children of Protestant Dissenting Ministers of the Three Denominations, established in 1733.

Horton (now Rawdon) the north, and so on. Like the Associations, they were ultimately given corporate membership of the Union alongside the local churches and the Associations.

A Baptist Irish Society was formed in 1814, to aid evangelistic efforts in that country. Fifty years later the Home Missionary Society and the Irish Society were united. In 1882, after several years of difficult negotiations, the Union itself undertook the work formerly done by both these agencies. A few years earlier, partly but not solely in order to increase the financial resources of the Union, personal membership had been instituted. These varied types of membership were somewhat anomalous, but this was characteristic of the age and the denomination. The results appear to have been on the whole advantageous rather than harmful. Disparate interests and activities were steadily drawn together and the Union became an effective central agency for witness and service, able to undertake further specific tasks on its own. In 1870, for example, the Union established an Augmentation Fund to supplement the stipends of the more inadequately remunerated ministers. Help of this kind had been available to ministers and churches of the Particular Baptist denomination in England and Wales since 1717 from the Particular Baptist Fund. The managers continued to make generous grants, but their resources were limited and they were bound also to aid a number of ministers and churches which had not joined the Union. The Augmentation Fund ultimately developed into the Sustentation Fund and this was in 1947 incorporated into a general Home Work Fund.

In 1876 the Union also sponsored an Annuity Fund for ministers. Several of the Associations had Annuity and Provident Funds of their own, but the growing movement of ministers from one part of the country to another made the administration of such local funds more difficult. A central denominational scheme was necessary. It was not until 1927, however, that a really comprehensive and satisfactory Superannuation Fund came into existence. The augmenting of stipends and provision for retirement made it imperative that the Union directly interest itself in the recognition and accrediting of ministers and this, in turn, brought it into closer relationships with the theological colleges.

Yet another line of activity was in the field of church building. The Baptist Building Fund, formed in 1824, had its own independent board of managers. Churches were able to borrow from this fund interest-free loans repayable over a period of ten years. When the New Connexion was united with the Union, the assets of a similar General Baptist Building Fund were handed over to the older and larger Fund. It was already clear, however, that greater resources were needed to help with church extension projects, particularly in growing urban areas. The Union itself therefore opened a Church Extension Fund from which outright grants could be made. Further aid of this kind was made available from the Twentieth Century Fund and from time to time the Union sponsored other schemes to aid the purchase of sites and the erection of buildings. So far, however, the denomination has not shown any clear conviction that the main burden should be lifted from the local church and neighbourhood.

For some years the Union also raised an Education Fund to help ministers with the education of their sons and daughters, though such aid never reached large proportions.

Throughout their history the theological colleges have been jealous of their independence, yet inevitably closely related to the life of the local churches and to general denominational developments. On a number of occasions, leaders of the Union—and the Union itself through its Council or Assembly—have discussed plans for a more unified scheme of ministerial training. In the early years of his secretaryship of the Union, Edward Steane made certain proposals with this object, but they proved unacceptable. In 1871 Dr. S. G. Green raised the matter, equally unsuccessfully. Fourteen years later, when the Union had grown in strength, and ministerial recognition and support at the denominational level were generally approved, another attempt was made, but it also failed. Eight or nine years later an officially sponsored plan which would have united the colleges at Rawdon and Manchester in a new Northern Baptist College, came very near to success, but in the end had to be abandoned. The original proposals relating to the Sustentation Scheme put forward by J. H. Shakespeare included the reorganization of collegiate training under the supervision of the Union. The colleges, however, preferred to set up an inter-collegiate board of their own to which the Union appointed representatives. The transfer of Regent's Park College from London to Oxford was accompanied by an agreement for co-operation with Bristol College and was followed by a steady drawing together of the staffs of all the colleges affiliated to the Union. At the same time it became clear that there must be closer co-operation between the colleges, the Associations and the Union in the approval of ministerial candidates. Young men are not now accepted by the colleges unless first approved, not only by the church of which they are members, but also by committees of the Associations acting on behalf of the Union.

With a number of other smaller societies the Union has had more or less close relations. One of these, the Baptist Total Abstinence Association, formed in 1874, was half a century later taken over by the Union. Others, which owed their origin largely to encouragement given by the Union—such as the Baptist Colonial Society and the Baptist Historical Society—still maintain an independent existence, as does the Baptist Men's Movement, though this has always been closely linked with the Missionary Society. By 1926, when the Total Abstinence Association was taken over, the Union had set up a number of departments of its own, concerned with ministerial recognition, and work among women, young people and lay preachers. It had also become responsible for an order of deaconesses. It had developed into an organization with large-scale activities and interests, and considerable financial resources, and was closely concerned with the life of the county Associations and the local churches at many different points. The one major society remaining independent was the Baptist Missionary Society.

In 1874 when the changes were first mooted which led to the British and Irish Home Mission Society being fused with the

Union, Dr. Richard Glover proposed that at the same time the overseas work of the denomination be more closely integrated with that of the Union. His proposals fell on deaf ears. The Missionary Society was then a much stronger body than the Union. It commanded larger support. As headquarters the Union had only a few rented rooms in the Baptist Mission House. With the erection of the Baptist Church House in 1903 and the subsequent growth in the responsibilities and resources of the Union, the problem of the right relationship between the Union and the Missionary Society assumed a new form. By the 1930s there was a widespread feeling that it would be advantageous if the two bodies were brought closer together and if some at least of their departmental activities were combined. A scheme for new joint headquarters was prepared. The particular scheme was rejected by the Assembly, but the problem of relationships remained and has gained a new importance and urgency, being no longer a merely domestic or denominational matter.

What has already been said indicates how the Union found itself committed to ever-extending responsibilities towards Baptist ministers and Baptist churches. But it found itself also called upon to represent Baptists in their relationships with other denominations. Baptists and Congregationalists have always felt themselves closely akin. The roots of both groups run back into the Puritanism and Separatism of the sixteenth and seventeenth centuries, and their general outlook and polity are similar. Till the end of the eighteenth century there were a number of Nonconformist churches which included in their membership both Baptists and Paedobaptists. With the formation of the Baptist Union and the Congregational Union denominational consciousness increased and some of the older joint fellowships divided into two separate churches, as was the case, for example, in Oxford. The two Unions developed side by side and by much the same stages. They campaigned together for full civil rights. For many years the *Baptist Union Handbook* contained a list of London Congregational ministers. In 1886 the two Unions held a united Assembly. A number of influential leaders in both denominations looked forward to a merging of the two bodies. There was even talk of a world organization, which might include both Baptists and Congregationalists. Early in the twentieth century a few "Union churches" were formed in new areas and these were affiliated to both Unions. By then, however, other influences were at work. Many Baptist churches no longer confined their membership to those baptized as believers and the Free Church Council movement had come into being.

This latter movement embraced Methodists and Presbyterians, as well as Baptists and Congregationalists, and was also shared in by Quakers. Local councils of Free Churches were united in a National Free Church Council, whose annual assembly became a kind of unofficial Parliament of Nonconformity. Many of the leaders hoped for a United Free Church and engaged in joint evangelistic campaigns. An even more significant development took place in 1916 when, in response to the lead given by the General Secretary of the Baptist Union and others, a Federal Council of the Evangelical Free Churches was formed, consisting of officially appointed representatives of the various denominations and with a Declaratory Statement of Common Faith and Practice. This step carried greater implications in respect of the status and function of the Congregational Union and the Baptist Union than it did in the case of the Methodist Conference or the Assembly of the Presbyterian Church of England. It meant that the two "Unions" were thought of as competent to enter into a federal relationship with bodies that regarded themselves as "churches" in a more unitary and theological sense. The Baptist Union had long had as one of its objects: "To confer and co-operate with other Christian communities as occasion may require." The joining of a Federal Council went beyond the original intention of these words, even if they could be stretched to include it. The truth was, of course, that by 1916, in response to the needs of the hour, the general sentiment of the denomination had moved ahead of the letter of the Union's constitution. The functions which the Union had gradually been called upon to exercise were bringing it closer to the position envisaged for an

Assembly, Association or Council in some of the Baptist Confessions of the seventeenth century. It had ceased to be a voluntary
society with strictly limited authority and aims.

These important developments received a further fillip in 1942
when the British Council of Churches was formed at a meeting
held in the Baptist Church House. The Baptist Union then took
its place as a constituting member side by side with the Congregational Union, the Methodist Conference, the General Assembly
of the Church of Scotland, the Church of England and a number
of other bodies and communions. Very various types of ecclesiastical organization granted one another a measure of mutual
recognition for purposes of common action and entered into an
association with one another, the theological implications of
which were left for later discovery and discussion.

The British Council of Churches was no isolated phenomenon.
It was but one of the expressions of that network of new relation-
ships between Christians comprehensively described as the
Ecumenical Movement. The Baptist Missionary Society had
been represented at the World Missionary Conference held in
Edinburgh in 1910 and co-operated in the formation of a Standing
Conference of British Missionary Societies and an International
Missionary Council. After some initial hesitation, the Baptist
Union committed itself to participation in the Faith and Order
movement. It shared in the Life and Work movement. Its
General Secretary served on the committee which drafted the
constitution of the World Council of Churches and representatives were sent to the assembly in Amsterdam in 1948 at which
this Council came formally into being. Here again, in an even
wider setting, the Union found itself accepted by other communions, whose pattern of churchmanship was very different
from its own. It committed itself with them to a fuller explora-
tion and expression of the meaning of the Church as the Body of
Christ. Following the "Lambeth Appeal to All Christian People",
issued by the bishops of the Church of England in 1920, the
Baptist Union was already involved, as the mouthpiece of the
Baptists of Britain, in "conversations" with official represen-

tatives of other churches with a view to closer understanding and fellowship.

Even if it were not in membership with the Free Church Federal Council (which now unites the National Free Church Council and the Federal Council of Evangelical Free Churches), the British Council of Churches and the World Council of Churches, the Baptist Union would be faced with theological questions as to its own nature and function. That it is in these new relationships gives additional point and urgency to such questions. A similar situation faces those of other traditions. All Christians are being driven to a re-examination of the doctrine of the Church and of the relation to it of their own forms of church life. Baptists have clearly to ask themselves whether the present structure of the Union is adequate for the responsibilities now placed upon it. Before they embark on any radical changes, however, it is well that they learn something of the history of the Union and reflect upon it.

It is important that its slow growth be remembered. The present forms and methods have been gradually developed to meet changing situations. It has always been itself a living, changing complex of relationships. Between 1813 and 1831 it gained the interest of only a small number of individuals and churches. Its continued existence was uncertain. For the next forty years its influence on the life of the denomination as a whole was relatively slight. In the last thirty years of the nineteenth century, however, the need for such an organization became increasingly apparent and it grew in importance. The "Down Grade" storm was successfully weathered and at a time of general denominational expansion the Union showed more initiative and vigour. Separate Baptist Unions were formed in Wales and Scotland, but these remained affiliated to the older body and co-operated closely with it on many matters.

The period from 1898 until the First World War was marked by rapid developments in many different directions. Not only had the Union by then secured the adherence of almost all the Baptist churches of this country; it was looked to as the natural centre of, and agency for, common effort of all kinds. In spite of the difficulties facing all the Churches during the past three or four decades, the Union has steadily increased the range of its influence and service. There has also been a gradual realization that more is implied by the linking together of local churches than appears to have been realized by the fathers and founders of 1812–13.

CHAPTER 1

THE FORMATION OF THE GENERAL UNION, 1812–13

I

THROUGHOUT the long reign of George III the leading Baptist church in London was that which met in Carter Lane, Tooley Street, Southwark, near the southern end of London Bridge, the old bridge, which was lined with houses and had fortified gates at each end. The Baptist meeting-house had been erected in 1757. It was, says Walter Wilson, "an oblong building, with galleries entirely around".[1] He goes on: "There is also a large baptistery, with every conveniency for baptizing." In the vestry hung a three-quarter painting of Dr. John Gill, who had been minister of the church for no less than fifty-one years. Gill was a contemporary of Samuel Johnson and John Wesley. His fame rested on his resolute and logical expositions of High Calvinism. In 1773 he was succeeded by a young Devonian, John Rippon, destined to exercise an equally lengthy ministry. Rippon increased the prosperity of the church, drawing "the most numerous" Baptist congregation in London, one that contained wealthy merchants and well-known professional men, among them Robert Bowyer, the painter of miniatures. Sought after as a preacher for special occasions, Rippon was also an indefatigable collector, editor and compiler. He was the recognized leader of the denomination in the metropolis. It was in his vestry, under his chairmanship and beneath the portrait of his venerable predecessor, that the formation of a nation-wide union of Particular Baptist churches was resolved upon. The meeting was held at 8 a.m. on Thursday, 25th June 1812.

George III had then been on the English throne for more than

---

[1] *Dissenting Churches of London*, IV, 1814, p. 213.

half a century. A few months earlier, owing to the King's recurrent mental breakdowns, his son had been made Prince Regent.
The Industrial Revolution was bringing rapid changes throughout England. The long-drawn-out struggle against Napoleon's
attempt to dominate the continent of Europe was not yet over.
At the time of the meeting in Carter Lane, English interest
centred in Portugal, from which country the troops commanded
by Viscount Wellington—that year made an Earl—were making
daring raids into Spain. That very month of June, Napoleon
began his ill-fated invasion of Russia.

How much the sixty or more Baptist ministers who crowded
the Carter Lane vestry spoke together about the war we cannot
know. News travelled slowly and the Continent seemed a long way
off. The threat of a French invasion was past. The assassination of
the Prime Minister, Spencer Perceval, the previous month and
attacks on machinery in the midland and northern counties are
more likely to have been topics of conversation. But the French
Revolution and the conquests of Napoleon had quickened interest in prophecy. Andrew Fuller had been taking his morning
congregation in Kettering through the Book of Revelation. He
was himself persuaded that the seventh trumpet spoken of in
chapter xi had sounded and that "the period of the vials" had
begun—"a period of ardent struggle, successful effort and
glorious victory" so far as Christians were concerned, and one
that would be followed—though not perhaps for a century or
more—by the millennium. "We are not likely to see the latter," he
wrote; "but we have entered, I think, on the former. It is ours to
work and war in this glorious cause."[2] Such views helped to
swell the rising tide of missionary enthusiasm. The day before the
Carter Lane meeting the ministers had attended special gatherings
in support of the mission to India. It is of these that they are certain to have talked.

The leaders of the Baptist Missionary Society, then twenty
years old, had arranged for special sermons on its behalf to be

[2] Letter to John Birt, of Hull, 7th March 1812 (*Baptist Magazine*, 1818, p. 333). Cp.
Fuller's *Expository Discourses on the Apocalypse*, 1815.

preached in London. The Society had originated in Northamptonshire and its affairs were still directed from Kettering, the home of its secretary, Andrew Fuller. Fuller had heard six months earlier that a "General Union" of the Baptist churches was being projected. He showed himself rather sceptical about it, as he was of anything centred in London.[3] He disliked the metropolis, much as did his slightly younger contemporary, William Cobbett. But the mission to India needed much more substantial support from the London churches than it had so far received, and special services had been arranged for June 1812. The historic Dutch Church in Austin Friars had been secured for the occasion. Fuller himself came up from Kettering. John Ryland was there from Bristol. They were no doubt very glad that so many ministers from the provinces had made the journey to London. The collections at the services totalled £320, which nearly equalled all that had previously been received for the mission from London in a year.

The need for the closer linking together of the Baptist churches and Associations of churches had been felt for some time. Through *The Baptist Annual Register*, which he had edited from 1790 to 1802, Rippon had done much to introduce Baptists to one another and to gather together the materials for their history. He had even projected some kind of world association which would include the Baptists of the United States and the Mennonites of Holland. He was the obvious chairman for a meeting to discuss the formation of a union of the ministers and churches of the United Kingdom. "Beloved at home, respected abroad and useful everywhere," so Rippon was described by his most

[3] See Ivimey, *History of the English Baptists* IV, 1830, p. 124 and note. In a letter to Christopher Anderson in January 1812 (now in the possession of the Baptist Missionary Society), Fuller had written: "There is a talk among the denomination of a general *union*, and of an annual meeting in London. Could we not have our collection in April, and the sermons for our public collection on a weekday, and so afford opportunity for all who chose it, to attend without leaving their own places? Could not this service be accompanied with a communication of intelligence? Would not this be a *seed* out of which would grow insensibly the object wished for, a union of the denomination, and a union in an object worth uniting in—the promotion of the kingdom of Christ?" When Ivimey first told him of the proposal of a General Assembly in the summer of 1812, Fuller had, however, commented: "You will only show the poverty of the denomination by such a meeting."

famous successor, C. H. Spurgeon.[4] His sermons and addresses
were said to have "vivacity, fervour, quaintness and point".[5] In
1812 he was sixty-one years of age. Spurgeon notes, however,
that Rippon was not often the initiator of new enterprises. Asked
on one occasion why he did not attend more denominational
meetings and take the lead, the Carter Lane minister is said to
have replied: "Why, I see the Dover coach go by my house
every morning, and I notice that the leaders get most lashed."[6]
The arrangements for the meeting to discuss the formation of a
General Union almost certainly owed as much to Joseph Ivimey
as they did to John Rippon.

Ivimey was a younger man, not yet forty. Since 1805 he had
been minister of the Baptist church which met in Eagle Street,
Holborn. Deeply interested in Baptist history, he had already
published the first of four substantial volumes on this subject.
Fuller, who in 1811 described Rippon as getting "old and ob-
stinate",[7] thought Ivimey "an excellent man".[8] In 1809 *The
Baptist Magazine* had been launched at Tiverton in the west
country. It was already clear that it would provide a useful and
effective channel for denominational information and exhortation,
replacing *The Evangelical Magazine*, which had been started in
1793 and had at first been supported by some Anglicans as well as
by Nonconformists, but which had passed more and more into
the hands of the Independents. In June 1811, Ivimey contributed
to *The Baptist Magazine* an article with the challenging title,
"Union Essential to Prosperity". Two months later this was
followed up by "An Address to the Baptist Denomination" by
B.D.[9] which appealed for immediate action. In the following
months there must have been discussion of the project by the
Baptist Board and other meetings of ministers. Letters must have
been sent to the provinces soliciting support. *The Baptist Magazine*

[4] *The Metropolitan Tabernacle*, 1876, p. 50.
[5] Stoughton, *History of Religion in England*, VII, p. 282.
[6] *The Metropolitan Tabernacle*, p. 52.
[7] Letter to John Sutcliff, January 1811. Rippon was then sixty, Fuller fifty-seven!
[8] Letter to William Ward, March, 1813.
[9] Probably Bourn Hall Draper (1778–1843), minister in Chipping Norton, and later in
Coseley and Southampton.

was able to announce, in its issue for June 1812, that the day after the missionary meetings a gathering would take place in Carter Lane "to take into consideration the proposed measure for an annual general association of the Particular Baptist Churches".

II

The twenty years prior to 1812 had been a period of quickened life and expansion for Nonconformists. Their evangelistic zeal had revived as a result of the Methodist movement and the influence upon them of the Great Awakening in America. They were able to adapt themselves more easily than the Church of England to the growth and shift of population. The Established Church had as yet done little to meet the spiritual needs of those in the new industrial areas. The tithe system was increasingly unpopular and the scandal of non-residence was bringing the clergy into contempt. They were further losing favour by opposition to the rising democratic spirit of the age. The Napoleonic era was a notable period of chapel-building so far as Dissenters were concerned.

In his *Annual Register* for 1794 and again in 1798 Rippon printed a list of Particular Baptist churches and ministers. In 1794, there were, he said, 326 churches in England and 56 in Wales; in 1798, 361 in England and 84 in Wales. Rippon made no estimate of the English membership, but stated that in Wales it had increased from 7,098 (1794) to not less than 9,000 (1798). Writing in 1798, he stated: "It is said that more of our meeting-houses have been enlarged within the last five years, and more built within the last fifteen, than had been built and enlarged for thirty years before—and yet, it is necessary for many more of our societies to lengthen their cords and strengthen their stakes." The process continued in the early years of the nineteenth century.

There is no record of exactly how many persons attended the meeting in the Carter Lane vestry in June 1812, but it is significant that at the close no less than sixty ministers "gave their names to the Secretary as favouring the proposed plan of union". If there

were other ministers present and any laymen, their names are un-
recorded. But the support of sixty ministers meant the actual
presence of a sixth or seventh of the ministers of the denomination, no mean total in days when travel was difficult and expensive. London and Southwark, where, according to Rippon's list,
there were in 1798 twenty-one Particular Baptist Churches, contributed eleven ministers to the company. Three of the eight
Middlesex churches were represented. The rest of the signatories
came from churches in Berkshire, Buckinghamshire, Cornwall,
Devon, Essex, Gloucestershire, Hampshire, Hertfordshire, Hunt-
ingdonshire, Kent, Norfolk, Northamptonshire, Oxfordshire,
Shropshire, Somersetshire, Suffolk, Sussex, Wiltshire and Wor-
cestershire. The county of Kent sent the largest single group. The
north of England was unrepresented. Rippon's 1798 list records
that there were nineteen churches in Lancashire and twenty-nine
in Yorkshire.

The list of names is an interesting one. The leaders of the Baptist Missionary Society were present—Fuller, from Kettering,
Ryland from Bristol, and Sutcliff from Olney. There was also
one other there who belonged to the much smaller company who,
twenty years earlier, in 1792, had responded to Carey's challenge.
This was Reynold Hogg, the first treasurer of the Missionary
Society, in 1812 minister of the church at Reigate. James Hinton
had come from Oxford and at the close of the business gave an
address on "The Nature and Advantage of Christian Union".
William Winterbotham, who between 1793 and 1797 had been
fined and imprisoned in Newgate gaol for sermons alleged to be
seditious, was there from Horsley in Gloucestershire. John
Stanger came from Bessels Green in Kent. He was then seventy
years of age. His father, grandfather and great-grandfather had
all been Baptist ministers. In 1787 Stanger had journeyed back
to his native village, Moulton in Northamptonshire, to share in
the ordination of young William Carey. Other notable figures
from the provinces were John Saffery, then engaged in an influential ministry in Salisbury, and Mark Wilks, of Norwich.
Those from the metropolis included the grave William Newman,

minister at Old Ford and president of Stepney College, founded only two years earlier; Timothy Thomas—"the man's broad open countenance revealed his generous and honest nature"[10]— minister since 1780 of the historic Devonshire Square church, which was still located in Bishopsgate, and a distributor to Baptists of the *Regium Donum*, the gift to Nonconformist ministers from the Royal purse; and, among the younger men, Francis Augustus Cox, who had settled the previous year at Shore Place, Hackney, and was destined to play a notable part in denominational and public affairs in the following decades. It can fairly be said that, apart from the absence of representatives from the north of England and Wales, the company included most of the better known ministers of the day with the exception of Robert Hall, then of Harvey Lane, Leicester, and Joseph Kinghorn, of Norwich.

The meeting approved nine resolutions.[11] It was agreed that "a more general Union of the Particular (or Calvinistic) Baptist churches in the United Kingdom is very desirable" and that churches and Associations be invited to appoint messengers to a meeting to be held a year later in June 1813. The objects of the Union were to be "the promotion of the cause of Christ in general; and the interests of the denomination in particular; with a primary view to the encouragement and support of the Baptist Mission". The "Associated Ministers in London" were to act as a committee and "all communications relative thereto" were to be addressed "(free of expense) to their Secretaries, Mr. Button, No. 24, Paternoster Row, and Mr. Ivimey, No. 56 Red Lion Street, Holborn". John Sutcliff and Robert Hall were to be asked to preach sermons at the 1813 gatherings, and, failing them, James Hinton and William Steadman, of Horton. When the resolutions had been passed and Hinton had given his address, the veteran John Stanger offered the concluding prayer and Rippon gave out the verses:

[10] C. H. Pike, *Ancient Meeting-Houses*, 1870, p. 58.
[11] The contents of the first Minute Book of the Baptist Union, with notes by Mr. Seymour J. Price, will be found in *The Baptist Quarterly*, Vol. IV (1928–9).

Lord, if we meet on earth no more,
O may we meet on Canaan's shore!
Leave guilt, and death, and sin behind,
And every bliss in glory find.

But if we longer here remain,
And ever meet on earth again,
May every heart inflamed with love
Be fitter for Thy courts above.

III

The decision to form a General Union was clearly in part the result of the developing activity of the Missionary Society and the fact that annual missionary meetings were to be held in London. But the advantages of co-operation for other purposes were in the minds of the promoters of the new society. In his introductory address Rippon mentioned a number of specific objects in addition to the support of the Mission. He instanced the Academies, the education of the children of deceased ministers, village preaching, Sunday Schools and new church buildings. An annual assembly, of the kind he hoped for, would be able to consider "*whatever* relates to the real interests of the denomination at home and abroad".

William Button, who was associated with Ivimey in the provisional secretariat, was a man of fifty-eight, who had been since 1774 pastor of a church in Dean Street, Southwark, a daughter church of that to which Rippon ministered. Button added bookselling to his pastoral duties and had a business in Paternoster Row, which a few years later involved him in financial difficulties and caused his retirement to Lewes. He was, however, active in the committee meetings which took place—usually in the Jamaica Coffee House, Cornhill—in the early months of 1813 in preparation for the first Assembly of the new Union.

They were busy months, particularly for those concerned with the mission in India. In March 1812, the printing works at Serampore were completely gutted by fire. Buildings, paper, type and

manuscripts were all destroyed. Fuller and his friends knew nothing of this when they met in Carter Lane on 25th June 1812, for
the news did not reach England until the following September.
It caused a wave of sympathy which brought contributions for
the repair of the damage from all parts of the country and from
many others besides Baptists. Then, in the spring of 1813, official
discussions began on a new charter for the East India Company.
Friends of the Mission had to engage in widespread agitation to
secure proper freedom for the work of their agents in the terri-
tories controlled by the Company. Fuller travelled frequently to
London for consultations with William Wilberforce and others
ready to champion the missionary cause in Parliament. Petitions
were organized and presented to the House of Commons. On
22nd June 1813, only two days before the General Union came
together for its first regular meeting, the terms of the new Charter
were debated in Parliament and Wilberforce made one of his
most notable speeches. There was also in those months exciting
news from the continent of Europe. Napoleon, in retreat from
Moscow, was facing the insurrection of the German states. There
was every prospect that his long career of conquest was at last
nearing its end.

Public affairs can hardly have been absent from the minds of
those who gathered for the Baptist meetings in June 1813. According to the arrangement made the previous year, John Sutcliff and
Robert Hall preached sermons on behalf of the Missionary
Society. In the evening a public dinner was held at the London
Tavern in aid of Stepney College. The following morning the
ministers and messengers met once more in Rippon's vestry.
Neither Fuller nor Ryland was present on this occasion; the
former was about to set out on his fifth journey to Scotland on
behalf of the Mission. But Stanger, Winterbotham and Saffery
were there again, as well as Sutcliff. In addition, there were a
number of important newcomers, including Francis Franklin, of
Coventry,[12] and ministers from Yeovil, Wokingham, Portsea,

[12] See George Eliot, *Felix Holt*, 1866, for a picture of Franklin under the name Rufus
Lyon.

Truro and Sheffield. Forty-five ministers set down their names as members of the new organization. This was fifteen fewer than the previous year, but a sufficient number to justify going on with the project. The resolutions that were passed must be quoted in full for they formed the initial constitution of the Union.

"1. That this Society of ministers and churches be designated 'The General Union of Baptist ministers and churches' maintaining the important doctrines of 'three equal persons in the Godhead; eternal and personal election; original sin; particular redemption; free justification by the imputed righteousness of Christ; efficacious grace in regeneration; the final perseverance of real believers; the resurrection of the dead; the future judgment; the eternal happiness of the righteous, and the eternal misery of such as die in impenitence, with the congregational order of the churches inviolably".

2. That ministers and churches, who may hereafter be desirous of uniting with this Society, be admitted, with the consent of the whole body, at the annual meeting.

3. That the formation of this Union be for the purpose of affording to the ministers and churches of the denomination the means of becoming better acquainted with each other, with a view to excite brotherly love, and to furnish a stimulus for a zealous co-operation in promoting the cause of Christ in general, and particularly in our own denomination, and especially to encourage and support our missions.

4. That an annual meeting of the Society be held in London, or elsewhere, on the Wednesday nearest Midsummer-day, in every year, at which two sermons shall be preached and collections made in aid of the Baptist Mission.

5. That the members of the General Union meet on the following morning at six o'clock to hear the report of the Committee, to transact the business of the Society, and to choose a Treasurer, Committee and Secretaries for the ensuing year.

6. That for the present year Mr. Burls be the Treasurer; that the associated ministers in London, who are members of the General Union, with one or two members from each of their churches who join the Union, be the Committee; and that Mr. Wm. Button, Mr. Joseph Ivimey, and Mr. Thomas Thomas be their secretaries, and that their meetings be open to all the ministers and messengers from the country belonging to the Union.

7. That it be recommended to the churches to establish Auxiliary Societies in aid of the Mission, and that our Academical Institutions; the Particular Baptist Fund; the Widows Fund; and the Baptist Society in London for the encouragement and support of itinerant and village preaching, are

justly entitled to the approbation and support of the denomination, and that the churches be requested to obtain subscriptions and make collections in aid of these several objects.

8. That auditors of the Treasurer's Accounts be annually appointed by the Committee, a correct statement of which together with a report of the Committee, and the minutes of business at the annual meeting, shall be printed, as soon as conveniently may be after the annual meeting and circulated among all the churches belonging to the Union.

9. That *The Baptist Magazine*, furnishing a most desirable medium of communication, respecting the state of our churches at home and providing a most seasonable aid to necessitous widows of deceased ministers to which purpose the whole profits are applied, is highly deserving the encouragement of the denomination; and that it be recommended to all our ministers and churches, to promote the circulation of it, to the utmost of their power.[13]

10. That this Society disclaims all manner of superiority and superintendence over the churches; or any authority or power, to impose anything upon their faith and practice; their sole intention is to be helpers together one of another, in promoting the common cause of Christianity, and the interests of the several churches of the denomination to which they belong.

11. That the monthly prayer meeting for the spread of the gospel that has for many years been observed in most of the churches, be recommended to be generally regarded on the first Monday evening in every month.

12. That the Sermons for the Mission be preached next year by our brethren Hinton and Steadman, in case of failure Bro. Saffery."

IV

It was a workmanlike constitution, characteristic of the age. The doctrinal basis, though presented in summary form and very different from the elaborate Confessions of Faith drawn up in the seventeenth century, closely followed that of most of the contemporary Associations of Particular Baptist churches. For example, when the Yorkshire and Lancashire Association was reorganized in 1787, "doctrines embodied in the Scriptures" were defined as:

"Three Equal Persons in one God; Election: Fall of Man: Redemption of the Church: Justification of Sinners: Regeneration: Obligation of Faith and

---

[13] *The Baptist Magazine* began publication in London in 1813.

Repentance: Baptism of Believers: Duty of Brotherly Love: Perseverance of the Saints: The moral law as a rule of moral conduct to Christian disciples: Resurrection of the dead: Final Judgment, Everlasting misery of the wicked and eternal happiness of the righteous."

The declarations of the Midland and Southern Associations were even more closely similar verbally to that of the new General Union. It was in terms such as these that the Calvinism of Particular Baptist churches was customarily defined.

The practical objects of the Union and the causes recommended for support deserve attention, as well as the explicit disclaimer of authority over the churches. It seems likely that the resolutions were drafted by Thomas Thomas, who was appointed secretary jointly with Button and Ivimey. Born in Aberdare in 1759, a nephew of a more famous Welsh minister—Joshua Thomas, of Leominster—Thomas Thomas had received training at the Bristol Academy and, after a first pastorate in Pershore, had ministered at the historic Millyard church, which had Seventh Day Baptist associations, and then at Peckham. In addition to his pastoral duties, he found time to keep a school in Mile End and to act as secretary of Stepney College.[14] Timothy Thomas, of the Devonshire Square church, was his brother. William Burls, who was made treasurer of the Union, was a deacon of the Carter Lane church. A successful merchant, living at No. 56, Lothbury, he was a firm friend of Fuller and the Baptist Missionary Society, a member of the Committee of the British and Foreign Bible Society, and later the first treasurer of the Baptist Irish Society.[15]

Rippon and Ivimey, in particular, must have felt a sense of satisfaction at the meetings of June 1812 and June 1813, and the promise they held for the future. A General Union had been formed. But both men knew a good deal about the denomination and its history. They must have been aware that little more than a seventh of the ministers had attended the meetings; that in other parts of the country there was considerable prejudice against

[14] *The Baptist Magazine*, June 1817, has a portrait of Thomas Thomas.
[15] See E. A. Payne, *The Excellent Mr. Burls*, 1943. From 1819–21 Burls was also co-treasurer of the Missionary Society with Thomas King, of Birmingham.

London; that the Union had to contend with a number of competing interests; and that earlier attempts at a General Assembly of the churches had failed. They knew the many cross-currents of thought and practice that flowed beneath the surface of the denomination.

Some account of the earlier attempts at a nation-wide union and of the general denominational situation is necessary if the subsequent history of the Union formed in 1812–13 is to be understood.

CHAPTER 2

EARLIER EFFORTS AT UNION

I

THE Union which Rippon and Ivimey took the lead in forming in 1813 was of Particular Baptist Churches, that is, those Calvinistic in their theology and congregational in their polity. There had been such churches in England and Wales for nearly two hundred years. A second and slightly older stream of Baptist life found expression in General Baptist churches, so-called because their theology was Arminian. These churches had a polity that was more connexional in character. As Dr. Whitley pointed out: "It is important to note that the various congregations were not thoroughly independent, being linked not only with local Associations, of which we trace at various times Staffordshire, Lincolnshire, Northamptonshire, Leicestershire, Buckinghamshire, the Western, the Northern, the Essex and the Kentish, but also into one General Assembly for all the kingdom."[1] Of this Assembly we have fairly complete minutes from 1689, as well as a number of earlier records. By 1813 there were serious tensions within the General Baptist body. The majority of the churches represented in the Assembly had become Unitarian in sympathy, but under the leadership of Dan Taylor a number of churches influenced by the Evangelical Revival had formed in 1770 a New Connexion and were meeting together separately. Since the New Connexion was destined ultimately to be merged with the Union formed in 1813, some account of the theory and practice of the General Baptist churches is desirable.

As early as 1626 churches in London, Lincoln, Sarum, Coventry and Tiverton joined in correspondence with Mennonite leaders

[1] *Minutes of the General Assembly of the General Baptist Churches*, 1909, p. xxvi.

in Holland. Early in the Commonwealth period thirty congregations in Leicestershire, Lincolnshire and nearby counties sent two representatives each to a meeting which drew up a statement of their common faith and practice.[2] In 1654 a gathering of "Messengers, Elders and Brethren" met in London and issued *The Humble Representation and Vindication . . . touching the Civil Government of these Nations*,[3] churches in London, Kent, Buckinghamshire, Northamptonshire and Lincolnshire being represented. We possess full minutes of a similar gathering in London in 1656. In 1660, in the anxious days which followed the restoration of Charles II to the throne, a General Assembly was again held in London. It claimed to represent the entire body of General Baptists in England, then said to number some twenty thousand members. Its *Brief Confession or Declaration of Faith*, to which forty signatures were attached, was formally presented to the new King.[4] Whenever possible, and often at the risk of imprisonment, the Messengers and Elders of the churches met together during the years when the so-called Clarendon Code was in force against Nonconformists. More than fifty representatives produced in 1678 *An Orthodox Creed, or a Protestant Confession of Faith*, closely modelled on the Westminster Confession.[5]

Article XXXIX of this Confession deserves special notice, as it sets forth the General Baptist attitude at the time to "General Councils, or Assemblies".

"General councils, or assemblies, consisting of Bishops,[6] Elders and Brethren, of the several churches of Christ, and being legally convened, and met together out of all the churches, and the churches appearing there by their representatives, make but one church, and have lawful right, and suffrage in this general meeting, or assembly, to act in the name of Christ; it being of divine authority, and is the best means under heaven to preserve unity, to prevent heresy, and

---

[2] W. J. McGlothlin, *Baptist Confessions of Faith*, 1911, pp. 95 f.

[3] W. T. Whitley, *Minutes*, etc., pp. 1–5.

[4] McGlothlin, op. cit., pp. 111 f.

[5] Ibid. pp. 124 f.

[6] The title "Bishop" was often applied to those more usually described as "Messengers". With this Article, Article XXXI of the Westminster Confession should be compared. See J. F. V. Nicholson, "The Office of 'Messenger' amongst British Baptists in the Seventeenth and Eighteenth Centuries", *Baptist Quarterly*, XVII, No. 5 (January 1958), pp. 206 f.

superintendency among, or in any congregation whatsoever within its own limits, or jurisdiction. And to such a meeting, or assembly, appeals ought to be made, in case any injustice be done, or heresy and schism countenanced, in any particular congregation of Christ, and the decisive voice in such general assemblies is the major part, and such general assemblies have lawful power to hear, and determine, as also to excommunicate."

As soon as William and Mary were on the throne and the Toleration Act had been passed, a General Assembly met in London. Unfortunately no list of those present has survived, though we possess a record of the proceedings prepared by Thomas Grantham, a leader in Lincolnshire and the eastern counties.

"The first thing Debated was the power by which General Conventions or Assembly were Called and it was conceived and by the Majority concluded that seeing no Church has Superiority in this Case the power of such Convening is Devised from the word of God and particularly from the 15th of the Acts of the Apostles And that wch. gives being to our present Assembly in the Necessity we find of it and the Agreemt. of the persons Concerned to Convene for the Help of all Churches whom they do represent."[7]

Other subjects discussed were marriage regulations, ordination and hymn-singing. A further meeting was planned for 1691. The subsequent history of this General Assembly was chequered, for there were several questions on which the representatives found it difficult to agree. During the early decades of the eighteenth century, it twice split in two and there were rival Assemblies. Many of the churches became infected with the spirit of the age and moved towards Arianism and Socinianism. The New Connexion, formed in 1770, quickly grew in size and importance, however. Its leaders were strongly evangelical in temper and its annual assembly became an important feature of its life. In the first few years a number of ministers were admitted to membership, even if their churches were unwilling to join the New Connexion. In 1795, however, at a meeting in Nottingham, it was decided that nobody could sit and vote except as the actual representative of a church. The annual "Association" as it came to be called, was then formally constituted an assembly of delegates.

[7] Whitley, *Minutes*, etc., p. 26.

In 1811, the older General Assembly of the General Baptists met in June in Worship Street, London. This was then the centre of the first General Baptist church brought back to England by Thomas Helwys in 1612. There appear to have been less than three dozen Elders and Representatives at the Assembly. The affairs of several local churches were reviewed and a strong appeal made for the Education Society which assisted with the training of ministers. Great satisfaction was expressed at the rejection by the House of Lords of the bill presented by Lord Sidmouth, which would have made it more difficult for dissenting ministers to secure licences to preach. In that same year, the New Connexion had its assembly in Melbourne under the chairmanship of Dan Taylor. Fifty-eight churches were represented by eighty-one delegates. It was reported that the total membership of the associated churches was 5,471 and that during the previous year there had been 339 baptisms.

Rippon and Ivimey must have known something at least of both these Baptist assemblies. They must also have had in mind previous attempts to draw together the Particular Baptist churches.

II

Here the problem was, in the nature of the case, more difficult, but the seventeenth century provided some interesting and significant happenings and declarations. The Particular Baptists stressed the autonomy of the local congregation in the appointment of officers and the management of its internal affairs, but they regarded some measure of mutual "communion" between churches as essential. For this purpose they favoured county and regional associations.

In 1644 seven London congregations issued a joint Confession of Faith and its importance may be seen from the fact that it was re-issued in 1646, 1651 and 1652.[8] In the preface they describe themselves as:-

[8] McGlothlin, op. cit., pp. 171 f.

2*

"Seven Congregations, who though we be distinct in respect of our particular bodies, for conveniency sake, being as many as can well meet together in one place, yet are all one in Communion, holding Jesus Christ to be our head and Lord."

The use of the phrase "for conveniency sake" is extremely significant. In the Confession itself, it is Article XLVII which shows how the congregations regarded themselves as related to one another:

"And although the particular Congregations be distinct and severall Bodies, every one a compact and knit Citie in itself; yet are they all to walk by one and the same Rule, and by all means convenient to have the counsel and help one of another in all needful affairs of the Church, as members of one body in the common faith under Christ their only head."

The united action of the London churches was followed a few years later by a group of churches in and near the county of Berkshire. We possess the joint declaration that they drew up after representatives had met at Wormsley and Tetsworth in 1652–3. It was supported, as was customary in seventeenth-century documents of this kind, by Scripture references, and need not here be reproduced in full. The points made are, however, of considerable importance for they indicate clearly the nature and purpose of the "Associations" which sprang up about this time in various parts of the country.

Particular churches "ought to hold a firm communion each with other" for three purposes:

(1) "in point of advice in doubtful matters and controversies"
(2) "in giving and receiving in case of want and poverty"
(3) "in consulting and consenting to the carrying on of the work of God, as choosing messengers, etc. and in all things also wherein particular members of one and the same particular church stand bound to hold communion each with other."

How far-reaching and comprehensive this last statement was intended to be is shown by the appending of six "Scriptural reasons". The first states boldly that "there is the same relation betwixt the particular churches each towards other, as there is betwixt particular members of one Church" and that "all the particular assemblies are but one Mount Zion". "Particular church communion (was) never appointed as a restraint of our love which should manifest itself to all the churches". The sixth reason is "to convince the world, for by this shall men know as by one mark that we are true churches of Christ".[9]

This Berkshire declaration does not stand alone. Three years later, in 1655, a number of churches in the Midlands united. They desired "a close communion with each other" for five purposes:

(1) advice, after serious consultation and deliberation, (2) the sending out of gifted men, (3) help in time of need, (4) joint carrying-on of the work of the Lord, and (5) watching over each other.

The Somerset Confession of 1656, probably drafted by Thomas Collier, who was described as "General Superintendent and Messenger to all the Associated Churches", was not quite so explicit or elaborate, but the duty of association is made clear in Article XXVIII:

"That it is the duty of the members of Christ in the order of the Gospel, though in several congregations and assemblies (being one in the head) if occasion be, to communicate each to other, in things spiritual and things temporal."[10]

These declarations imply a doctrine of the Church very different from the individualism and independency that came to be favoured in later generations. It may be that the persecution which followed the Restoration and the promulgation of the Clarendon Code led to a greater emphasis on local autonomy and that this resulted in a growth of the independent spirit. The Second London Confession, adopted in 1677 and reaffirmed at the Assembly of 1689, seems to indicate this. In the course of the Article on the Church, it is said:

"As each Church, and all the members of it, are bound to pray continually for the good and prosperity of all the churches of Christ in all places; and upon

[9] E. A. Payne, *The Baptists of Berkshire*, 1951, pp. 147–8.
[10] McGlothlin, op. cit., p. 210.

all occasions to further it (every one within the bounds of their places, and call-ings, in the exercise of their gifts and graces) so the Churches (when planted by the providence of God so as may enjoy opportunity and advantage for it) ought to hold communion amongst themselves for their peace, increase of love, and mutual edification."[11]

In the sentences that follow the chief emphasis is laid upon the settling of difficulties or differences, "either in point of doctrine or administration". It is made clear that the messengers of the churches "are not entrusted with any Church-power properly so called; or with any jurisdiction over the churches themselves, to exercise any censures either over any churches or persons; or to impose their determination on the churches or officers".

It might have been better if the more theological statements of the previous generation had been adhered to or studied, but it is to be noted that, as soon as conditions allowed, the summons went out for a General Assembly. When the Toleration Act had been passed, seven London ministers—among them William Kiffin, Hanserd Knollys and Benjamin Keach—united in a circular letter to all the Calvinistic Baptist churches in England and Wales, inviting them to send representatives to a meeting in London in September 1689. They were asked to consider "the low estate of the churches" and to devise means of securing a more numerous and better equipped ministry. One hundred and seven churches responded, though the narrative of the proceedings gives the names of the messengers from only ninety-four of them. Seven Welsh churches were represented. The Assembly of the General Baptists had met the previous May. The Particular Baptist Assembly reaffirmed the 1677 Confession of Faith and set forth its decisions in a General Epistle to the Churches.[12]

The first of the resolutions makes clear the limited authority that was felt to be possessed by the Assembly.

"That we disclaim all manner of superiority and superintendency over the churches, and that we have no authority or power to prescribe or impose any

[11] McGlothlin, op. cit., pp. 267–8. Cp. A Somerset Confession of 1691, Crosby, *The History of the English Baptists*, Vol. IV, 1740, appendix, p. 31.

[12] See Rippon, *Baptist Register*, III, pp. 260 f. for the text of the summons and IV, Supplement, for the Confession, General Epistle and Narrative of Proceedings.

thing upon the faith or practice of any of the churches of Christ. Our whole intendment is to be helpers together of one another, by way of counsel and advice, in the right understanding of that perfect rule which our Lord Jesus, the Bishop of our souls, hath already prescribed, and given to his churches in his word."

Nevertheless, the Assembly discussed and recommended the grouping together of churches under one minister; the adequate support of pastors and their ordination. It decided that Baptists who were cut off from local Baptist fellowships might fitly attend the ministry of Independents and Presbyterians. It advocated the enforcement of discipline within the churches, even to matters of long hair, periwigs and apparel, as well as the strict observance of the Lord's Day. More significant was the agreement of the representatives that "a public fund or stock was necessary", for the help of churches otherwise unable to support a pastor, for the payment of ministers engaged in evangelistic and church extension projects, and for ministerial training. It was thought that the fund could be raised by a free-will offering, paid over quarterly to London as a result of "an annual collection made in the several churches, of a half-penny, penny, twopence, threepence, fourpence, sixpence per week, more or less, as every person shall be willing". The fund was to be administered by nine brethren, "all living in and about London". The General Epistle called for a general fast on 10th October 1689.

The meeting of 1689 was a promising one. The proposals made were bold and foreshadowed many of the activities of the Union formed in 1812-13. The number of churches represented was far larger than at the meetings more than a century later in Carter Lane, and there were ministers and messengers present from the north of England and from Wales. It did not prove possible, however, to maintain an annual General Assembly, partly no doubt because communication and travel were difficult and partly because of internal stresses and the general decline in religious enthusiasm.

Like the General Baptists, the Particulars were not agreed at the end of the seventeenth century, and for some years afterwards, as to the propriety of congregational singing. On a number of practical matters some were stricter than others. Important as London already was in the national life, it must have seemed remote and uncongenial to many of the Baptists of the provinces. Within a year or so, it was decided that the Assembly should meet in two sections, one in London at Whitsun, the other in Bristol at Easter, with fraternal delegates as liaison officers. The London Assembly of 1692, which decided on this arrangement, declared that the two assemblies should not be accountable to one another "any more than churches are" and that "no churches make appeals to them to determine matters of faith or fact, but propose or query for advice".[13] By the end of the seventeenth century, the meetings in the west of England had become to all intents and purposes a continuance of the Western Association, whose origins went back to Commonwealth times. The London meetings quickly declined in importance and, though an effort was made to revive them in 1704, they gradually petered out. The early decades of the eighteenth century were unfavourable for adventurous or united undertakings. Thomas Crosby, whose *History of the English Baptists* appeared in 1740, speaks of General Assemblies being "changed into Associations" and gives as reasons, first, the difficulty of travel and, secondly, the "churches being settled in peace and unity".[14]

The main practical achievement of the period was the establishment in 1717 of the Particular Baptist Fund, gathered and administered in London, but used to aid students and poorer ministers in all parts of the country. Apart from this, such united denominational activity as there was among the Particular Baptist Churches remained in the channels of local Associations. Of these the most important were the Western, the Midland, the Northern and that centred in Berkshire and Oxfordshire. Even these Associations found it difficult, and sometimes impossible, to hold a regular annual gathering.

In the second half of the eighteenth century, however, there

[13] T. Crosby, *The History of the English Baptists*, III, p. 265.
[14] Op. cit., IV, p. 3.

came a new wave of religious interest and zeal. The formation in 1764 of a new Association, known as the Northampton Association, marked a turning-point in the life of the Particular Baptist churches. The nucleus consisted of six churches, two in Northamptonshire itself, three in Leicestershire and one in Buckinghamshire. Within eight years, the number had grown to fourteen and before long the Association stretched from Nottingham to St. Albans. Within this large area many new churches were formed as a result of an evangelistic movement, which owed less to the example of the Wesleys than it did to the Great Awakening in America with which Jonathan Edwards was associated. The movement was contemporaneous with the development of the New Connexion among the General Baptists. The Northampton Association soon had a remarkable group of leaders. Robert Hall, the elder, and John Collett Ryland were followed by younger men—John Sutcliff, Andrew Fuller, the younger Ryland, the younger Hall and, last but not least, William Carey. Contact with these men played an important part in causing Abraham Booth, of Kirkby Woodhouse, to leave the General Baptists and join the Particulars, a notable change, for Booth was to become an outstanding figure in London after his removal there in 1769.

It was within the Northampton Association that in 1792, in response to the pleadings of Carey, there was formed the "Particular Baptist Society for Propagating the Gospel among the Heathen", soon familiarly known as the Baptist Missionary Society. The flame of missionary enthusiasm, once alight, spread far beyond the boundaries of the Northampton Association. Auxiliary societies were formed—in Birmingham, in Bristol, in the north and elsewhere. The Association had already set going other important influences. In 1784 a Call to Prayer was issued, which resulted in the spiritual quickening of many ministers and churches.[15] It was inspired by Jonathan Edwards's account of an earlier prayer movement and his pamphlet was reprinted by John Sutcliff in 1789. Fuller had published *The Gospel Worthy of all Acceptation* in 1784, a plea for a more evangelical Calvinism.

[15] E. A. Payne, *The Prayer Call of* 1784, 1941.

When he began to travel about the country in the interests of the Missionary Society, "Fullerism" became a revivifying impulse north, south, east and west. A new concern for itinerant preaching and village evangelism showed itself in many different places.

The formation of the Northampton Association had been followed by the establishment of a Norfolk and Suffolk Association in 1769. The Particular Baptist churches of Kent and Sussex drew together. Several of the older Associations began to revive. The closing decades of the eighteenth century and the early years of the nineteenth saw a general quickening of religious life. In this London followed rather than led, but once the new impulses were felt in the metropolis, the need for bolder and more united planning was soon recognized.

John Rippon's long ministry at Carter Lane began in 1773. In 1787 he published the first edition of his *Selection of Hymns*, based upon, but supplementing the collections of Isaac Watts's compositions. This quickly secured acceptance among the Particular Baptists. From 1790 to 1802 his *Annual Register* played an important part in making churches and Associations aware of one another and of their fellow-Baptists overseas. After Rippon, the most influential London minister was Abraham Booth, pastor of the church meeting in Prescot Street, Goodman's Fields. In 1797 Booth took the lead in forming "The Baptist Society in London for the Encouragement and Support of Itinerant and Village Preaching", later known as the Home Mission Society. John Rippon, William Button and Thomas Thomas, all of whom were involved, as we have seen, in the meetings of 1812–13, were associated with Booth in this earlier enterprise, which in part grew out of evangelistic journeys made by Saffery, Hinton and others in the early years of the Missionary Society. Preaching missions were undertaken by agents of the Itinerant Society in Shropshire, Herefordshire and Wales and before long grants were being made to ministers for new evangelistic work in almost every part of the kingdom. A new era of Baptist advance had begun.

III

These developments formed part of the background to the effort to establish a General Union of the Particular Baptist churches. There was also a new concern for a properly trained ministry. When the General Baptists appealed for their Education Society in 1811 they said: "Every other Denomination of Protestant Dissenters is sensible of the utility of learning to the proper discharge of the duties of the Christian Ministry and their attention is of course directed to this matter with an increasing degree of zeal and activity".[16] This was certainly evident among the Particular Baptists. The oldest Baptist Academy, that at Bristol, had been reconstituted in 1770. A Northern Education Society, formed in 1804, had established an Academy at Horton, near Bradford. The Welsh churches had opened a college at Abergavenny in 1807. Three years later London, after various abortive efforts, had its Baptist Academical Institution at Stepney.

It was an age of societies—missionary societies, education societies, Sunday School societies, Bible societies, tract societies and the like. All this quickening of activity throughout and beyond the denomination needed some co-ordinating centre, some common planning. Behind the efforts of Rippon, Ivimey, Thomas Thomas and their associates lay this increasingly clamant need.

Their task was not an easy one, however. Ministers, churches and Associations had become content with and jealous of their independence. They were shy of one another. There were deep cleavages of theological outlook and church practice even within the ranks of the Particular Baptists. Fuller's evangelical Calvinism was by no means universally accepted. Indeed, controversies over it continued in many parts of the country for several decades, causing divisions in local churches in not a few instances. The Calvinistic churches as a body were saved from any trend towards Unitarianism. Fuller published the first edition of his *Calvinistic and Socinian Systems Examined* in 1793. In the following

[16] W. T. Whitley, *Minutes*, etc., p. 302.

years he engaged in a vigorous exchange of letters with William Vidler, who, starting as a General Baptist minister in Battle, later became widely known in London as a Unitarian and a Universalist. What most sharply divided the Calvinistic Baptists—and even those sympathetically disposed towards "Fullerism"—was the question of "terms of communion". Should the Lord's Table be closed against any who had not been baptized as believers? Could there be any church fellowship inclusive of Baptists and Paedobaptists?

The issue was an old one. It had caused contention in the seventeenth century, John Bunyan pleading that "differences of judgment about water-baptism" should be "no bar to communion", William Kiffin taking a more rigid line. "Mixed, or free communion" churches were to be found in many parts of the country, but they were by no means universally approved. Abraham Booth argued against them with Robert Robinson, of Cambridge, and with the Rylands. Fuller himself was not happy about them.

The controversy flared up again within a year or so of the meetings of 1812–13, and thus exposed the serious differences of opinion and practice among those whom it was hoped to unite. In 1815 Robert Hall, then minister of Harvey Lane church, Leicester, published a substantial treatise *On Terms of Communion with a particular view to the case of the Baptists and Paedobaptists*. Abraham Booth had died in 1806, but Hall's work was professedly a reply to Booth's *Apology for the Baptists*, which had first appeared in 1778. Joseph Kinghorn, of Norwich, stepped into the breach in defence of close communion and for several years he and Hall engaged in pamphlet warfare. Joseph Ivimey was a close communionist[17] and he found himself involved in public controversy with young Francis Augustus Cox, of Hackney. The matter was to remain a troublous one for several generations. Where it was joined with suspicion of "Fullerism", it was liable to precipitate division within local congregations and

[17] His distinguished predecessor, Dr. Andrew Gifford, minister at Eagle Street from 1735–84, had been an open communionist.

the establishment of Strict Baptist churches, out of fellowship not only with the General Union but also with the older Associations.

In 1805, William Gadsby (1773–1844) had become minister of a chapel in Back Lane, Manchester. He was a working-class preacher of considerable power and a determined Calvinist of the old school. He took his church out of the Yorkshire and Lancashire Association and became the leader of the strictest of the Strict Baptists with an influence which spread to many other parts of England through his periodical *The Gospel Standard*. In 1828–9 "Fullerism" and the communion issue were to be the main causes of the break-up of the Norfolk and Suffolk Association, and the establishment of another separated group of Strict Baptist churches. The practice of close communion was slowly abandoned by most, but not all, the churches in fellowship with the Baptist Union. As late as 1841, however, the Eagle Street church refused to grant a transfer to one of its members, who desired to join the Devonshire Square church, because the latter practised open communion. Close communion has continued to be the practice in most of the Baptist churches in Wales.

These internal stresses help to account for the fact that, even in a period of chapel-building and renewed activity in many directions, the project of a General Union drew together only a relatively small company. Rippon and his friends had set their hands to a difficult task. They were helped by the fact that Nonconformists generally were showing a renewed determination to combine in agitation for the removal of the civil disabilities from which they continued to suffer. Earlier efforts to secure the repeal of the Test and Corporation Acts had failed. A Tory oligarchy was in power, opposed alike to the claims of Roman Catholics and Dissenters, to any reform of Parliament and to attempts by wage-earners to combine in order to secure better conditions. But popular support for all these measures was slowly rising. Lord Sidmouth's attempt to place new restrictions on the activity of Dissenters was defeated as a result of the promptness with which petitions were signed and sent up to Parliament. In 1813 William Smith's Trinity Act was passed. This gave legal toleration to Unitarians and opened for them a considerable period of influence in public affairs. The disabilities, large and small, under which the older Nonconformist bodies suffered, remained un-remedied, however, but the new Methodist societies were gradually aligning themselves with the Dissenters.

As Rippon reflected on the situation, he must have been well aware of the difficulties which would confront the new General Union. But he felt that the times were propitious for the drawing together of the Particular Baptist churches and perhaps knew of parallel developments on the other side of the Atlantic. The second half of the eighteenth century had seen a number of new Baptist Associations formed on the American continent. When the Warren Association, centred in Rhode Island, was formed in 1767, one of its promoters had used language which is an interesting echo of that used in some of the seventeenth-century Confessions.

"For, as particular members are collected together and united in one body, which we call a particular Church, to answer those ends and purposes which could not be accomplished by any single member, so a collection and union of churches into one associational body may easily be conceived capable of answering those still greater purposes which any particular Church could not be equal to. And, by the same reason, a union of associations will still increase the body in weight and strength, and make it good that a threefold cord is not easily broken."[18]

In 1799 the Philadelphia Association issued a call for a General Conference of Baptists covering all the Associations in the United States. It was not immediately acted upon, but in May 1814, less than a year after the formation of the General Union in this country, a "General Missionary Convention of the Baptist Denomination in the United States for Foreign Missions" met. It was composed not of state conventions or associations, but of individuals. It prepared the way, however, for later denominational developments in America and was, like the General Union, a sign of the times.

[18] Dr. Samuel Jones to James Manning. See W. W. Barnes, *The Southern Baptist Convention*, 1954, p. 2.

CHAPTER 3

DIVIDED INTERESTS, 1814–31

I

THE first main period in the history of the General Union ran from its formation until 1831–2, when there took place a re-organization so substantial as to be almost a new beginning. Enough has been said to make clear that difficulties were to be expected. Perhaps the most notable thing about this early period was that the Union did not peter out or disintegrate. A somewhat similar Congregational Union, formed in 1808 to promote the spiritual growth of the confederated churches and the evangeliza-tion of neglected districts, met with considerable public criticism, languished and in 1827 was merged with a Home Missionary Society started in 1819. Of this Congregational Union, R. W. Dale said: "The Union justified neither the hopes of its founders, nor the fears of its foes; it had no vital force, and soon ceased to exist."[1]

Baptists were more fortunate, perhaps because they were more accustomed to Associations, Connexions and Assemblies. John Stoughton, a nineteenth-century historian, who was himself a Congregationalist, makes an interesting comment on the stronger denominational consciousness shown by Baptists during the years 1800–20:

"There is more unity in Baptist history than in the history of Independents during the early part of the century. Baptists had stronger sympathies with each other; for their denominational zeal rallied round one distinct institute, the name of which ever shone on their banners. They, for the most part, co-oper-ated more intimately, and with less diversity of organization and action, per-haps with a greater amount of *esprit de corps*; moreover, to any one writing

[1] *History of Congregationalism*, 1907, p. 688.

43

their history at the period, they supply links of connection in three controversies, which they carried on without destroying denominational unity. The hyper-calvinistic controversy, the communion controversy, and the Serampore controversy were so many family discussions."[2]

The controversies to which Stoughton alludes all involved persons prominently connected with the General Union, and though they may be described as "family discussions", they caused considerable dissension and distress. H. W. Clark, a later historian of Nonconformity, also a Congregationalist, carries Stoughton's remarks a little further:

"Any breaking out of internal disputes within a religious body necessarily leads to an adoption of the method of 'definition of differences' by the parties *within* the Church, and if the Church have any tendency in that direction already, must accentuate it as regards the Church's self-definition *as a whole* against other Churches at its side. And any Church so placed must be more open to pressure of any kindred influence from beyond itself. Within the Calvinistic Baptists that was the posture in which things stood."[3]

The disputes and differences among the Particular Baptists undoubtedly hindered the development of the General Union. The records of the period suggest, however, that even more operative adversely were other interests and distractions, some within the denomination itself, others relating to Nonconformity as a whole.

Throughout the period, Joseph Ivimey remained one of the secretaries of the General Union and for ten years of it the sole secretary. Stoughton described him as "a good man of contracted views".[4] A more detailed description is given by F. A. Cox, his opponent on the question of close communion. "He was a man peculiarly devoted to the interests of the denomination to which he belonged," says Cox, "so much so, that notwithstanding considerable generosity of mind, he often made himself suspected of a party spirit. . . . His heart was catholic, but his temper sectarian . . . He suffered considerable disadvantage from a want

[2] *History of Religion in England*, VII, pp. 261–2.
[3] *History of Nonconformity*, II, 1913, pp. 344–5.
[4] Op. cit., VIII, p. 145.

of early education; but he had read and thought much, and a certain rudeness of manner was compensated by the warmth of his heart, and the energy of his conduct."[5] It was this energy that probably preserved the General Union during its early uncertain years, for though he had many other interests—perhaps too many —Ivimey went on summoning an annual meeting, even though it sometimes secured little support and was overshadowed by the larger gatherings in aid of other causes.

II

The second Assembly of the General Union met in Dr. Rippon's vestry on 23rd June 1814. Three weeks earlier the war against Napoleon had been brought to an end by the Treaty of Paris. Napoleon was in custody on the island of Elba. London had been giving an almost hysterical welcome to the Czar Alexander of Russia while preparations were being made for the Congress of Vienna. He and his sister, and a number of other European rulers and statesmen, left the capital that very day. But there was to be an unexpected and unwelcome interlude. A few months later, the exile escaped and made his way to France again. Military operations had to be renewed. There was no doubt talk in Carter Lane on 23rd June of affairs on the Continent and the prospects of peace, but the main interests there were again domestic and denominational.

The previous day sermons had been preached on behalf of the Baptist Missionary Society by William Steadman, of Bradford, and John Saffery, of Salisbury. Of the former, F. A. Cox says: "His appearance was uncouth, his manners unattractive; and yet his real goodness, his excellent sense, and his affectionate spirit, ensured him everywhere a welcome reception."[6] As minister of the Westgate church and tutor at the Academy in Little Horton,

---

[5] *History of the Baptist Mission*, I, 1842, p. 434. George Brookes, of Bewdley, writing in 1839, said: "Rev. Mr. Ivimey believed, as did also the late Rev. Jas. Dore, that when a man ceased to be a strict Baptist, there is no resting place for his feet till he finds himself a strict Papist."

[6] Op. cit., I, p. 437.

Steadman had become an influential figure in Baptist circles. Saffery was "a plain but powerful advocate of the mission in the pulpit",[7] highly esteemed by his friends. Both Steadman and Saffery were among the forty-six ministers—one more than the previous year—who attended the meeting of the General Union. The Minute Book also records the presence of some twenty laymen. Six or seven churches, represented at the preliminary meeting in 1812, but not in 1813, had delegates there. Another fifteen or sixteen churches were represented for the first time. On the day of the missionary sermons, John Sutcliff had passed away in Olney and this accounted for the absence from Carter Lane of his close friend and collaborator, Andrew Fuller. Perhaps for the same reason, John Ryland also was absent. Of the newcomers, Steadman was not the only one from the north. William Angus, a layman from Newcastle, was there. The presence of younger ministers such as John Dyer, of Reading, and William Gray, of Chipping Norton, was also significant, for they were subsequently to play important parts in the life of the denomination. The veteran, John Stanger, was at Carter Lane once more and, as before, Rippon took the chair. *The Baptist Magazine* for June 1814 had printed an "Address to the Denomination" on the proposed activities of the General Union. It had been drafted by Rippon, William Newman, Thomas Thomas and James Upton, of Church Street, Southwark, and was followed up at the meeting itself by the decision to send to leading ministers throughout the country a Circular Letter signed by the secretaries.

On the whole, the officers must have felt that satisfactory progress had been registered. Three months earlier a new denominational society had been formed, the Baptist Society for the Propagation of the Gospel in Ireland, later known as the Baptist Irish Society, which was destined to become closely linked with the fortunes of the Union. Saffery had visited Ireland in 1813 on behalf of the Baptist Missionary Society. His reports on the social and religious condition of the inhabitants caused widespread concern. Of the eleven Baptist churches founded in the seventeenth

[7] Op. cit. I, p. 287.

century and then enjoying considerable prosperity, only five remained. The London ministers, who met monthly at the Jamaica Coffee-House, off Cornhill, led by Ivimey and Button, summoned a meeting in the Eagle Street church, in December 1813, to consider what could be done to foster evangelical witness in the neighbouring island. Four months later, in April 1814, at a meeting in the New London Tavern, Bishopsgate, with the active encouragement of Fuller, the Baptist Irish Society came into existence. Ivimey was appointed secretary.[8] This society became a further channel for the rising tide of evangelistic zeal.

The following year the third Annual Assembly of the Union was held, again in June. The battle of Waterloo had been fought four days earlier, but news of Wellington's victory was probably not known to the ministers and their friends. There was a larger attendance than formerly, but the meeting mourned the loss of Andrew Fuller, who had died the previous month, prematurely worn out by his many labours. For thirty years he had been a dominating figure among the Baptists, widely respected as a preacher, theologian and controversialist, as well as the honoured secretary of the Missionary Society. On this occasion, the meeting of the General Union was held in Eagle Street, Holborn, and Dr. Ryland was in the chair. The delegates reaffirmed the advantages of meeting together and decided that for the future the gathering should be called "The General Meeting of the Particular (or Calvinistic) Baptist Denomination". The London ministers were requested to prepare "a general account of the state of religion in the Churches of the metropolis and its vicinity". The most interesting proposal in 1815 concerned, however, the procuring of a place of worship in London "for the use of the denomination, sufficiently large to contain the congregation usually assembling at our annual meetings, and other purposes." It was suggested that the building should be vested in trustees, two-thirds of whom should be selected from London churches,

---

[8] Ivimey remained secretary until 1833. From 1814–30, William Burls was treasurer. An Irish Evangelical Society was formed by Congregationalists in 1814. It became closely associated with the Congregational Union in 1840.

and that the London friends proceed at once to draw up detailed plans. Since Baptists had not a large enough meeting-house of their own, the missionary sermons for 1815 had been preached in the Dutch Church in Austin Friars, in the Jews' Chapel, Spital-fields, and in chapels belonging to the Countess of Huntingdon's Connexion. The Baptist Itinerant Society had arranged a break-fast gathering in the New London Tavern.

In 1816, though Dr. Rippon returned to the chair, the General Union found another meeting place, Elim Court Chapel, in Fetter Lane. Walter Wilson describes the chapel as

"a square, substantial brick-building, with four galleries, extending round the place; and behind the pulpit is placed an organ. In this appendage, it differs from most other places of worship among the recognized Dissenters. As the building is raised several feet from the ground, the space underneath is formed into a vault for the burial of the dead. In a small adjoining yard there are also some vaults devoted to the same purpose."[9]

Abraham Austin had been minister there since 1785. At one time a General Baptist, he and his church had broken away from the old General Baptist Assembly. At the 1816 meeting of the General Union a special collection was taken for the proposed central building and a committee of laymen was appointed to receive further contributions. We hear nothing more about this project and know little of what took place in 1816, except that interest-ing reports were given of the state of affairs in different parts of the country and that they were regarded as encouraging.

The annual meeting in 1817 was held once more in Carter Lane at 8 a.m. The missionary sermons had been preached the previous day by Joseph Kinghorn, of Norwich, and William Winterbotham, the one at Spa Fields, the other in Sion Chapel. The most interesting proposals discussed by the General Union on this occasion related to a Loan Fund for the building and repair of meeting-houses. The scheme was put forward by a layman, John Marshall.[10] Little came of it at the time, but William New-

[9] *Dissenting Churches of London*, III, 1810, p. 474.
[10] See *The Baptist Magazine*, 1817, pp. 313–14, 355–9.

man, of Stepney College, kept the proposal in mind and out of it there developed seven years later the London Baptist Building Fund, destined to become a strong and beneficent denominational agency. Newman had reasons for satisfaction, for the Particular Baptist Fund had received a number of generous bequests and had been able to increase its grants considerably, particularly those to Stepney College. The Missionary Society was enlarging its activities and the report of the third annual meeting of the Irish Society, held the day after the Union meeting at the City of London Tavern, makes it clear that this society also was rapidly gaining considerable popular support.

III

The first Minute Book of the Union ends with the record of the 1817 meeting. What happened in the immediately ensuing years is best gathered from other sources. It was a difficult period in public affairs. The end of the long-drawn-out struggle with Napoleon was followed by severe economic depression and widespread distress. The closing years of the long reign of George III and the decade during which George IV was on the throne do not form a very glorious chapter in British annals. There was growing need of reform in almost every department of government, but changes came only after much agitation. General conditions were unfavourable to the swift development of a nation-wide organization.

Other and more immediate causes may have militated against the effectiveness of the General Union in those years. William Button had probably little part in the secretarial arrangements after his departure from London. Thomas Thomas died in 1819. Joseph Ivimey, left as sole secretary, was much occupied with other matters. The preface to the second volume of his history had been dated the very day the Baptist Irish Society was formed. The third volume was completed by the end of 1822. In 1819 Ivimey had added to his responsibilities the joint secretaryship of the Baptist Widow and Orphan Society and had begun his

pamphlet warfare with F. A. Cox on open communion. The
Baptist Missionary Society had come to recognize the need for
adequate leadership in London. After Fuller's death Ryland and
Hinton were appointed to manage the affairs of the mission,
though Fuller himself had hoped that Christopher Anderson, of
Edinburgh, would succeed him. But Ryland lived in Bristol and
Hinton in Oxford, and the arrangement was soon seen to be unsatisfactory. In 1818 John Dyer was elected as the first full-time
secretary and two years later headquarters were established in the
metropolis, rooms being rented in Wood Street, off Cheapside.[11]
A few years later offices were secured in Wardrobe Place, Doctors' Commons. Then came a spell in Fen Court, Fenchurch
Street. This, however, is to anticipate. What the denomination as
a whole might have done, if the plans of 1816 had been carried
out, was in the end undertaken by one denominational society,
which gradually drew to itself as tenants some of its sister organizations, including the General Union itself.

Though the Missionary Society was about to enter upon a
difficult phase in its history, the main enthusiasm at the annual
meetings in London gathered about its services, and to a lesser
extent about those of the Irish Society. Nevertheless, the General
Union continued to hold its own meeting each year. At Carter
Lane in 1819, at 8 a.m., there is said to have been a considerable
attendance, though the committee of the Missionary Society was
meeting at the same time, with William Ward, of Serampore,
present. In 1820 the Union tried holding its gathering on a Tuesday evening. William Steadman was again present on this occasion and Ivimey read a report on the condition of the London
churches. It was agreed that ministers who wished to join the
Union should be sponsored by three of their brethren, a rule
which remained in force until the whole question of the recognition and accrediting of ministers was taken up seriously at the
end of the century. In 1821 the Union again met at the early hour
of 8 a.m. but it was agreed that the two hours then available were

[11] For brief accounts of Fuller, Ryland and Dyer, see E. A. Payne, *The First Generation*,
1936.

insufficient for the proper transaction of the business. Rippon apologized for not having prepared "the Epistle for the Yearly Meeting". His address was taken up with the importance of catechizing, special mention being made of Dr. Ryland's re-issue of one of the pamphlets of his father on evangelical religion. Early in 1822 Ivimey narrowly escaped death through taking by mistake nearly an ounce of laudanum. Soon afterwards his health began seriously to fail. In 1823, the year the aged John Stanger died, there was no public announcement of the Union's meeting sent to *The Baptist Magazine* and the attendance was probably very small. That year the London ministers transferred their monthly meeting from the Jamaica Coffee House to the new missionary headquarters in Fen Court and George Pritchard, pastor of the church meeting in Keppel Street, Holborn, became joint-secretary with Ivimey of the Irish Society.

In 1824 a development took place of considerable importance for the future. In November, the London Baptist Building Fund was commenced. Its object was to help with the erection of meeting-houses "in any part of the United Kingdom". "The new society aimed," it was said, "at abolishing the inconvenience and many serious evils created by the numerous personal calls on wealthy Londoners by country ministers begging for their churches". For a hundred years this had been the recognized method of securing help for the building of country chapels. William Carey had resorted to it while at Moulton. But it was a method obviously open to abuse. At the inaugural meeting of the new Fund, Benjamin Shaw, the treasurer of the Missionary Society, presided. James Hargreaves, minister of the church in Little Wild Street, became secretary, and the committee consisted of a group of laymen and "all ministers contributing to the society". Ivimey, Newman, Pritchard and James Upton, senior, were among those who supported the Fund in its early years. After ten years the word "London" was deleted from its title, but not until 1857 were grants to London churches allowed.

In the eighteen-twenties the Missionary Society was involved in unfortunate controversy with William Carey and the group of missionaries whose work was directly based on Serampore. Ever since the death of Fuller there had been misunderstanding and tension. Had John Dyer gone to India, as was at one time suggested, much of the subsequent trouble might have been avoided. The visits to this country of Ward in 1819 and of John Clark Marshman in 1822 did little to remove the difficulties. The death of Ryland in 1824 and of Saffery in 1825 meant the loss of two wise counsellors personally known to the pioneer missionaries. In 1826 Joshua Marshman came back to England. The annual meetings of the Society at which he was present were shadowed and anxious ones. The consultations which followed led to a deadlock and in 1827 the Missionary Society and the Serampore Mission separated. John Foster, the essayist, described the action of the committee as "one of the most odious and wicked proceedings to be found in any modern ecclesiastical annals," but both bodies had considerable popular support and for ten years had a separate existence. Inevitably the differences which had arisen had an unfortunate effect on the effort to draw the churches together.

The work of the Irish Society continued to awaken considerable public interest. Of its annual meeting in 1827, it is recorded: "Many thousands were assembled even before six o'clock to breakfast, and when the doors were opened at seven o'clock, the large room at the City of London Tavern was soon filled".[12] Four years later, another interest was added to those that had become familiar—the Mission, the Itinerant Society, the Irish Society and the Academies—and to the public issues of the day. In May 1831 a "Society for diffusing the Gospel through the Continent of Europe" was formed. F. A. Cox and J. Baylis were appointed joint-secretaries. Joseph Gurney became treasurer and on the committee appear the familiar names of Ivimey, Dyer and Murch and those of two newcomers, Stovel and Steane, who were to play important parts in the affairs of the Union in subsequent decades.

---

[12] *The Baptist Magazine*, 1827, p. 329. In the same week Robert Hall preached for the Missionary Society and for Bristol College and then for Edward Steane. At Denmark Place, Camberwell, hundreds failed to get in. "We hope never to witness so disgraceful a scene at any place of religious worship", said *The Pulpit*, 30th June, 1827, p. 34.

By then Nonconformists had at last won their long battle against the Test and Corporation Acts. In 1820 they had had to resist a proposal which would have fastened fresh restrictions on their progress. Henry Brougham, later to become Lord Chancellor, but then a rising young politician prominently engaged in the defence of Queen Caroline, put forward an education bill which would have placed rate-supported schools completely under the control of the clergy of the Church of England. In the face of vigorous opposition the Bill was withdrawn, but the Protestant Dissenting Deputies and the Protestant Society for the Protection of Religious Liberty, formed in 1811, judged that the time was ripe for a new campaign for the redress of the grievances of Nonconformists. So long as the Test and Corporation Acts of the seventeenth century remained on the Statute Book, even if they were not vigorously applied, they were a threat to and a slur upon Dissenters. Over seven years of vigorous campaigning proved necessary.[13] At length, however, through the influential backing of Lord John Russell and other Whig politicians, success was achieved. The Duke of Wellington and Sir Robert Peel withdrew their opposition. The newly enthroned Archbishop of Canterbury and a number of bishops agreed to the repeal of the Acts and in May 1828 this received the Royal Assent. To mark this notable victory a public dinner was held in the Freemason's Tavern. There were four hundred guests present under the chairmanship of the Duke of Sussex, one of the King's brothers, and the Baptist, F. A. Cox, of Mare Street, proposed a special vote of thanks to those bishops and clergy who had supported the Nonconformist cause. G. M. Trevelyan says that repeal was mainly of symbolic importance and not of great immediate effect, "for until the Parliamentary and Municipal elections had been democratized, Dissenters had little chance of holding office."[14] But the measure gave widespread satisfaction and it marked a stage towards the full political emancipation of Nonconformists and gave them greater confidence.

[13] See B. L. Manning, *The Protestant Dissenting Deputies*, 1952, pp. 220–53.
[14] *History of England*, 1926, p. 631.

IV

It is clear that these other interests and causes militated against the rapid development of the General Union, which had no clearly articulated programme of its own. The individual societies occupied most of the time and energy of the leaders and also of the rank and file. This is clearly illustrated in the case of Francis Augustus Cox, an interesting and influential figure throughout the period and one who had shared in the formation of the General Union.

Cox, who was born in Leighton Buzzard and inherited property from his grandfather, is described as "the active, busy, zealous worker in all philanthropical and religious movements".[15] His church had become an important one. In 1825 he was appointed one of the secretaries of the Home Missionary Society, which then had twenty-five agents in various parts of the country. But Cox's main activities went in other directions. He was closely associated with the Protestant Society for the Protection of Religious Liberty. This body, in addition to its work for the repeal of the Test and Corporation Acts, aimed at the reform of the marriage, burial and University laws and regulations. In conjunction with the Dissenting Deputies, it had secured in 1812 the repeal of the Quakers' Oaths, the Conventicle and the Five Mile Acts. It helped to secure freedom for missionary work when the East India Company's Charter was renewed in 1813. It led the opposition to Brougham's Education Bill in 1820. In the following years it became "a recognized power in the State"[16] and the leaders of the Whig party formally identified themselves with it.

Cox was also a leading member of the United Committee, national in character and for the first time uniting Methodists with the older Dissenting bodies in public agitation, which directed the closing stages of the campaign for the repeal of the

[15] Skeats and Miall, *History of the Free Churches of England*, 1891, pp. 471–2. Cp. Stoughton, op. cit., VIII, pp. 146–7.

[16] Skeats and Miall, op. cit., p. 457. Cp. Manning, op. cit., p. 46: "The organization was novel in two ways—first, it was national; second, it united the Methodists for the first time with the older Dissenting bodies."

BAPTIST LEADERS OF THE EARLY NINETEENTH CENTURY

EDWARD STEANE, D.D.
SECRETARY OF THE UNION
1835–1882

JOHN HOWARD HINTON, A.M.
SECRETARY OF THE UNION
1841–1866

Test and Corporation Acts. Hence his prominent part at the celebration dinner. He became one of the distributors of the *Regium Donum*. He served on the committee which arranged for the celebration of the third centenary of the Reformation (1817). He interested himself in the Society for Promoting Ecclesiastical Knowledge, which issued pamphlets and books on church establishments and property and on the principles of dissent. He had a considerable share in the starting of University College and London University (1827)[17] and later became a prominent member of the Religious Freedom Society (1839–43), the Evangelical Voluntary Church Association (1839) and the British Anti-State Church Association (1844). In 1845 Cox led the opposition to the Maynooth College grant and also gave his support to the Anti-Corn Law League. All his life he was a keen supporter of the Baptist Missionary Society, writing the valuable two-volume history of its first fifty years. He represents the manifold interests of an able Nonconformist minister resident in the metropolis.

The same may be said of Cox's friend, Dr. Thomas Price, "to whose sagacity, wisdom and judgment the civil liberties of Dissenters will always owe the profoundest obligation."[18] Price was minister of Devonshire Square Church, Bishopsgate, from 1827 to 1837, in succession to Timothy Thomas. A leader of the Religious Freedom Society and a vigorous opponent of slavery, he was also one of the editors of *The Eclectic Review*. Halévy comments somewhat severely on this *Review*. He says:

> "Readers of this excellent periodical will look in vain for an article of mystical aspiration or religious meditation. Under colour of making war against clericalism, embodied in the Establishment, it spoke of nothing but free trade, the franchise, and the individual's political RIGHTS, and thus, instead of making Radicalism Christian it ended by secularizing Christianity."[19]

When founded in 1804, the object of *The Eclectic Review* had been,

---

[17] This brought him into touch with Brougham, who, when he became Lord Rector of Glasgow University in 1824, conferred an LL.D. on Cox. Another notable Baptist contribution to the cause of education was John Foster's *Essay on the Evils of Popular Ignorance* (1820), which was several times reprinted and often quoted.

[18] Skeats and Miall, op. cit., p. 472.

[19] *History of the English People*, 1951 edition, IV, p. 390.

3

according to Robert Hall, "to counteract the irreligious bias which seems to attach to almost all literary journals".[20] The contributions of John Foster and Josiah Conder hardly merit Halévy's strictures. Most Baptists, however, preferred *The Baptist Magazine*.

The General Union had to face these many competing claims from other societies and causes. What should be noted is that during the twenty years from 1812–32, difficult as they were, Baptist churches steadily increased in number and vitality. Association life was reviving. A new Association, the Southern, came into existence in 1823 and, five years later, the Norfolk Association, having shed a number of Strict Baptist churches antipathetic to "Fullerism",[21] began its separate course. In 1831 the Monmouthshire Baptist Association was formed by thirty churches, most of which used the Welsh language in worship.

The position of the Church of England was becoming more insecure and unsatisfactory. Its diocesan organization bore little relation to the growth and movement of population. Its spiritual life was at a low ebb and it appeared to be the champion of privilege and repression. Marsh, Bishop of Peterborough, declared in 1831 that "if we except the period which preceded the Church's overthrow in the time of Charles I, there never was a time when the clergy were assailed with so much calumny and so much violence as they are at present".[22] Two years later, Thomas Arnold wrote: "Nothing, as it seems to me, can save the Church but an union with the Dissenters".[23] Arnold proceeded to put forward a scheme for comprehension based on an episcopate acting on the advice of councils composed of both laymen and clerics. The scheme appealed neither to his fellow Anglicans nor to Dissenters, but is an illustration of the widespread concern about the future of the Established Church.

G. M. Trevelyan describes the general circumstances of the time in these terms:

[20] Letter to Olinthus Gregory, 30th October 1804.
[21] These formed the Suffolk and Norfolk (New) Association of Strict Baptist Churches in 1829.
[22] Quoted by W. L. Mathieson, *English Church Reform*, 1928, p. 45.
[23] Ibid., pp. 71 f.

"The mass of unregarded humanity in the factories and mines were as yet without any social services or amusements of a modern kind to compensate for the lost amenities and traditions of country life. They were wholly uncared for by Church or State; no Lady Bountiful visited them with blankets and advice: no one but the Nonconformist minister was their friend: they had no luxury but drink, no one to talk to but one another, hardly any subject but their grievances. Naturally they were tinder to the flame of agitation. They had no interest or hope in life but Evangelical religion or Radical politics. Sometimes the two went together, for many Nonconformist preachers themselves imbibed and imparted Radical doctrines. But the political conservatism with which the Wesleyan movement had started was not yet exhausted, and acted as a restraining element."[24]

There were, however, many cross-currents in evangelical circles. A notorious episode of the period was that in which Edward Irving was the central figure. As a young man of thirty, Irving came to London in 1822 and at once attained outstanding success as a popular preacher, first at the Caledonian Church and then at a large new building in Regent Square. But he was quickly drawn into the "Albury Circle", a group of evangelicals, which, at the invitation of Henry Drummond, M.P., met to discuss "Unfulfilled Prophecy" and the Second Coming of Christ. In his preaching Irving came to lay increasing emphasis on preparations for the Second Coming and on gifts of the Spirit. In April 1831 cases of "speaking in tongues" began to occur and much popular excitement followed. Irving was cast out of the National Scotch Church and died in 1834, a broken and tragic figure, leaving as his legacy the Catholic Apostolic Church and a wider revived interest in prophecy and ecstatic phenomena.

Baptists were not at the time seriously affected by this movement. They were, however, influenced by the growing demand for reform in all branches of the national life and were conscious of their growing strength. New and younger leaders were emerging. Robert Hall, the famous preacher, a man of varied and extraordinary powers, died in 1831. The following year, Joseph Kinghorn, of Norwich, passed away. Rippon and Ivimey must have felt that they were survivors of a vanishing age

[24] *English Social History*, 1944, pp. 476–7.

Though its direct achievements were few, the General Union also had survived; but it needed reorganizing. The Congregationalists had decided to make a new effort to form a national union, and in 1831 set up a provisional committee. That same year, at the annual meeting of the General Union, it was decided that the time had come for radical changes in its structure and functioning.

CHAPTER 4

NEW BEGINNINGS,
ACHIEVEMENTS AND DIFFICULTIES, 1832–63

I

"We are anxious," Joseph Ivimey had said in 1811, "to see such a Union prevail in our Denomination as shall most effectually continue all our efforts in the cause of Truth and Righteousness at home, and give ten-fold vigour to our exertions on behalf of the heathen abroad." In practice the General Union had achieved relatively little. The Baptist Missionary Society had quickly established itself in the confidence of the churches and kept this confidence in spite of its unfortunate breach with the Serampore missionaries. It had built up an organization of Auxiliary Societies in all parts of the country and had set up a headquarters in London. The Home Missionary Society and the Baptist Irish Society had grown in strength. They, like the Particular Baptist Fund and the Baptist Building Fund, pursued each its own objects. The colleges were independent societies, each with its own local constituency. The annual meeting of the General Union was a mere shadow of the larger gatherings that met about the same time on behalf of other causes. It had become little more than a social gathering for such ministers as cared to attend. It had, in the words of a Baptist historian, "no practical aim, no permanent offices, no inspiring leaders",[1] and if this verdict is a little too severe, it is not far from the truth. By the beginning of the 1830s it was high time that the whole basis of the Union was re-examined.

Reform was in the air. Sir Walter Besant argued that the

---

[1] W. T. Whitley, *History of British Baptists*, 1923, p. 266. Ivimey himself admitted that the "good design" of the Union "was never fully realized". See *History of the English Baptists*, IV, 1830, p. 382.

eighteenth century should be regarded as continuing till the accession of Queen Victoria. There were few changes in manners, customs or prevalent ideas between 1700 and the close of the third decade of the nineteenth century. A significant turning-point came with the accession of the new and popular King, William IV in 1830 and the twin agitations that reached their peak in the following years, that for the abolition of slavery and that for parliamentary reform. Baptists supported both these causes. Their missionary interest in Jamaica had made them vividly aware of the evils of slavery. They had always been champions of civil and religious liberty. In 1821 Robert Hall had reissued his *Apology for the Freedom of the Press*, first published in 1793, because it had been suggested that he had renounced his earlier political opinions and because he believed that "only radical reform could save the country from certain ruin". *The Baptist Magazine* saw the second reading by the House of Commons of the first Whig Reform Bill in 1831 as "the finger of God". Changes were indeed at hand in the whole structure of English society. Nonconformists looked forward to the redress of their continuing grievances. Many anticipated that among the changes that would come would be the ending of the established and privileged position of the Church of England. Both Baptists and Congregationalists felt the need for more effective national organizations.

So far as the General Union was concerned, the first move for a review of the situation came at the annual meeting of 1831, which was held in the Blackfriars church, the month in which Lord John Russell introduced his second Reform Bill. James Upton, of Church Street, who had been present at the first meeting of the Union in 1813, suggested that the Baptist Board, that is, the London ministers' fraternal, should consider the denominational situation and prepare a new plan of action. As a result, in 1832, a few days after the Reform Bill had at last passed the House of Lords and received the Royal Assent, a revised constitution for the Union was adopted. Its objects were re-defined as follows:

"1st. To extend brotherly love and union among the Baptist ministers and churches who agree in the sentiments usually denominated evangelical.

2nd. To promote unity of exertion in whatever may best serve the cause of Christ in general, and the interests of the Baptist denomination in particular.

3rd. To obtain accurate statistical information relative to Baptist churches, societies, institutions, colleges, etc., throughout the kingdom and the world at large.

4th. To prepare for circulation an annual report of the proceedings of the Union, and of the state of the denomination."

Thirty years later, the vague terms in which the first of these objects is expressed came under criticism. John Howard Hinton, who had by then been one of the secretaries of the Union for more than twenty years, himself spoke severely of the phraseology used. Recalling the discussions, however, he declared: "What a poverty-stricken resolution it is that defines these objects, was as strongly felt then as it has often been felt since; but it was absolutely *all* that the assembled brethren would bear."[2] Hinton was labouring under a sense of frustration and misgiving. His words are perhaps hardly fair to what was gained by the decisions of 1832. The doctrinal declaration of 1813 had been of a familiar Calvinistic pattern. "Fullerism" had provided a bridge between the Particular Baptist churches and those of the New Connexion of the General Baptists. By omitting the older theological formula and speaking only of "the sentiments usually denominated evangelical", the way was opened for the adherence to the Union of churches belonging to the New Connexion. The process thus began which resulted sixty years later in the complete merging of the two groups of Baptists.

The very different action of the Congregationalists should, however, be noted. When the Congregational Union was formed in May 1832, it was said to have seven objects. The first was "to promote Evangelical Religion, in connection with the Congregational Denomination". The next four objects are very similar to those adopted the same year by the Baptist Union. Then come two others:

[2] Chairman's Address, 1863.

"6. To inquire into the present methods of collecting funds for the erection of places of worship, and to consider the practicability of introducing any improved plan.

7. To assist in maintaining and enlarging the civil rights of Protestant Dissenters."

But the following year the Congregational Union adopted an elaborate "Declaration of the Faith, Church Order and Discipline of the Congregational, or Independent Dissenters".[3] The Savoy Declaration of 1658 was regarded as "though most orthodox, too wordy and too much extended for our purpose". Dr. Peel describes the new statement as "a diluted Calvinism", popular rather than scholastic, the product of preachers rather than of theologians. But it provided Congregationalists with a standard which they were ready to reaffirm fifty years later. It is interesting to speculate whether, had Baptists agreed upon a similar statement in 1832, they would have been able to avoid the sad breach in their ranks which occurred in 1887. They were, however, subject to more theological cross-currents than the Congregationalists.

In preparation for the 1832 meeting of the General Union, Joseph Belcher, then minister in Chelsea, prepared a careful statistical report, published in the July issue of *The Baptist Magazine*. It compared the number of Particular Baptist churches in England and Monmouthshire in 1790 and 1832, and concluded that there had been a threefold increase in the forty-two years. Belcher's survey dealt with the counties one by one. Yorkshire, where there were sixty churches, had the largest number. Somersetshire came next with forty-eight. In London there were thirty-nine. Belcher noted that progress in the metropolis had not been as rapid or satisfactory as in other parts. The total Belcher gave for 1832 was 910 churches, some twenty more than the figure given by a Congregationalist investigator for 1829.[4] Congregationalists had at the time three or four hundred more churches than had Baptists. There were about three times as many Methodist

[3] See Dale, *History of Congregationalism*, pp. 700–709. Peel, *These Hundred Years*, pp. 69–74.
[4] Peel, *These Hundred Years*, p. 20 n.

chapels, belonging to the various groups into which the original Wesleyan movement had already divided.

It was felt that the kind of information Belcher had collected should be regularly and systematically brought together. It continued what Rippon had done forty years earlier in his *Register*. Belcher was appointed secretary of the reorganized General Union together with Joseph Ivimey, who was nearing the end of his life.

II

The anti-slavery campaign was at its height in Britain. The abolitionists were much aided by Baptist missionaries from Jamaica. William Knibb had reached England early in June, 1832, and the historic meeting in Spa Fields chapel at which he refused to be silenced took place the evening before the reconstitution of the Baptist Union. Knibb played an important part in the election campaign that followed the passing of the Reform Bill. Among the London Baptist ministers, Thomas Price and Charles Stovel were his close friends and collaborators. The meetings Knibb addressed in all parts of the country between June 1832 and August 1834, and his evidence before committees of both Houses of Parliament, contributed materially to the ending of slavery in the British colonies. They also aroused concern at the attitude to slavery of many of the Baptists in the United States, and it was decided to raise a fund to send James Hoby and F. A. Cox to the triennial American Convention of 1835 with a "fraternal expostulation". This was a delicate mission, for the two British Baptists found themselves in Richmond, Virginia, among sturdy opponents of the anti-slavery movements which were agitating the American nation.[5] "It would seem to me," wrote John Foster, the essayist, to J. P. Mursell, of Leicester, "that the great absurdity was the *project itself*. For if the commission did (Drs. C. and H. did not,

[5] See Cox and Hoby, *The Baptists in America*. Isaac Taylor Hinton, brother of J. H. Hinton, was pastor of the church in Richmond, Virginia, from 1833–5. An American Baptist Home Mission Society, with headquarters in New York, had been formed at the Triennial Convention in 1832.

however, understand it so) combine the two objects, an amicable fraternization with the Baptists at their great convention, and a full, loud declaration against slavery in that assembly, it is quite clear the thing was impracticable; the whole thing would have been blown up at once."[6] From the United States Cox travelled up into Canada, finding there nearly a hundred Baptist churches.

The proposal for this mission to the New World had come in the first instance from the Baptist Board. According to J. H. Hinton, the churches which contributed to the cost were there-after asked for subscriptions to the Baptist Union. The first list of churches belonging to the Union was published in 1834 and, said Hinton, "these, without exception, are attached to it not by any act of adhesion on their part, but solely by the fact of having contributed to the expenses of Dr. Cox and Dr. Hoby in their voyage to the United States, a contribution which was sagaciously, but arbitrarily (and very much to the surprise of some parties) assumed to constitute a link 'connecting themselves with the body'."[7]

Whether or not this is the whole story, a subscription was cer-tainly instituted about this time, and during the eight years of Belcher's secretaryship considerable progress was made in shaping the Union into a more effective denominational instrument and slowly gaining the adherence to it of the churches in all parts of the country. James Upton had presided over the annual meeting in both 1831 and 1832. The following year it was possible to meet in the new chapel in Park Street, near the end of Southwark Bridge, to which Rippon's congregation had moved from Carter Lane. Rippon's mental energy and bodily strength had greatly declined, but he was once more called to the chair and it was fit-ting that he had lived to see the Union at last well-established. The ministers took breakfast together at 7 a.m., the meeting be-ginning an hour later. To judge by a critical article in *The Baptist Magazine* a few months later, the attendance was still not very large. Belcher's report that year was felt to be incomplete. But it

[6] 19th October 1836. See Arthur Mursell, *James Phillippo Mursell*, 1886, p. 51.
[7] Address to the Baptist Union, 1863.

has to be remembered that Englishmen had still to depend on coaches for distant travel and that the postal service was expensive and somewhat uncertain. The writer of the article suggested that all the existing Baptist Associations should be dissolved since half the churches were not in membership with any of them, and that they should be replaced by a series of District Conventions or Fellowship Meetings, open to all Calvinistic Baptist churches. There might then be a Triennial Meeting of the whole body, with collections for a general fund to meet travelling expenses. These proposals were not adopted. The progress made was of a different and less radical kind.

When Ivimey died in 1834, William Murch, of Stepney College, became co-secretary, and the following year Edward Steane, of Camberwell, was also appointed, thus beginning a notable official connection with the Union, which lasted nearly half a century. F. A. Cox presided at the annual meeting in 1834. For the succeeding ten years, brethren from the provinces were called to the chair, a clear sign that the Union was taking on a more national character. Three names stand out. In 1837 John Howard Hinton presided. He was ministering in Reading at the time, but a few months later moved to London to become pastor at Devonshire Square and in 1841 replaced Joseph Belcher as joint-secretary of the Union with Edward Steane. In 1840 James Acworth was called to the chair. Four years earlier he had succeeded William Steadman as president of the Horton Academy. For the next twenty years and more he proved a staunch friend of the Union, occupying the chair again in 1856, 1859 and 1861, and doing much to secure the interest of the Baptists of the north of England. Hardly less significant was the fact that in 1842 John Gregory Pike, of Derby, the leader of the General Baptists of the New Connexion, was invited to preside over the annual gathering. An annual pastoral letter was then being sent out to the churches. The committee met quarterly, with the treasurer, Mr. James Low, in the chair. Low served as treasurer for thirteen years. He had joined Rippon's church in 1810 and in the closing years of his life became one of Spurgeon's closest friends and supporters at the Metropolitan Tabernacle. Joseph Belcher had rendered useful service to the Union. In 1843 he left England and, after a short spell in Nova Scotia, settled in the United States. There he became widely known as a pastor, writer and editor, dying in Philadelphia in 1859.

The coming together in the secretariat of the Union of Steane and Hinton coincided with other significant denominational changes. In July 1841 John Dyer, the secretary of the Baptist Missionary Society, died in tragic circumstances. His newly appointed colleague, Joseph Angus, had to take the lead first in arranging the jubilee celebrations of the Society and then in the erection of new headquarters in Moorgate. The specially built Mission House was available for the annual meetings of the Baptist Union in 1844. The following year the meetings were held for the first time in the provinces, thus fulfilling the original intention that the Union should meet "in London, or elsewhere".

Leeds was the place chosen and the delegates met in the South Parade Church, the meetings taking place at the end of May. Visitors were allowed in the gallery for the business session at which Hinton presented the annual report and James Low the accounts. Resolutions were passed against the continued payment of the *Regium Donum*, which had become a form of state aid distasteful to dissenters, and against the proposed Maynooth Grant for a Roman Catholic University in Ireland. The formation of the Hanserd Knollys Society, to further the study of Baptist history, was welcomed, though the name was queried. The need for a denominational Manual and for details regarding chapel building was stressed. In a public meeting Charles Stovel, of London, Charles Birrell, of Liverpool, and Hinton took part, as well as ministers from the north of England.

The following year meetings similar in pattern were held in Birmingham,[8] and in 1847 in Norwich. *The Baptist Record*—a monthly periodical started a few years earlier and similar in style and content to *The Baptist Magazine*—commented somewhat

---

[8] The Congregational Union had had an autumn session in Birmingham in 1839 with 138 delegates present.

scathingly on the Birmingham meetings, comparing them un-favourably with those of the Congregational Union, which it thought better prepared and more purposeful.

"With us (it was said) . . . the whole affair is most fortuitous. A delegate detects himself asking silently the question, For what *purpose* are we gathered? and following this with another. Are the authorities themselves quite clear upon the matter? . . . Do the Committee consider it quite enough to run down to Birmingham or elsewhere, just audit the accounts, and then return? Why are so few there, but because no one thinks it worth while to travel many miles without a purpose; and because few churches will pay their pastors' or their delegates' expenses to a meeting so destitute of all explicable meaning."[9]

There was no doubt some point in these criticisms, for the Norwich meetings were attended by only some fifty ministers and delegates. The Baptist Missionary Society, the Irish Society and the Home Missionary Society still held their own meetings in London in April.

After these three experimental visits to the provinces, the Union remained in London for the next nine years, holding its assembly in the Moorgate headquarters of the Missionary Society. There the Union rented an office, though it still had no full-time secretaries. It was decided to publish a Manual (later the annual Handbook) and to begin the building up of a library. This project had the cordial support of E. B. Underhill, who had taken the lead in establishing the Hanserd Knollys Society.

Underhill was an honorary secretary of this society throughout its eight or nine years of activity. He had as colleagues first Benjamin Davies, of Stepney College (until his departure for Canada), then William Jones, of the same college, and on the latter's death, James Hoby. The detailed secretarial work was done by George Offor, junior (1787–1864), well known for his edition of the works of John Bunyan. The society aimed at the publication of two or three octavo volumes annually and offered these for a subscription of ten shillings and sixpence. Ministers were given a free copy of each volume, if they secured ten subscribers, and another

[9] Op. cit., p. 772.

free copy was offered to any Sunday School which could collect ten subscriptions. The volumes published were:

> *Tracts on Liberty of Conscience*, edited by Underhill, 1846.
> *The Broadmead Records*, edited by Underhill, 1846.
> *Bunyan's Pilgrim's Progress*, edited by George Offor, 1847.
> *Roger Williams' Bloudy Tenent of Persecution*, edited by Underhill, 1848.
> *John Canne's Necessity of Separation*, edited by Charles Stovel, 1849.
> *The Martyrs' Mirror*, edited by Underhill and Millard, Vol. I, 1850.
> *The Works of Charles Du Veil*, edited by F. A. Cox.
> *The Martyrs' Mirror*, Vol. II, 1853.
> *The Fenstanton, Warboys and Hexham Records*, edited by Underhill, 1854.
> *Confessions of Faith*, edited by Underhill, 1854.

An edition of the works of Henry Danvers, undertaken by W. H. Black, pastor of the Mill Yard Seventh Day Baptist Church, seems never to have been completed. In 1848 Underhill gave a series of lectures on Baptist History in a number of Lancashire churches. Much valuable material, as well perhaps as the records of the society, perished when Offor's library was destroyed by a fire at Sotheby's in 1865.

When, in 1849, Joseph Angus left the secretaryship of the Missionary Society for the presidency of Stepney College, Frederick Trestrail and E. B. Underhill were appointed in his place. For the following twenty years and more, Trestrail and Underhill directed the growing foreign missionary interests of the denomination. Angus became one of the most influential Baptist leaders until the end of the century and a well-known public figure.[10]

The Baptist Irish Society, which Trestrail left, had been passing through a difficult period. George Pritchard had resigned the secretaryship in 1835 and was succeeded by Samuel Green, minister of the church in Walworth Road, Southwark. Trestrail was appointed in 1843, when Green resigned. The Society faced a heavy deficit and the famine in Ireland, which followed the

---

[10] For brief sketches of Underhill and Angus, see E. A. Payne, *The Great Succession*, 1938. Both appear in the *Dictionary of National Biography*. For Trestrail, see his own *Reminiscences of College Life in Bristol* and *The Short Story of a Long Life*, 1892.

failure of the potato crop in 1846 and 1847 brought much of its work to a standstill. In these and the ensuing years the Baptist churches in the south and west of the island lost by death and emigration more than 3,000 adherents. Thereafter Baptist work was chiefly concentrated in the north.

Baptist responsibilities and interests were, however, enlarging. The visit of Cox and Hoby to the United States directed attention to the New World, to which a steady stream of emigrants was proceeding. The reunion of the Serampore Mission with the Missionary Society in 1837 gave a great fillip to foreign missions. The Cameroons became a new field of activity. Conditions in Europe also became a matter of concern. A Baptist Continental Society was formed and agents were ordained for work in France and among the Mennonites. In 1834, with the baptism in Hamburg of Johann Gerhardt Oncken, the modern Baptist movement on the Continent began. In 1840 one of Oncken's chief collaborators, G. W. Lehmann, of Berlin, came to London and was ordained by J. H. Hinton and others in the Salters' Hall church.

III

There was still much to distract attention from the Baptist Union. But during the thirty years from 1830 to 1860, it was not so much the work of the older philanthropic and religious societies as public affairs, particularly those bearing on ecclesiastical matters. There were many of these.

Within a few years of the repeal of the Test and Corporation Acts, Dissenters began to organize petitions to Parliament in favour of a general registration of births, deaths and marriages, and the right to baptize, marry and bury according to their own forms, and in favour of admission to the older Universities without religious tests. Some urged that all these reforms should be granted in one comprehensive measure. This the Government resisted. Political changes, as well as the opposition of vested interests of various kinds, caused delays in dealing with any of the

Nonconformist grievances. In 1836, however, the Tithe Commu-
tation Bill was passed, and this was followed soon afterwards by a
Registration Act and a Marriage Act. Next came the Established
Church Bill, which reorganized the dioceses of the Church of
England, a Plurality Bill, and a bill dealing with Cathedral Reform and the setting up of the Ecclesiastical Commission. This
legislation of 1836–40 placed the Church of England on its present
basis and may not unfairly be said to have "saved" the Establishment, though this was not evident at the time. Indeed, most
Nonconformists still believed that the Establishment was doomed.
They continued to form societies which aimed at ending the
State connection, and became the more vocal and determined as
the Oxford Movement developed. John Keble had preached his
famous Assize Sermon on 14th July 1833 and the following September John Henry Newman began the publication of the
Tracts for the Times.

As the "hungry 'forties" drew nearer, agitation against the
Corn Laws increased. Cobden and Bright appealed successfully to
Nonconformists for active support of the Anti-Corn Law League.
Its meetings were often held on chapel premises, particularly in
the north of England. The General Body of the Protestant Dissenting Ministers of the Three Denominations lent its support
to the cause, though it claimed to be abstaining from party
politics. In August 1841 no less than 645 ministers met in Manchester, of whom 182 were Baptists.[11] This was a far larger number than had so far attended a meeting of the Baptist Union.
Benjamin Evans of Scarborough, Thomas Price and F. A. Cox
were among the Baptist ministers who were subsequently active
on behalf of the League. At the same time men like J. H. Hinton,
J. E. Giles of Leeds, and J. P. Mursell of Leicester, were supporting
the suffrage demands of the Chartists.

During these years Nonconformity in general strengthened its
hold on the growing population, particularly in the Midlands
and the North of England. Then came a temporary set-back.
"For English dissent as a whole the years immediately before and

[11] R. G. Cowherd, *The Politics of English Dissent*, 1956, pp. 134 f.

after 1850 were," says Halévy, "a period of decline."[12] Between 1844 and 1848 there had been a second period of railway investment and speculation, under less scrupulous auspices than the earlier one of 1836-7, when the promoters had been mainly wealthy Dissenters, like the Baptist, Samuel Morton Peto.

In 1844—in spite of the opposition of the Church of England, the Methodists and the Dissenting Deputies and their denominations—Peel's Government passed the Dissenters' Chapels Act which secured Unitarians in the possession of the chapels they held, unless the trusts were quite explicitly against them. It was in the following year that John Henry Newman joined the Church of Rome. His action helped to draw together the individuals who promoted the Evangelical Alliance in 1846. They included both Anglicans and Dissenters, Edward Steane, the Secretary of the Baptist Union, being prominent among the latter. The British Anti-State Church Association (later known as the Liberation Society) was already in existence. It claimed that in the General Election of 1847 twenty-six of the candidates returned were in favour of the disestablishment of the Church of England and no fewer than sixty-two opposed to the further State endowment of religion. The so-called "Political Dissenters" were gaining strength. Their leader, Edward Miall, editor of *The Nonconformist*, had been a Congregational minister. From 1852 to 1856 he sat in Parliament as member for Rochdale, together with some forty more avowed Dissenters. Founded in 1841, *The Nonconformist* had as its slogan "The Dissidence of Dissent and the Protestantism of the Protestant Religion". Nonconformist grievances and disabilities were provocatively stated and even magnified, that they might be redressed. England was at this time, as G. M. Trevelyan has said, less class-conscious than "church-and-chapel" conscious.[13] The main appeal of Nonconformists was, however, to the rising and growingly prosperous middle class, which had secured political power as a result of the Reform Bill of 1832 and the hardly less important Municipal Corporations Act of 1835.

---

[12] *The Age of Peel and Cobden*, 1947, p. 330.
[13] *English Social History*, p. 515.

The annual assemblies of the Baptists and the Congregationalists, which had attacked slavery and continued to speak in favour of disestablishment, free-trade, some further extension of the franchise and the political rights of the individual, showed, it must be confessed, little or no interest in legislation to improve working-class conditions. In spite of their part in the repeal of the Corn Laws, they were lukewarm about the Ten Hours Bill. "The Nonconformist clergy befriended the poor against the land-owner," say the Hammonds; "the Church clergy befriended the poor against the manufacturer.[14]

For all the Churches new issues of a more theological character were emerging. The refusal of the Bishop of Exeter in 1847 to institute George Gorham as vicar of Brampford, because of the latter's repudiation of the doctrine of baptismal regeneration, caused controversy and litigation in the Church of England which dragged on until 1850 and had wide repercussions. The Papal Bull of 1850 re-establishing the Roman hierarchy in England was a further cause of public excitement. Nor were Nonconformists without their own domestic controversies. New views of Biblical inspiration and authority were finding advocates. The hymns of T. T. Lynch provoked the "Rivulet Controversy" within the Congregational body,[15] and in 1851–2 young William Hale White (Mark Rutherford) was expelled from New College, London, for opinions judged to be incompatible with his candidature for the ministry. A few years earlier, George Dawson, an able and original preacher, had to leave the church in Birmingham of which James Hoby had once been minister, because his Christology appeared too "liberal" to his fellow Baptists. For the remaining thirty years of his life Dawson drew an eclectic congregation of his own to an independent church in Birmingham.

The sixth decade of the century closed with a series of shocks to the general peace of mind. First came the Crimean War. This was opposed by Cobden and Bright, but—in the words of John

---

[14] *The Bleak Age* (Pelican Edition, 1947), p. 202.
[15] Spurgeon wrote in the *Christian Cabinet* a review of Lynch's book, which the author described as "impertinent without being malevolent".

Morley—"the army of the Nonconformists, which has so seldom been found fighting on the wrong side, was seriously divided."[16] The war with Russia was followed by the Indian Mutiny, at the close of which a Baptist, Sir Henry Havelock, became almost overnight a popular though posthumous hero. At a memorial service conducted in Bloomsbury Church by William Brock, more than a thousand persons are said to have been turned away and the sermon had to be repeated the following Sunday.[17] During these years cholera was rife in many of the larger English cities and took a heavy toll of life. Then came blows to the dominant systems of thought. George Eliot had followed up her translation of Strauss's *Life of Jesus*, which appeared in 1846, with a translation of Feuerbach's *Essence of Christianity* (1854).

"My aim has been," wrote Feuerbach, "to change my readers from friends of God to friends of man, from believers to thinkers, from devotees to workers, from candidates for the next world to students of this one, from Christians whose creed makes them half animal, half angel, to men who are complete men."[18]

But in 1859 Charles Darwin published *The Origin of Species*, which, whilst it precipitated a controversy destined to occupy the next thirty years, linked man firmly with the animal kingdom. *Essays and Reviews*, published by a group of Anglican scholars in 1860, showed how serious were the new challenges to popular religious beliefs. The violent outcry the book provoked showed how unprepared were most of the clergy and the general public for the intellectual changes that were at hand.

IV

Baptist life was inevitably affected by the general conditions of the time—political, intellectual and religious. For a dozen or more years after the reorganization of the Union in 1832, there was a

---

[16] *Life of Cobden*, 1906 edition, p. 619.
[17] J. G. Pollock, *Way to Glory, The Life of Havelock of Lucknow*, 1957, pp. 1–2. A Havelock Scholarship Fund was established in his honour, the Principal of Regent's Park College being the chairman of the trustees. Of Brock's sermon, expanded into a biographical sketch, 46,000 copies were sold.
[18] Quoted by H. R. Mackintosh, *Types of Modern Theology*, 1937, p. 127.

steady growth in the number of churches and in membership. Towards the end of the eighteen-forties, there was some decline. Writing on the state of the denomination in 1846, *The Baptist Record* declared:

"There are many indubitable signs of spiritual depression, of diminished vitality and power. Nor is this state of things confined to ourselves; wherever the results of close observation have been made known, we are called to notice the same melancholy fact."[19]

The previous year the Baptist Building Fund had received a substantial legacy from Dr. William Newman, of Stepney College, and turned its activities from small grants for new buildings to more substantial loans, with most satisfactory results, but there was considerable concern at the size of chapel debts throughout the denomination as a whole.

The year 1848 brought an event that caused much public excitement. The Hon. and Rev. Baptist Wriothesley Noel, of St. John's Chapel, Bedford Row, left the Church of England and became a Baptist. The reason he gave for his secession was the state connection of the English Church, though he was opposed to political agitation against it. For the next twenty years Baptist Noel ministered in the John Street Baptist Chapel, becoming in due course President of the Baptist Union.[20] A number of other Baptists had no scruples about joining in the activities of the "Political Dissenters". Among the more prominent of these was J. P. Mursell, of Leicester, who became one of the most zealous coadjutors of Edward Miall.

In the early eighteen-fifties several important denominational developments took place. In 1852 a sharp temporary increase in numbers was registered through accessions from the Methodists, who were passing through a period of stress and controversy. At the beginning of 1855 the first issue of *The Freeman* appeared. This weekly Baptist paper, launched by a Leeds printer, mainly

[19] Op. cit., p. 657.
[20] Joseph Parker, *A Preacher's Life*, p. 396, speaks of hearing Noel speak in the Free Trade Hall, Manchester, in support of the North in the American Civil War. He spoke, says Parker, "in his own plaintive and gentle way".

at the instance of Dr. Benjamin Evans of Scarborough, was destined to become of considerable influence and importance in the subsequent decades. The initial statement of its editorial policy deserves quotation in full:

> "Regarding the interests of the Baptist denomination as in no way separate from those of the whole church of Christ, and yet as constituting a field of spiritual effort to which Baptists are bound, by conscientious obligations, to devote their energies, the promoters of 'The Freeman' design it to be at once DENOMINATIONAL AND CATHOLIC—a position which, in their view, involves no contradiction, unless fidelity to minor truths is held to be absolutely inconsistent with a strong and cordial attachment to those more comprehensive principles which unite in 'one body all of every name who profess allegiance to the common Lord'."

That Baptists were growing in confidence and were desirous of widening their contacts was further shown by the moving of Stepney College to new premises in Regent's Park, so as to be nearer London University. The annual denominational meetings in the spring, however, still awakened only fitful interest. The meeting of the Baptist Union in 1855 was described as "interesting, but thinly attended". The public gathering in support of the Irish Society two days later drew only "a very thin sprinkling of people". Of the Missionary Society's meeting in the Exeter Hall it had to be said: "We should like to have seen a larger assembly". The following year the attendance was somewhat better and it was noted that "several ladies were present during the preliminary engagements of the day". In 1857 the meetings of the Union were held in Nottingham with a view to "more extended intercourse with the General Baptist Association", the name adopted by the churches of the New Connexion. A new hymnbook was about to appear. Rippon's *Selection* of 1787 had passed through many editions and had been enlarged, but it had as rival *A New Selection*, issued by John Haddon in 1828, the profits of which went to the widows and orphans of ministers and missionaries. In 1858 the Psalms and Hymns Trust was formed and an influential committee, led by S. G. Green, produced a collection of 1000 hymns which quickly became popular and continued in use into the twentieth century. In the first twenty-one years, 900,000 copies of *Psalms and Hymns* were sold and £10,000 was distributed to widows and orphans.

Most Baptist churches had by this time shifted their second Sunday service from the afternoon to the evening. The change had become general in the 1830s. In the evening, it was claimed,

"an audience of a more miscellaneous kind was obtained, and the ministry insensibly assumed a more varied character. Subjects arising out of common life, or relating to public questions and prevalent social discussions, were handled in a manner calculated to interest the most careless persons, and to win their confidence in religious teachers.[21]

Frequently the discourses delivered in the evenings were described as "lectures". The larger churches in the towns and cities began to have a considerable number of auxiliary societies and organizations attached to them. One such church in Liverpool, for example, in addition to three Sunday schools and six Bible classes, had a Savings Bank, a Women's Institute (with classes in reading, writing, arithmetic, sewing and singing for girls and women over fifteen years of age), a Clothing Society, a Dorcas Society, two Book Societies for the reading of essays and discussion, a Mutual Improvement Society for young men, a Mothers' Association and a Tract Visiting Society.[22] Pews or sittings were allotted in return for seat "rents" collected quarterly, but in even the largest churches—such as the one just mentioned:

"certain sittings are allotted at the smallest sums convenient to the poor, and some are free, that everyone may have a place."

Only at the Communion Service was it customary to take up a collection. Contributions to objects other than the support of the minister in the six years 1853–8 averaged—in the case mentioned —£613, of which £183 went to foreign missions, £50 to the Irish mission and £20 to two of the colleges.

[21] C. M. Birrell, *Life of William Brock*, 1878, p. 116. Writing in 1812, Bogue and Bennett suggest that the change began with the Calvinistic Methodists and say: "It is devoutly to be wished that it may not gain ground." See *History of Dissenters*, IV., pp. 344 f.
[22] See the Manual of Pembroke Chapel, Liverpool, for 1860.

In these middle years of the century there came to the pastorate of a number of Baptist churches ministers who were to make their pulpits famous, exercising from them considerable influence on denominational and public affairs. In 1838 Charles Mitchell Birrell had begun a forty years' ministry at Pembroke Chapel, Liverpool, built by a group who believed in "open communion". He was soon joined in that city by another famous Baptist preacher, Hugh Stowell Brown. In 1843 John Turland Brown was called to College Street, Northampton, the church of the Rylands, where he was to remain until 1894. In 1848 Bloomsbury Baptist Church was opened and William Brock came from Norwich to be its first minister, quickly drawing a large congregation.

The erection of the Bloomsbury Church owed much to the efforts of Sir S. Morton Peto, a well-known contractor and Member of Parliament, of whom it was said: "He gave a new direction and a greater breadth of view to all departments of Christian activity throughout the whole Baptist community". Peto was from 1853–5 and again from 1863–7 chairman of the Dissenting Deputies. He was also for many years treasurer of the Baptist Missionary Society. What is generally known as "Sir Morton Peto's Act", passed by Parliament in 1850, simplified the duties of trustees of Nonconformist chapels and made easier the appointment of new trustees. It was Peto who, in 1855, transformed the Regent's Park dioscura into Regent's Park Chapel, where not only the communion table but membership was of the "open" kind. William Landels was called from Birmingham to be the first minister there and his ministry lasted nearly thirty years.

Three other notable and lengthy pastorates began in the same period. In 1851 Charles Williams settled in Accrington, soon becoming an acknowledged leader in the north. Seven years later, Alexander McLaren moved from Southampton to an open membership church in Manchester. He was to remain in active service until 1903, outstanding as a preacher and expositor, broad in his sympathies, a believer, as he himself said, in "denominational walls" but not in "the broken bottles on the top". John

Clifford, who came as a young man to Paddington the year
MᶜLaren settled in Manchester, continued as pastor there until
1915, remaining active and influential in denominational affairs
and a well-known public figure until his death in 1923.

Most significant of all was the arrival in London in 1854 of
Charles Haddon Spurgeon. He was then only twenty years of
age and came to the church in New Park Street—the church of
Gill, Rippon and Angus—which seemed then to be a declining
cause. Within a few months he had achieved sensational popular
success. Services were held in the Exeter Hall, while the chapel
was enlarged. Then the Surrey Gardens Music Hall had to be
hired. At last, in 1861, after various other expedients had been
tried, the great Metropolitan Tabernacle was built, with seats for
3,600 persons and additional accommodation for 1,000 more. For
the next thirty years Spurgeon preached there to overflowing
congregations.

The era of the great Victorian preachers had begun, and among
them Baptists, led by Spurgeon and MᶜLaren, had an outstanding
place. New efforts to reach the non-church-going sections of the
population were undertaken and, in the very years when new
intellectual challenges to religion began to show themselves, a
widespread popular movement of spiritual quickening appeared,
which has come to be known as the "Second Evangelical Revival". The Religious Census of 1851—the details of which were
not published till three years later—showed how many people
there were who not only did not attend public worship, but
could not because there was no accommodation for them. On
the whole the results of the Census were more encouraging to
Nonconformists than to Anglicans, but the former had no reason
for complacency. It appeared that the Particular Baptists had
1,374 chapels in England and 373 in Wales. The New Connexion
had 179 chapels in England and 3 in Wales. There were still 93
chapels belonging to the Old General Baptists, that is, those who
had become Unitarians. The sittings in Baptist chapels were said
to total 752,343, but only 39 per cent of them were occupied at
the most numerously attended service on the day of the Census.

The course and influence of the Second Evangelical Revival has been traced by Dr. Edwin Orr.[23] Beginning in the United States in 1857–8, it resulted the following year in many instances of spiritual quickening in Ulster, Scotland and Wales. In 1860 special prayer meetings were organized in London and, under the leadership of the famous Lord Shaftesbury, a series of Theatre Services were held. At a number of other centres in the metropolis, and throughout the country, popular evangelistic services took place. The supporters of the Evangelical Alliance were to the fore in these efforts, but the movement had the support of other circles as well. Most Baptists co-operated wholeheartedly. Baptist Noel, Brock and Landels had already shared in the Sunday evening services in the Exeter Hall, originally promoted by Lord Shaftesbury, but from which Anglicans withdrew because of the objections of the local incumbent. They and other Baptist ministers assisted in the Theatre services. All such efforts had the encouragement of Spurgeon. *The Freeman* published favourable reports of what was going on in different parts of the country. Throughout what Dr. Orr calls 'the Revival decade', that is, from 1860–70, there was a notable growth in the number and strength of Baptist churches. Those affiliated to the Baptist Union gained, he estimates, over 43,500 members in the first seven years. The impact of the movement on the Welsh Baptist churches was particularly strong.

In his detailed study of London Baptist life, Dr. Whitley states that "the number of churches founded between 1860 and 1870, and the number surviving, has never been equalled before or since". "But," he continues, "while they were as busy as beavers, they were as unsociable as otters; they multiplied at an unprecedented rate, but each was isolated at first."[24] This comment has to be borne in mind in considering the relative ineffectiveness of the Baptist Union throughout the three decades under review.

[23] *The Second Evangelical Awakening in Britain*, 1949.
[24] *The Baptists of London*, 1928, p. 79.

V

Throughout the greater part of this period Steane and Hinton were the joint-secretaries of the Union. Both were men of considerable ability and influence. Some further personal details about them may help to an understanding of the situation.

Edward Steane was a native of Oxford and had been a pupil in James Hinton's school. After training at Bristol College and Edinburgh University, he became minister of the church at Denmark Place, Camberwell. He is described as

"a gentleman of singular administrative abilities and of admirable judgment; few could excel him in the faculty of drawing a resolution, or preparing a report; and none could surpass him in the skill and sympathy to follow, and while following, to influence, the moods of a meeting. Had he been a diplomatist or a politician, his qualifications must have placed him high in either vocation."[25]

In fact, he rarely took part in political movements. In 1860, both the Baptist Union and the Congregational Union sent out circulars asking for petitions to Parliament in favour of the Abolition of Church Rates Bill. The following year Steane was to be found at the numerously attended Anti-Church Rates Conference. But his main interests lay in other directions. Skeats and Miall speak of his having "a cosmopolitan interest in the Gospel".[26] Stoughton describes him as "a man of broad, catholic sympathies".[27] It was Steane who came forward as the leading Baptist protagonist when the Baptist Missionary Society found itself in controversy with the British and Foreign Bible Society over the right rendering of the Greek word *baptizo*. Baptists felt that it should be translated in new versions by some word meaning "to dip or immerse" rather than being merely transliterated. Steane drafted the memorandum setting out this view and it was presented to the Bible Society on 6th January 1840 in the name of the Baptist Union. When it was rejected, Steane took the lead in the formation of a

[25] *London Quarterly Review*, Jan., 1875.
[26] Op. cit., p. 699.
[27] Stoughton, op. cit., VIII, p. 147.

separate (Baptist) Bible Translation Society and accepted first the secretaryship and later the treasurership. The new society quickly gained the support of the churches, operating side by side with, but independently of, the Baptist Missionary Society.[28]

A few years later, Steane joined with Joseph Angus, then secretary of the Missionary Society, in calling a conference on education for the ministry. He urged that the four existing theological colleges should be reduced to two, giving their time to theological studies in the strict sense, but each having associated with it an institution for teaching literary and scientific subjects. A second conference was held but showed no disposition to accept Steane's bold proposal, though all the colleges were facing financial difficulties and needed additional staff because of the demands made on tutors for elementary instruction.[29] Until 1845 the Missionary Society either sent its candidates to the colleges for training and supported them, or, more commonly, paid the Colleges for the students they took up and sent abroad. When W. H. Pearce appealed for ten missionaries for India and when, later, William Knibb appealed for ten missionaries for Jamaica, each missionary taken from the Colleges cost the Society £150 to £200. Following the B.M.S. Jubilee this was changed and the Colleges, sometimes by special scholarships, prepared men for the mission field as well as the home ministry, bearing the cost out of their own resources. The denomination was not at the time sufficiently united for a scheme such as that urged by Steane and Angus, though its adoption then might have brought considerable advantages.

Steane's main interests, beside those of his pastorate, were already being drawn in another direction. In 1845–6 he joined with Sir Culling Eardley, an Anglican philanthropist, in the establishment of the Evangelical Alliance. A union of evangelicals had been proposed by Thomas Chalmers, of Glasgow, when he lectured in London in 1838, and the following year the Evangelical Voluntary Church Association was formed; it had Sir Culling

[28] American Baptists had had a similar controversy with the Bible Society in 1837.
[29] *The Baptist Record*, 1846, pp. 357 f., 391, 491.

Eardley as treasurer and Dr. Cox as one of its secretaries, while Steane and Angus were on the committee. A wider project was urged by John Angell James, the Congregationalist of Carr's Lane, Birmingham, in his contribution to *Essays on Christian Union*, published under Scottish auspices in 1845. It was Steane, however, who had "the lion's share in shaping the constitution of the Alliance and a chief part in its early administration".[30] Chalmers had favoured "co-operation immediately, with a view to incorporation afterwards", that is, *rapprochement* between the churches as such, but the Evangelical Alliance was finally based on the membership of individual Christians belonging to different churches.[31] Of the Conference of 1846, at which the Alliance was formed, Steane himself said:

"It has required incessant thoughtfulness and the most watchful care lest an indiscreet word spoken or sentence written should wound the sensitiveness or offend the prejudices of the curiously mixed and balanced ideas of which our association is composed—Churchmen and Dissenters, Presbyterians and Methodists, Establishmentarians and Voluntaries."[32]

Steane became the first editor of the Alliance's journal, *Evangelical Christendom*. He found himself frequently drawn into conferences both in England and on the Continent as the new organization widened the range of its interests.

The co-operation of evangelicals probably interested Steane more than any purely denominational activities. Ruth Rouse argues that the Alliance pursued incompatible objectives. "From its beginnings it combined the aim of uniting Christians in the bonds of brotherly love with the aim of combating popery and Puseyism."[33] This tension was to remain unresolved. Steane's achievement was, however, no mean one. Many of his fellow Dissenters—and not a few Baptists among them—were devoting

[30] J. W. Ewing, *Goodly Fellowship*, 1946, p. 136.

[31] The Southern Baptist Convention was formed in 1845, following differences in the General Baptist Convention for Foreign Missions over slavery and other matters; it was a union of churches and associations, not of individuals.

[32] Quoted in *A History of the Ecumenical Movement*, 1954, p. 320.

[33] Ibid., p. 323.

their energies to the Liberation Society and to various semi-political activities. Moreover, there were some Baptists who drew the lines of legitimate co-operation much more narrowly than did Edward Steane. In 1841 a Baptist Tract Society had been formed by those holding "strict communion" views, and four years later a Baptist Evangelical Society came into existence, also on a strict communion basis, the Rev. William Norton, of whom more will have to be said later, being active in both societies.

Steane became a widely respected figure in the religious life of his time. In 1857 the Archbishop of Canterbury, Dr. Sumner, invited him to Lambeth Palace, together with Jabez Bunting, the Methodist leader. They met in the Guardroom, and in the presence of a number of bishops, Bunting was asked to offer prayer. High Churchmen criticized the proceedings as nothing but "Spurgeonism in the Church", but the meeting was a significant one.

By this time Steane's health had begun to fail, though he lived on for another quarter of a century. The more active leadership in Baptist affairs had already passed largely into the hands of John Howard Hinton. "The churches will ever be indebted to the venerable John Howard Hinton (*clarum et memorabile nomen*)", said a Baptist historian writing in 1868.[34] And when Hinton died, a few years later, it was truly said that the Union "owed its preservation in times of comparative feebleness to his perseverance. . . . Without the meed of much popular sympathy, he toiled for its fuller organization and development, and laid down the principles and methods which are now more widely appreciated."[35]

A contemporary has left a vivid description of Hinton:

"His was not a figure which could easily pass unnoticed. When he rose, six feet in height, of spare and severe form, his countenance calm and thoughtful, touched with sadness, hardly lighted by eyes which seemed to turn inwards rather than outwards, and to see the truth rather than men, the first sentiment awaked was reverence bordering on dread. When the sentences began to come they were clear and convincing in their logic, uttered in the shrill tones of a

---

[34] J. M. Cramp, *Baptist History*, p. 478.
[35] *The Baptist Handbook*, 1875. See also *Dictionary of National Biography*.

nervous temperament, and sometimes flung defiantly at the audience as if intended to arouse more than conciliate. But his nature was, to those who knew him intimately, full of tenderness, and a sympathy singularly prompt and delicate."[36]

Seven years older than Steane, he had been educated at the same institutions—James Hinton's school in Oxford, Bristol College and Edinburgh University. As a young minister, he shared enthusiastically in the anti-slavery struggle. Close friendship with William Knibb helped him to produce an admirable biography of the missionary champion. Hinton was present in Nottingham in 1834 at the first general conference which called for the disestablishment of the Church of England. In 1836 he was one of the founders of the Church Rate Abolition Society and in 1839 of the Religious Freedom Society. In 1842 he served the National Complete Suffrage Union as a lecturer.[37] He followed closely the events which caused Thomas Chalmers to form the Free Church of Scotland in 1843 and it is not without significance that the Baptist Union, of which Hinton had by then become co-secretary, was the only representative body to send delegates to the conference held in London in April 1844, at which the British Anti-State Church Association was formed. This society remained one of Hinton's major interests until 1855, by which time he, like several other Baptists, had become somewhat troubled by Edward Miall's political activities.

Hinton stood with his colleague, Steane, in support of the Evangelical Alliance. "Whatever tempests may beset its course," he said in reply to critics, "I would rather go to sea in this little bark and risk perishing in it, than stand upon the shore, an idle or an indifferent spectator."[38] He developed a deep interest in the Baptist communities on the continent of Europe, visiting Holland and Germany in 1851 and Sweden in 1858. He was always an ardent advocate of the work of the Baptist Missionary Society. His pastorate at Devonshire Square was an important and exacting

---

[36] See E. A. Payne, *The Baptists of Berkshire*, pp. 101–2.

[37] This Union had been formed by Joseph Sturge, the Birmingham Quaker.

[38] Quoted by J. W. Ewing, *Goodly Fellowship*, p. 15.

one, but he was ceaselessly busy with his pen, writing much on theological questions[39] and co-operating with his brother, Isaac Taylor Hinton, in a history of America. But amid all these varied activities, the affairs of the Baptist Union had a special place in Hinton's affection, and its debt to his patience and persistence was a great one.

VI

The difficulties which he faced, he himself set out in an important address delivered when he occupied the chair of the Union in 1863.[40] Hinton was then seventy-two years old and about to resign the pastorate at Devonshire Square. He was obviously more than a little depressed and regarded what he said as his swan-song.

"Denominational union among Baptists," he said, "has been slow in manifestation, and difficult of cultivation. We have long been a divided body, and we are so still; and if any progress at all has been made, it is unquestionable both that much remains to be done, and that the most recent efforts have met with little success. . . . The Baptist denomination, while in name *one*, is in *fact* many. If it were an evil spirit it might say, 'My name is Legion.' Let us glance for a moment at its several parts.

"In the first place, it is divided into two by a difference of doctrinal sentiment, some churches holding the Calvinistic system, some the Arminian. These constitute respectively the General Baptists and the Particular Baptists, bodies distinguished, not, as has been sometimes supposed, by preaching open and strict, or general and particular communion; but by maintaining the doctrines respectively of general and particular redemption. Of these two bodies the larger, or the Particular Baptists, is itself divided by a doctrinal diversity, according as the Calvinistic system has been found capable of being modified into two forms, which have been called High and Moderate Calvinism.[41]

"The Particular Baptist body is further divided by a practical diversity on the subject of Communion. It contains churches which restrict fellowship at the Lord's Table to persons who have made profession of their faith by Baptism,

[39] See *Theological Works*, in seven volumes, 1864–5, in which Hinton himself collected what he regarded as his more important theological writings. Hinton was generally regarded as Fuller's successor as a theologian. "He who was rebuked by his elder brethren for innovations in doctrine is now rebuked for his vindication of orthodoxy," said Daniel Katterns in 1861. (See *Baptist Magazine*, 1861, p. 259.)

[40] I may, perhaps, be allowed to record the fact that my grandfather, Philip Griffith acted as Minute Secretary on this occasion.

[41] Hinton suggested as alternative names Owenism and Fullerism.

and churches who admit to Communion professed believers in Jesus, although unbaptized. These are called respectively Open-Communionists and Strict Communionists. . . . We have then six parties."

After referring to the legal obstacles to full union between General and Particular Baptists, because of the terms of their trust deeds, Hinton spoke of a suggestion which had been made two years earlier by the General Baptist Association that there should be some further steps towards closer union. He pointed out that the Particular Baptists had no organization exactly parallel to that of the General Baptists or able to speak for them. Not even the local Associations could do this. "Fully one-third of the Particular Baptist Churches are not in any Association at all," he declared. So far as the Baptist Union was concerned, it had to be remembered that less than half of the Particular Baptist churches belonged to it. Of the churches then in membership with the Union a third were General Baptist.

Two organized groups of Strict Baptist churches have already been referred to, namely, those sometimes called "Gadsbyites" and those associated with the Norfolk and Suffolk Strict Baptist Association. William Gadsby was succeeded by his son, and in the middle of the century the group secured notable reinforcement through the baptism of William Tiptaft and J. C. Philpot, two Anglican clergymen. Philpot, who had been a fellow of Worcester College, Oxford, became the editor of *The Gospel Standard*. The Norfolk and Suffolk Strict Baptists had their own publications, *The Gospel Herald* (1833) and *The Earthen Vessel* (1845). They were more prepared for closer co-operation with one another than were the Gadsbyites. In the main, however, the Strict Baptist churches lived an independent, isolated life, and when they tried to combine, soon found themselves involved in theological controversy. In 1846 an "Association of Strict Baptist Ministers and Churches in and about London" was formed. It secured the adherence of only seven churches and a dozen or so ministers, the latter including William Norton, the editor of the Baptist Tract Society. Meetings were held bi-monthly for six years. But early in 1849 eleven Strict Baptist Churches, most of which had remained aloof, formed "The New Association of Particular Baptists in London" (the name was changed in 1851 to "The Association of Baptists holding Particular Redemption and Practising Strict Communion"). In 1852 the rival Associations decided to unite, but "the marriage was not a success: the parties were in death-throes almost before the close of the honeymoon".[42] Within a year or so, all co-operation ceased.

The differences among Particular Baptists were clearly very serious. Hinton did not feel that much could be expected from a general appeal for greater tolerance and charity, for the differences came from strongly-held convictions. The title "Baptist Union" was a "magnificent designation". It was, in Hinton's view, the result of Joseph Belcher's desire to link the enlarged meeting of the Baptist Board held in 1833 with the annual meetings of ministers, which had begun in 1812-13. What Hinton felt about this and the inadequacy of the 1833 Constitution has already been quoted.

"Happily for the denomination, as I think," said Hinton, "the Baptist Union has continued in existence until now, and has been useful; but its existence has been a continual struggle, and even by those who learn only by experience, it must be expected to be so still."

He clearly feared that pressure for closer union between General Baptists and Particular Baptists would increase the divisions among the latter. "A just object would seem to be to engage Particular Baptists to be united among themselves; they might then, perhaps, be willing to approach somewhat nearer to the General Baptist brethren."

Hinton declared that he spoke as he did with reluctance and that not all his hearers would agree with him. No doubt he underestimated what he had himself accomplished, as he certainly failed to foresee the remarkable progress that was made by the Union in the next two decades. For that he can hardly be blamed. The differences among Particular Baptists had but recently been exposed in the famous Norwich Chapel Case, which had led in

[42] For further details see S. J. Price, "The London Strict Baptist Association, 1846–53", *Baptist Quarterly*, Vol. IX (1938), pp. 109 f.

the end to an appeal to a Court of Chancery and an important judgment by the Master of the Rolls. The point at issue had been the legitimacy of open communion in St. Mary's Church, Norwich, the trust deeds of which were admittedly of the Particular Baptist variety.

As already noted, Joseph Kinghorn, minister at St. Mary's from 1790 to 1832, was a "Strict Communionist" and a vigorous opponent of the position taken by Robert Hall. Trouble arose in the Norwich church when Kinghorn's successor, William Brock, who had never made any secret of the fact that he believed in open communion, began first to administer the Lord's Supper in his own house to persons who had not been immersed as believers, and then arranged a special service for them in the chapel on the third Sunday of the month. A group of members, together with two of the trustees, endeavoured to stop these services and threatened legal proceedings against Brock. No such step was actually taken, however, and in 1848 Brock resigned on receiving a call to the new church in Bloomsbury.

Fresh trouble developed in 1857, following the admission to communion of a new member who had not been baptized because she had produced a medical certificate that the state of her health made it inadvisable. George Gould, who had succeeded Brock as minister, declared his view that baptism ought not to be regarded as "a term of communion in the Lord's Supper". The church members at St. Mary's voted for open communion by a considerable majority, but offered to provide a special afternoon service each month for the celebration of the Lord's Supper by baptized believers only. Many of the strict communionists then withdrew altogether from attendance at the Lord's Supper and the question arose whether they could any longer be regarded as or allowed to remain members of the church. This issue was anxiously canvassed outside Norwich. Among those consulted were Steane, Hinton, Thomas Price, Baptist Noel, William Landels and Joseph Angus. All advised in the negative. Attendance at the Lord's Supper was, in their view, a mark and duty of church members. Angus, by then Principal of Regent's Park College, had secured the adoption of open communion at New Park Street—Rippon's old church—while minister there. There had been a general move in this direction in many parts of the country. But the Rev. William Norton, one of the Norwich trustees who had opposed Brock in 1845,[43] together with a fellow trustee and two of the church members, filed a bill of complaint against Gould and the other seven trustees.

The preliminaries of the case occupied many months. It was regarded as a test action, legal and theological arguments on both sides were marshalled with care and at great length.[44] Judgment was finally delivered by the Master of the Rolls on 28th May 1860. He ruled that strict communion was not a fundamental principle of the faith of Particular Baptists and that "it is established that each congregation was, from the earliest times, at liberty to regulate its practice, either to the Strict Communion or to Free or Mixed Communion as it might seem best to such congregation".

By 1860 a majority of the Baptist denomination had come to favour open communion. But the Norwich Chapel Case inevitably aroused strong feelings on both sides. Hinton's address from the chair of the Union in 1863 can be properly understood only in the light of the Norwich dispute and its repercussions elsewhere. His uneasiness, even his pessimism, were not unnatural. There were other tensions as well. More liberal ways of thought were undermining the older expressions of Calvinism. In 1860, when the Church of England was seriously rent by the storm over the publication of *Essays and Reviews*, Nonconformists anxiously

[43] In the same year he had also publicly attacked the tutors of the colleges at Haverfordwest and Pontypool for believing in and practising "open communion". See D. M. Himbury, *The South Wales Baptist College*, 1957, p. 49. The stages by which many Baptist churches were changing their practice may be illustrated by what happened at Beechen Grove, Watford. In 1824 a proposal for open communion was defeated by 27 votes to 14, with 5 abstentions. Five years later it was agreed by 29 votes to 14 to admit "brethren of the Independent denomination" to "occasional communion". In 1837 it was agreed to extend this privilege to "all whose lives and conversation give evidence of faith in Christ" and in 1855 the church decided, with only one dissentient, in favour of "open membership", the choice of the minister and the use of the property being secured by Deed of Trust to a majority of the Baptist members.

[44] See *Open Communion and the Baptists of Norwich*, with an introduction by George Gould, 1860, and *Norwich Chapel Case*, edited by William Norton, 1860.

debated J. Baldwin Brown's *Divine Life in Man*. A favourable review in *The Freeman* drew protests from both Joseph Angus and Spurgeon. Hinton himself regarded it as completely unsatisfactory in its treatment of the Atonement. Two years later the bicentenary of the Great Ejection of 1662 was celebrated. The Baptist Union urged a wider basis of celebration than that originally suggested and a Central United Committee was formed at a meeting in the library of the Moorgate Mission House, with Samuel Cox as secretary and Sir Morton Peto as treasurer. But Spurgeon stood aloof from the celebrations.

Hinton was also no doubt aware of some of the difficulties that were facing American Baptists. Those linked in the Southern Convention were embarrassed by the rise of what was called "Landmarkism". The movement was based on the view that the only true New Testament churches were Baptist churches, all others being mere human societies. The only validly ordained gospel ministers were therefore Baptist ministers. They ought not ever to preach in other pulpits, it was urged, nor ought ministers of other denominations to preach in Baptist pulpits. "Non-affiliation in pulpit ministry" or "non-pulpit affiliation" became a popular slogan. Many Baptists in the Southern States also rejected what was called "alien immersion", that is, baptism on profession of faith performed by a minister who had not himself been baptized as a believer. Some Baptists were taking up an anti-convention and anti-board attitude. The only activities they would recognize were those undertaken directly by the local church. The Southern Convention avoided making any particular view on these matters a test of fellowship, but they could not but hinder and weaken its work.

As events proved, Hinton had served the denomination in this country better than he knew. He had held together the Union during years of rapid change in all spheres of life. But if it was to serve the growing number of Baptist churches and the needs of the new age that had come to birth it needed further reorganization. That task Hinton knew he must leave to others. A word of caution was, he felt, necessary.

Chapter 5

REORGANIZATION AND PROGRESS, 1864-76

I

HINTON's address, from which quotations were given in the previous chapter, was delivered from the chair of the Baptist Union fifty years after the first annual assembly in the Carter Lane vestry. Much had happened between 1813 and 1863, but it is clear that Hinton would not have favoured any elaborate jubilee celebrations of the kind which the Baptist Missionary Society had arranged in 1842. Hinton was troubled and disappointed. He had succeeded in keeping the Union in being, but he feared for its future if too big a strain was put upon it, and not without reason. Of the thirty-seven Baptist Associations, only thirteen contributed to the funds of the Union in 1863. These Associations comprised in all 1,270 churches, only sixty of which sent a subscription to the Union. There were fifteen personal subscriptions, none of them large. The total income of the Union for 1863 was exactly £90 and the audited accounts showed a deficit of £49.[1]

Taken alone, however, these figures would give a quite misleading picture of the denominational situation, and of the growing strength and community sense which were to provide the basis of the progress made in the immediately succeeding decades.

Of the thirty-seven Associations the largest was the General Baptist Association with 147 churches scattered in various parts of the country. The Associations of Particular Baptist churches were county or regional bodies. The largest was that of Glamorganshire with 109 churches. Next to this came the Carmarthen and Cardiganshire Association with 76 churches. The London

---

[1] The Congregational Union had in 1848 abandoned an attempt at a fixed subscription. Its income in 1859 was £193.

Association had not yet been formed, though the ministers of
the metropolis met regularly in the Baptist Board. The total
membership of the 1,270 churches was given as 136,825, a more
than threefold increase since statistics had first been collected in
1834. Hinton had made clear, however, that many of the Particular Baptist churches were not in membership with any Association. The 1851 Census of Public Worship had revealed 366,000
people present at the most numerously attended Baptist services,
and the number must have increased substantially by 1863.

Moreover, though the Union's income was small, its relationship to the other Baptist societies was a strategic one. Its committee was the one body which united the main interests of the
denomination. In addition to the officers, there were eight official
members and thirty-one others elected annually at the suggestion of a Nomination Committee, which was instructed to secure
proper representation from the provinces. In 1836 the eight
official members were the two honorary secretaries of the Baptist
Building Fund, the two secretaries of the Baptist Missionary
Society and the secretaries of the Bible Translation Society, the
Baptist Irish Society, the Particular Baptist Fund and the General
Baptist Missionary Society. The Baptist Home Missionary
Society was at the time without a secretary. Had one been in
office, he would have been a member of the Baptist Union Com-
mittee. The main streams of corporate denominational life flowed
through these societies. The income of the Baptist Missionary
Society in 1863 was nearly £31,000, though the year closed with
a deficit of £1,200. The Translation Society received £1,800,
the Baptist Irish Society £2,500, the General Baptist Missionary
Society £4,700 (ending the year with a deficit of £1,100), the
Home Missionary Society £1,300. Mr. George Lowe was
treasurer both of the Home Missionary Society and of the Union.
The Home Missionary Society, the Irish Society and the Translation Society each had offices in the headquarters of the Baptist
Missionary Society at 33, Moorgate Street, as did the Union itself.
Of the thirty-one elected members of the committee of the Union,
eleven came from the provinces. Most of them served also on the

committees of one or more of the societies. Only three were laymen.

There were a number of other denominational agencies. A Society for Aged and Infirm Baptists, of which Dr. F. W. Gotch, of Bristol College, was secretary, assisted some twenty-seven beneficiaries with grants of £18 each, while a National Society of the same kind, formed in 1858 and directed from Birmingham, was run on the lines of a mutual benefit society and already had 142 members. The profits of *The Baptist Magazine*, of Rippon's *Selection of Hymns* and of a new Baptist hymnbook, published in 1860 and entitled *Psalms and Hymns*, were available for the widows of Baptist ministers and missionaries. The help available from these various funds was not adequate to the need, but they were evidence of a growing sense of responsibility. By 1863 *The Freeman* was in its ninth year of publication and was growing in influence. General editorial oversight was given by Dr. Joseph Angus, of Regent's Park College, much of the detailed work being done by Wm. Howie Wylie, who also assisted with *The Christian World*. The circulation of these two weekly papers did much to strengthen denominational sentiment.

The fourteen volumes of the "Bunyan Library" which appeared between 1861 and 1865 must also have had an influence of a similar kind. Issued by J. Heaton & Son, a publishing firm owned by Baptists, the series was for "the publication and republication of standard works by eminent Baptist authors". They were more popular in character than those issued a dozen years or so earlier by the Hanserd Knollys Society, though they included another edition of the Broadmead Records, and the two important volumes, *Early English Baptists*, by Dr. Benjamin Evans.[2] Volumes were devoted to the life and writings of Robert Robinson, Andrew Fuller, John Foster and the famous Welsh preacher, Christmas Evans. Missionary interests were represented by an abridgement of J. C. Marshman's *Life and Times of the Serampore*

[2] Fifty years later Champlin Burrage in *Early English Dissenters*, 1912, commended Evans as "much the ablest of the early English Baptist historical writers". He had "the mind of a true historian" and drew on documents from the Mennonite archives in Amsterdam which opened "a whole new field of research".

Missionaries and by a life of Adoniram Judson. J. H. Hinton prepared for the series an edition of *Principles and Practices of Baptist Churches* (1858) by Francis Wayland, the President of Brown University, Rhode Island, and also a History of Baptism. Taken together, the volumes represented the most comprehensive and successful single Baptist publication enterprise either before or since.

The theological colleges must also be remembered as important centres of denominational life and interest. In 1863 there were six of them. The oldest was at Bristol. In 1856 Dr. Angus had succeeded in moving Stepney College to Holford House, Regent's Park, where better use could be made of the facilities of London University and the doors could be opened to lay students. Spurgeon had established his own college for training preachers in 1856, classes being held from 1861 in the premises of the newly-built Metropolitan Tabernacle. The Northern Baptist Education Society had moved to new buildings at Rawdon, near Leeds, in 1859. There were also colleges in Haverfordwest, Pontypool and Llangollen. Plans were being made for a new College in Bury (later Manchester).[3] There was no dearth of ministerial candidates and the standard of training was improving. The instructions to students at Regent's Park College required them to be indoors by 10.30 p.m., forbade them to go to theatres and similar places of entertainment, ordered them to wear slippers in the bedroom and "as far as practicable" in their studies. The drinking of beer and wine was still customary in theological colleges, as among ministers and church members generally, though the temperance movement was beginning to gain strength.[4]

All these societies and agencies contributed to the intricate and interwoven pattern of Baptist life. The need for closer co-ordination was being increasingly felt.

So far the Baptist Union had not undertaken any special enter-

[3] The lead in this was taken by Dr. Benjamin Evans, of Scarborough, and a number of others who favoured "close communion".

[4] Though Joseph Livesey, a Baptist, and six other men of Preston signed the first total abstinence pledge in 1832, and the United Kingdom Alliance was formed in 1853, it was not until 1874 that a Baptist Total Abstinence Association came into existence.

prises of its own except the collection of statistics and other information, the fostering of relationships with Baptists overseas by correspondence and occasional visitation, and the representation of Baptist views on public questions. The Protestant Dissenting Deputies remained active in defence of the civil rights of Nonconformists and the promotion of legislation to extend those rights. The Liberation Society continued its agitation for the disestablishment of the Church of England. The Baptist Union frequently allied itself with these bodies, but the need for a more effective and independent channel for mobilizing and expressing denominational opinion was obvious. Resolutions on public questions took up an increasing amount of time when the committee of the Union met and at the annual assembly. In 1863, for example, when Hinton delivered his address, resolutions were passed about the distress caused by depression in the Lancashire cotton-trade; about the burial laws; about livings in the patronage of the Crown; and about religious tests at the Universities of Oxford and Cambridge. The last of these subjects had come to touch Baptists in a new and more personal way. They recognized the sacrifice Joseph Angus had made when, as a youth, he refused a scholarship at Cambridge because it would have involved subscription to the Thirty-nine Articles. In 1858 H. M. Bompas had been denied a Cambridge Fellowship because of his loyalty to Baptist principles, and the sons of John Aldis, the minister of the King's Road church, Reading, had begun to win a series of brilliant academic successes at Cambridge, the full fruits of which they could not enjoy. At the 1863 meeting the committee of the Union reported that during the preceding months it had protested against Bishop Colenso's attack on the Mosaic authorship of the Pentateuch and had addressed to the Baptists of the United States a letter expressing sympathy with those working for the emancipation of the slaves.

II

Hinton accompanied his chairman's address with an intima-

4*

tion that he must resign the active duties of the secretaryship of the Union. He was about to give up the pastorate at Devonshire Square. He was, however, pressed to continue in office as an honorary secretary, with Edward Steane, and did so for a further three years. The Union decided to appoint an Acting-Secretary at a salary of £50 a year.

The choice fell on James Henry Millard, B.A., then forty-four years of age. A Baptist minister, like his father before him, Millard had been trained at Stepney College. From 1844 to 1858, he had been pastor of the church in Huntingdon. Then for five years he ministered to the Maze Pond church in London. Early in 1863 he had been persuaded to return to Huntingdon. For the next dozen years or so, Millard was the key figure in the affairs of the Union, although throughout that period, and indeed beyond it, Edward Steane remained in office as honorary secretary.

Millard's influence was quickly felt. Writing in 1869, J. M. Cramp, after paying tribute to all that Hinton had done, continued: "But it is to the zeal and perseverance of the junior secretary, the Rev. J. H. Millard, that the Union is indebted for much of its new and more vigorous life".[5] When Millard died in 1883, it was said:

"To his care and zeal the Union owes no small amount of the success which has distinguished its labours in recent years; and if it is now a power amongst us, it owes no inconsiderable part of its influence to his courtesy and wisdom."[6]

He proved himself the right man for years of transition, successfully directing changes which transformed the older, rather nebulous organization into a far more effective and powerful denominational agency.

It was clear when Millard was appointed that changes were necessary. A forward move was overdue, but the difficulties

[5] *Baptist History*, pp. 478–9. The publication of this book was an important denominational event. Cramp (1796–1881) was one of the first students at Stepney College and became President, first of a Baptist College in Montreal and then of Acadia College (now University), Nova Scotia. He presented the Baptist story "from the foundation of the Christian Church".

[6] *Baptist Handbook*, 1884.

which Hinton had indicated showed that care and discretion would be required. Steane's health was failing and, though remaining honorary pastor of the Camberwell Church, he had decided to move out to Rickmansworth. He offered his valuable library to the Union. This was a munificent gift. Plans were at once made to form under the auspices of the Union "a depository and complete collection of all documentary and historical works relating to the Baptist denomination". The project could count on the support of E. B. Underhill, one of the secretaries of the Baptist Missionary Society, in whose headquarters the collection had to be housed, for, as already noted, he had himself a keen interest in Baptist history. It was not, however, easy for a secretary of the Union, resident in Huntingdon, to supervise such an enterprise and there was also competition from private collectors, chief among them Joseph Angus, who was building up the library of Regent's Park College as well as his remarkable personal collection of books and documentary material.

It was along other lines that the most effective advance was made. At the time of Millard's appointment, suggestions were put forward for a more adequate Ministerial Provident Society and the committee was instructed to publish papers on this matter. It was also proposed that an autumn session of the Union should be held in the provinces. Another significant resolution, passed unanimously, was as follows:

"That the attention of the Committee be called to the list of Baptist ministers who are accredited members of the Union; and that they be requested to consider whether any alteration in the principles on which their names are inserted in the list, or removed from it, can be made with a view to the increased efficiency of the Union."

Hardly less important, in view of these indications that new and enlarged activities were in prospect, was the resolution:

"That in view of the present state of the finances of the Union, the Session recognizes the necessity of more *general and systematic* contributions from the churches throughout the denomination, and trusts that the increasing activity and efficiency of the Union will stimulate the liberality of the wealthier brethren in particular, so that no deficiency of Funds shall hereafter be experienced."

When the annual meetings of the Union were held in the library at Moorgate Street a year later—in April 1864—it was clear that a new chapter had begun. Seven additional Associations had joined the Union during the preceding months. One hundred and forty-five churches had contributed to the funds, instead of only sixty, and the personal subscribers numbered more than fifty. It proved possible that year to implement the suggestion that an autumn session be held, and in October between three and four hundred ministers and delegates met in Cannon Street Chapel, Birmingham. At the close of the business, what was described as an "experimental meeting" was held in the Wycliffe church. The chairman of the Union for the year was the forthright James Phillippo Mursell, of Leicester. In his address in Birmingham he set forth what he thought should be the immediate aims of the Union:

"The raising of funds for the erection of meeting-houses in populous and necessitous districts; the supercession, on practicable, sound and safe principles of the distinction between General and Particular Baptists,[7] the removal of all national and ecclesiastical exactions from education, which in the hands of a great party is worked adversely to the principles and interest of Dissent; and the establishment of a denominational fund for the relief of the widows of ministers and of superannuated labourers."

These matters became, in effect, the main planks in the Union's programme, though some of them were not carried to a successful issue for more than a generation.

At the close of 1864 the Baptist Irish Society, like the Home Missionary Society, found itself without a permanent secretary. At the annual meetings the following spring it was agreed that

[7] Dr. Thomas Thomas, of Pontypool, speaking from the chair of the Union in 1872, quoted these words of Mursell's, and regretted that more had not been done to carry them out. "Our communion is becoming closer and more frequent. Not only are members of churches freely transferred from one section to the other, but brethren, if eligible for office in other respects, are, irrespective of sentiment, elected to be deacons in the churches to which they are transferred. Further still, General Baptist Churches are quite accustomed to choose Particular Baptist pastors; and a proportionate, but not an equal, number of General Baptist pastors are settled over Particular Baptist Churches."

the two societies should unite under the name "The British and Irish Baptist Home Mission". The object of the new organization was to be "the diffusion of the Gospel of Christ in Great Britain and Ireland". The amalgamation was a wise step in the co-ordination of denominational effort. For the next nine years the Rev. Charles Kirtland, who had been deeply stirred by the Ulster revival of 1859, proved an energetic secretary. Much good work was done through grants to men engaged in itinerant preaching and church extension, and it was later recognized that Kirtland's service made the subsequent transfer of the control of the enterprise to the Baptist Union itself "comparatively easy".

III

These were promising and important developments. But the Baptist figure in the limelight on a stage much larger than a merely denominational one was C. H. Spurgeon. After ten years in London, he was the best known and most influential evangelical preacher of the day and regularly drew congregations of several thousand people not only to the Metropolitan Tabernacle but wherever he went. Spurgeon had his own college. He was about to start an orphanage. Even those Baptists whose methods were more staid than his and whose preaching was on different lines, recognized that, though still only thirty years of age, Spurgeon was giving the whole denomination a fame it had not enjoyed since the days of Robert Hall and William Carey.

In 1864 Spurgeon touched off a public controversy which had widespread repercussions and considerable influence on ecclesiastical relationships. The way in which Nonconformists had celebrated the bicentenary of the Great Ejection of 1662 had caused some cooling off of the close friendship which had marked evangelicals, whether Anglicans or Dissenters, in the early decades of the century. In a sermon on Mark xvi. 15–16, afterwards widely circulated in print, Spurgeon attacked the doctrine of baptismal regeneration. The vigour of his strictures on the Church of England caused distress, not only to evangelical Anglicans like

Lord Shaftesbury, but to the former Anglican, Baptist Noel, and to not a few of Spurgeon's close friends and admirers. It became necessary for him to withdraw for a time from the already weakened Evangelical Alliance. William Landels and a number of other Baptist leaders supported Spurgeon and the controversy, which occupied many months, served to focus attention on the denomination. It also tended, as *The Freeman* put it, to make Spurgeon "the head of a denomination *within* a denomination",[8] and set the young preacher on a course which nearly caused the disruption of the Union some twenty years later. Spurgeon became a challenging personal force on the fringe rather than in the centre of the life of the Union, though at the time in no way hostile to it.

Spurgeon did not often deal with public affairs in his sermons, but throughout his life he identified himself with the Liberation Society. Speaking under its auspices in 1866, he urged the friends of voluntaryism not to be afraid of being called "political Dissenters". Following the appointment of J. Carvell Williams as chairman of its parliamentary committee, the fortunes of the Liberation Society seemed to be reviving. Gladstone had committed himself to the disestablishment of the Irish Church, and the number of Nonconformists in Parliament was increasing. Spurgeon allowed the annual meetings of the Society to be held at the Metropolitan Tabernacle and, even if he did not himself attend, sent messages of support. John Bright, Joseph Chamberlain and, in later years, Asquith, Campbell Bannerman and Lloyd George, were present at meetings of this kind.

Of far greater importance from the denominational point of view was the fact that in 1865 Spurgeon joined with William Brock, of Bloomsbury, and William Landels, of Regent's Park Chapel, in the formation of a new London Baptist Association. Reporting on the inaugural meeting, at which Spurgeon presided, *The Freeman* declared:

"The brethren assembled represented wellnigh every shade of opinion

[8] 1865. Quoted by Fullerton, *C. H. Spurgeon*, 1920, p. 308.

amongst us, although, if any party predominated, we should say it was that of our Strict Communion brethren. Still, it was most apparent that the ruling wish of all present was to give as little place as possible to differences of opinion, and rather to find the common basis on which they could practically agree. We are thankful, too, that the basis of this new Association is so broad. It does not rest in a creed, but simply with wide basis of evangelical sentiment."[9]

This was the spirit which animated J. H. Millard as he strengthened the Union itself. The chairmen—or Presidents, as they came to be called—of the ensuing years were successively Joseph Angus, John Aldis, the Hon. Baptist Noel, F. W. Gotch, of Bristol College, William Brock, William Robinson, of Cambridge, C. M. Birrell, of Liverpool, Thomas Thomas, of Pontypool, E. B. Underhill, Charles Stovel, Alexander MᶜLaren, of Manchester, and, in 1876, William Landels—a wide variety of men from different parts of the country, all of them occupying important positions. Their willingness to serve enhanced the standing of the Union and their presidential addresses received increasing attention.

The meetings held in London in the spring could no longer be accommodated in the Moorgate Street building. In 1866 Upton Chapel, Lambeth, was used and for the next four years the Baptist chapels in John Street and in Walworth Road. The Baptist Missionary Society decided to sell the Moorgate Street property and while new and spacious headquarters were being built in Castle Street (later Furnival Street), Holborn, found temporary accommodation in John Street. From 1871 onwards, for several years the Union held its annual assembly in the library of the new Mission House.[10] In 1875 the Bloomsbury Church became for the first time the scene of the meetings. This was to be the main meeting-place for over fifty years, save for certain special sessions held jointly with the Congregationalists in 1886, 1888 and 1901.

[9] Quoted by Fullerton, op. cit., p. 309, but there were a number of Strict Baptist churches which were not prepared to join the London Baptist Association; these formed themselves on 10th March 1871 into the Metropolitan Association of Strict Baptist Churches—a body not linked in any way with the Baptist Union. Twenty-seven churches, with an estimated membership of 7,000, formed the Association.

[10] The writer's grandfather was again Minute Secretary in 1871. The Memorial Hall, Farringdon Street, was built by the Congregational Union in 1873–5.

The increasing attendance which necessitated these changes was an evidence of the success attending Millard's efforts to strengthen the Union. From 1864 autumn sessions in the provinces were held regularly, the towns chosen after Birmingham being Bradford, Liverpool, Cardiff, Bristol, Leicester, Cambridge, Northampton, Manchester, Nottingham, Newcastle-on-Tyne, Plymouth and then Birmingham once more. Slowly but surely the Union was making itself known in all parts of the country and gathering to itself fresh support. "The isolation which has so long characterized our body is fast yielding to a genial growth of Christian love," said the editor of *The Baptist Magazine*. "The annual meetings in London never fully accomplished this; but these autumnal meetings are diffusing through our churches a spirit of brotherly affection."[11] Each year additions to the membership figures were reported. In 1874 the number of Baptist churches was given in the *Handbook* as 2,606 (1,946 in England, 528 in Wales, 96 in Scotland, and 36 in Ireland) and the total number of members as 244,416. "During this decade," say Skeats and Miall, "the Baptist denomination . . . steadily increased in numbers and influence, partly owing to the popularity of Mr. Spurgeon, partly to the growing strength of the Baptist Union of Great Britain and Ireland, and indirectly to the great success of the Baptist Missionary Society."[12]

IV

The events of "Black Friday", 11th May 1866, when Messrs. Peto and Betts (with which Sir Morton Peto was associated) and a number of other firms had to go into voluntary liquidation, left little mark on the increasing prosperity of the Baptist denomination. Nor was its position harmed by the public controversy—in which E. B. Underhill was involved—following the savage measures taken by Governor Eyre to suppress an outbreak of

---

[11] *Baptist Magazine*, November 1868, p. 689. The meetings in Bristol that year were particularly successful, being attended by 650 delegates.

[12] Op. cit., p. 605.

violence at Morant Bay, Jamaica. Nonconformity was a growing power in the life of the nation. New opportunities of influence came as a result of the Second Reform Bill, that of 1867, which gave household suffrage in the boroughs. Dissenters were ranged almost solidly behind the Liberal Party and helped to carry Gladstone to power in 1868. Gladstone's first and greatest ministry was in office from 1868 to 1874 and put through an important series of reforms, many of which concerned Nonconformists very closely. The abolition of Church Rates in 1868 brought to an end one of their chief grievances.

Of even greater significance, however, was the Education Act of 1870, which provided for the first time a national system of primary schools, and was followed by the abolition of religious tests at Oxford and Cambridge. Nonconformist opinion had changed. A few years earlier it had vigorously opposed any state intervention in education, largely because this appeared to involve its control by the Anglican Church.[13] Now, however, the need for state aid was recognized, but full public control was demanded. Many of the provisions of Forster's Education Act were regarded as unacceptable, particularly those dealing with denominational schools, and R. W. Dale, of Birmingham, led a campaign against them. But the setting up of local School Boards gave Nonconformists many new opportunities of public service. The effect of the opening of the Universities was not to be felt fully for a generation or more, but it registered an important step towards civil and religious equality in Britain.

The eighteen-seventies were important years in the development of Trade Unions and Co-operative Societies and in both of these movements Nonconformists played a part, though their communities belonged on the whole to the middle classes.

The growing strength of the Baptist churches was seen in several directions. In 1866 it was decided to form a separate Union for the churches of Wales and the Welsh-speaking churches of Monmouthshire. While maintaining close links with

---

[13] This had been the basis of the proposals of Brougham in 1820 and of Sir John Graham in 1843. See B. L. Manning, *The Protestant Dissenting Deputies*, 1952, pp. 333 f.

the Baptist Union of Great Britain and Ireland, the new Union was able to care for the needs of the Welsh churches, whether Welsh or English-speaking, in a way that could not be done effectively from London. In 1857 a Monmouthshire English Baptist Association had been formed of churches which were the result of the large influx of English people into the county. This Association adhered to the Baptist Union of Great Britain and Ireland and encouraged the individual churches to join. Many of these came to practise open communion, whereas the churches of the older Monmouthshire Baptist Association, and most of those of Wales, maintained close communion.

In 1869 a Baptist Union of Scotland came into existence. A Scotch Baptist Association, mainly of Highland churches, had been formed as early as 1835 and in 1842 had changed its name to the Baptist Union of Scotland, but the larger churches held aloof. In 1852 it became no more than an association of individuals and four years later lapsed altogether. The revived Union grew out of a Baptist Association for the Education of Young Men for the Ministry and consisted at its formation of fifty-one churches with 3,500 members. It was agreed in 1872 that the Welsh and Scottish Unions should be recognized as affiliated to the Baptist Union of Great Britain and Ireland. There were also a number of changes in the English Associations, the boundaries of several of them being re-drawn. Buckinghamshire churches formed a separate Association in 1867, while two years later those of Essex formed an Association in place of the Essex Baptist Union, which had lapsed in 1864 after a somewhat chequered existence of nearly seventy years.

A change in the treasurership occurred in 1869 following the death of the "zealous and liberal" George Lowe, F.R.S., who for twenty years had cared for the Union's slender finances. John Sands was appointed in his place. There was general agreement that the Baptist Union must undertake responsibility for nation-wide schemes to aid ministers and their dependants. In 1866 John Aldis and Joseph Angus suggested that every minister whose ministerial income was over £150 a year should voluntarily contribute 10 per cent of the excess to augment the salaries of his poorer brethren. William Landels and others contended that such a scheme must be combined with a stricter control of entrants to the ministry.[14] Nevertheless, in 1870, an Augmentation Fund was started on a voluntary and independent basis, help being gathered from various sources by a strong committee, and a few years later the Union itself undertook to sponsor the appeal and administer the scheme.

William Landels was an influential figure in Union affairs throughout Millard's secretaryship. By birth a Scotsman, and with considerable gifts as a preacher and speaker, he had come to London in 1855 after pastorates in Cupar and Birmingham. At Regent's Park Chapel he ministered to a large and prosperous congregation. His chairmanship of the Union in 1876 coincided with the launching of an appeal for a denominational Annuity Fund for ministers. Several of the Associations had Provident and Annuity Funds of their own, but the benefits that could be offered were not large and the increasing movement of ministers from one part of the country to another made the administration of the funds difficult. Landels threw himself enthusiastically into the campaign already initiated by C. M. Birrell, Alexander McLaren and Charles Williams, of Accrington, an important group of northern Baptist leaders. By the close of Landel's year of office £52,000 had been promised towards the capital sum required, nearly £9,000 being contributed by Lancashire and Cheshire Baptists.

Landels is said to have made the Union "the centre of a real brotherhood", particularly through his work for the Annuity Fund. He was later described as one of those who "brought the Baptist Union out of obscurity and placed it in a position from which to make its voice heard".[15] Nevertheless, in spite of the

---

[14] See T. D. Landels, *William Landels, D.D.*, 1900, pp. 200 f. In 1869 a speech by Landels advocating a period of probation on the field before marriage for young missionaries caused sharp controversy, but the proposal was shortly afterwards adopted by the Missionary Society. With the sending to China of Timothy Richard in 1869 a new chapter in Baptist missionary history was about to begin.

[15] Charles Williams, quoted in *William Landels, D.D.*, p. 336, by T. D. Landels.

progress that was being made, the general income of the Union in 1874 was still no more than £352. Many of the leaders in the north of England were becoming somewhat restive, though they had to admit that the churches of Lancashire and Cheshire had contributed only £24 to the Union, while giving £2,312 to the Missionary Society. Words uttered from the chair by Alexander McLaren in 1875 represented a growing dissatisfaction with the existing situation:

> "I trust (he said) that we may do something at these meetings to make this Baptist Union more of a power. Hitherto it has done little. We might address it with Wordsworth's question to the cuckoo—
>
> *Shall I call thee bird,*
> *or but a wandering voice?*
>
> But I for one hope these days are over, and that real work will increasingly mark its meetings."

McLaren pleaded for a bolder strategy, particularly in parts of the country where Baptist witness was weak. He urged the need for an Augmentation Fund which would provide a minimum ministerial stipend of £120 a year and for other nation-wide developments. But if these things were to be accomplished, the machinery of the Union had to become more representative and democratic. The constitution needed re-examination. Of this many had been conscious for some years.

A period of considerable outward progress had, however, coincided with one of much intellectual and spiritual questioning. Baptists were probably slower than those in some other Churches to open their minds to the new critical study of the Biblical documents. They shared the widespread reluctance shown by avowed Christians to accept the scientific theories as to the origin of man put forward by Charles Darwin. When in 1866 there appeared anonymously a study of Christ which attempted to make Him comprehensible as an historical character—the famous *Ecce Homo*—Lord Shaftesbury described it as "the most pestilential book that has ever been vomited forth from the jaws of hell". Few of those who regarded themselves as evangelicals were at the time ready to welcome Seeley's approach. On the other hand, it was some time before they were ready to approve the American evangelists, Moody and Sankey, who paid their first visit to England in 1873.[16] The increase in ritualistic practices in the Church of England caused general concern. It was hoped, however, that the Public Worship Regulation Act, promoted in 1874 by Archbishop Tait and strengthened through the efforts of Lord Shaftesbury, would check what were regarded as dangerous Romeward tendencies.

The years of Millard's secretaryship of the Baptist Union were the years when the keener minds were debating the essays of Matthew Arnold and R. W. Emerson, the one condescending, if not contemptuous, towards Nonconformity, the other the reverse. John Stuart Mill and John Ruskin were among the writers with a large following. Robert Browning exercised an influence over Nonconformists which Silvester Horne thought greater than that of either Dale or Spurgeon.[17] Women's suffrage and Socialism began to be talked of by a few daring spirits. Among the students in the theological colleges and the younger ministers there were many who felt dissatisfied with the older and more rigid theological formulae, particularly those relating to eternal punishment.

A Baptist minister who was attracting much attention was John Clifford. As well as being of radical social and political sympathies, he was clearly influenced by newer ways of thought in religion. Clifford, a General Baptist from the Midlands, was only two years younger than Spurgeon and had come to London in 1858. While attracting growing congregations to his church in Praed Street, Paddington, he achieved a remarkable series of successes at London University. In the ensuing years, Clifford and Spurgeon were to be the outstanding representatives of two trends within the denomination, the one liberal, the other

[16] Among the most outspoken critics were Strict Baptists like J. K. Popham (1847–1937), then minister in Liverpool. F. B. Meyer, then in York, was one of the first Baptist ministers to befriend Moody and Sankey. Trained at Regent's Park College, Meyer had served for a time as assistant to C. M. Birrell in Liverpool.

[17] *Popular History of the Free Churches*, 1903, p. 421.

conservative, yet both claiming and rightly claiming that they were evangelical.

V

At the autumn meetings of the Union in Northampton in 1871, a proposal by S. R. Pattison for setting up a standing Arbitration Committee to deal with disputes "cognizable by law within or respecting any Church in the Baptist Union" was approved. On the same occasion the question of the revision of the Constitution was first broached publicly. One of the younger ministers, T. Vincent Tymms, who had recently become pastor of a new and promising church in a growing district in North London, moved that the matter be studied by a committee consisting of Charles Stovel, Jesse Hobson and Upton Davies, and this was agreed.

Stovel was by then one of the veterans of the denomination and a formidable personality. For nearly forty years he had ministered to London's oldest Baptist church. The Union, the Missionary Society, the Particular Baptist Fund and the Building Fund had all had his steady and influential support. The stream of pamphlets and articles which came from his pen had helped to make him a well-known public figure. "With him," said Joseph Angus, "all questions were momentous; every field of conflict was a Thermopylae; every struggle was for life." In politics and religion Stovel was a staunch nineteenth-century independent. He linked the committee with the reorganization of the Union in 1831–2. The other members were younger men. Jesse Hobson was a grand-nephew of William Carey and for a time combined with a London pastorate the secretaryship of the Star Life Assurance Company.

Their report came before the spring assembly of 1873, when E. B. Underhill was in the chair. There was general agreement that the Union should in future be known as the Baptist Union of Great Britain and Ireland. The other proposals provoked considerable discussion and a special meeting was called to consider them on 10th July 1873. According to *The Freeman*, not a large number of ministers and delegates attended, but those who did were fairly representative of the different opinions and practices in the Union. The area of discussion had been enlarging. The British and Irish Home Mission had been finding its work increasingly difficult, in spite of Charles Kirtland's efforts. Clearly the needs of the new and rapidly-growing centres of population in England were not being met. There were sixteen towns with a population of over 15,000 which, according to the Handbook, had no Baptist church, forty towns with a population of over 10,000 and 183 towns with a population of over 4,000. A bolder plan for denominational extension was needed.

The Freeman, however, was advocating a full and frank report about chapel debts. "Zeal without knowledge is loading our denomination with buildings disproportioned both to our needs and our resources," it declared. A partial return from London had been obtained a few years earlier and this showed that every church member was having to pay an average of two shillings per annum in interest alone. "If the burden falls in equal proportion upon the denomination at large, we are devoting every year more than the general receipts of the foreign mission to interest on mortgages and notes of hand." The Building Fund had only some £20,000 available for loan purposes.

Church extension could not be satisfactorily tackled unless the denominational organization was strengthened. The closer linking of the British and Irish Home Mission with the Union found general favour, but there were difficulties in the way of carrying it into effect immediately. The changes agreed upon in 1873 concerned the basis of the Union and the composition of the assembly and the committee.

The alteration of the basis is said to have been due mainly to the insistence of Charles Stovel. The reference to "evangelical sentiments" was removed and in its place there was substituted this Declaration of Principle:

"In this Union it is fully recognized that every separate church has liberty to interpret and administer the laws of Christ, and that the immersion of believers is the only Christian baptism."

The dropping of the older phrase caused regrets in certain

quarters and awakened suspicions which, fourteen years later, at the time of the Down Grade controversy, bore unfortunate fruit. On the other hand, by 1873 the phrase had become ambiguous and was liable to misrepresentation and misuse. The new formula was felt to safeguard the independence of the churches against anything approaching synodal action on the part of the Union. By removing any attempt at a credal definition, the fellowship of "strict" and "open communion" churches was maintained, as well as making easier that between those with Calvinistic and Arminian trust deeds. The objects of the Union were at the same time extended in their range by a reference to co-operation with other Christian communities. A formal declaration against the Union of Church and State was also added.[18]

The Union was to remain a union of churches, but the colleges, Associations and certain other institutions were given a recognized place in its membership. The Assembly was made to consist of three distinct classes of persons—representative, personal and honorary. The ministers of churches in membership with the Union were made *ex officio* members of the Assembly, together with the heads and tutors of affiliated colleges. Churches, associations and recognized societies were given the opportunity of sending representatives in addition, the number being based on their size. The proposal to institute *personal* membership of the Union was keenly contested at the special session in July, 1873. But, said *The Freeman*, "the fact that such had long been informally permitted by the Executive and would be carefully controlled by the committee, secured its hearty adoption". There had been personal members of the Congregational Union since 1864.

It was proposed that cards be issued to those entitled to attend

[18] The change in the Basis of the Baptist Union should be compared with what happened in the Congregational Union in 1877-8. At the autumn meetings in Leicester in 1877 an "unofficial" conference took place under the leadership of J. Allanson Picton, a man of decidedly "liberal" theological views. There were protests at what had taken place and at the Assembly in 1878, in spite of the objections of the Chairman, Baldwin Brown, the delegates affirmed the loyalty of Congregationalists to "Evangelical Religion" and referred to the 1833 "Declaration of Faith and Order". Spurgeon, writing to Henry Allon, expressed his satisfaction at what had been done. See Albert Peel, *These Hundred Years*, pp. 271-2.

the Assembly. This, it was believed, would have the effect of relegating to the spectators' gallery "a large number of loose materials—'neither flesh, fish, fowl, nor good red herring' ". Honorary members were to be elected by ballot on the proposal of the committee. This committee also was in future to be elected by ballot and a record of the attendance of members placed annually before the Assembly. A minimum subscription of half a crown was agreed upon.

The new proposals were not without their anomalies. They were, however, an attempt to deal with a changing situation and a move towards a more truly representative organization. One of the younger ministers from Bristol, Richard Glover, urged a much more comprehensive and fundamental reorganization of the structure of denominational life. Before leaving Scotland, Glover had taken a leading part in the formation of the new Baptist Union in that country. In an address at the autumn meetings in Newcastle in 1874 he put forward "A Plea for the Union of our Leading Societies", urging that the Baptist Missionary Society as well as the British and Irish Home Mission should be fully united with the Baptist Union in the interests of denominational extension at home and abroad. His paper was delivered "with great spirit" and the discussion that followed was "decidedly animated". To most of his hearers, particularly the older ones, the suggestion appeared far too revolutionary. A new relationship between the Home Mission and the Union might be necessary and desirable, though even this was not to be accomplished easily. The Missionary Society was a strong and well-organized body with increasing commitments in India and China and a growing interest in Africa. Its leaders were inclined to look rather condescendingly on a sister organization, which still needed no more than a few rooms in the new Mission House as its offices and whose secretary lived in Huntingdon. Thirty years later, however, Richard Glover reaffirmed his belief in the proposals he made in 1874, and it is at least arguable that the adoption at that time of a more comprehensive scheme would have been in the best interests of all concerned.

A further attempt to bring the colleges closer together had also ended in failure. A plea put forward by Dr. S. G. Green at the spring assembly in 1871 was referred to a special committee, which reported to the autumn assembly in Manchester in 1872.

"From the replies received, it appears that the officers of several of these Institutions do not consider that the time has yet come for the introduction of any scheme of united action which shall embrace all the Colleges of the Denomination . . . The replies, however, received from the Officers of the Colleges at Bristol, Rawdon and Regent's Park, lead your Committee to believe that it would be possible for these three Colleges to agree upon a course of combined action which would materially increase the efficiency of their work."

A scheme was therefore drawn up and the three Colleges referred to were recommended to appoint a representative Board to carry it out. Nothing further appears to have resulted, however.

The reorganization of the basis and machinery of the Union in 1873 was, however, an important step forward. Slowly but surely the Union was—as Millard's successor put it—"reducing the disjointed parts of our denomination to unity of feeling, and a sense of common interest".[19] Millard himself had played a notable part in preparing the way for the changes. He continued in office while they were put into effect. But stronger leadership in London was clearly needed. A general quickening of the religious *tempo* was observable in many quarters. Of this the response secured by Moody and Sankey at their meetings in 1875 was but one indication. "This is a solemn time to live in," said a Baptist observer at the time; "every church seems to be up and at work." Spurgeon, writing of the meetings of the Baptist Union, said: "The numbers attending, and the harmony exhibited, appear to increase every year."[20]

[19] *Handbook*, 1879, p. 29.
[20] *Sword and Trowel*, 1875, p. 292.

CHAPTER 6

SUNSHINE AND CLOUD, 1877–87

I

IN order to smooth the way for the closer linking of the British and Irish Home Mission with the Baptist Union, J. H. Millard held both secretaryships for a few months and then resigned that of the Union. Samuel Harris Booth was appointed to succeed him and was destined to serve the Union—with an early and comparatively short break—for the ensuing twenty-one years.

Booth was described by Dr. Richard Glover as "one of the best men ever made by grace and nature in happy combination" and as "an admirable man of business". He had need of all his gifts, for he had to steer the Union through a period of rapid change in public affairs and in the religious temper and outlook of most of the population of Britain. It was he who was in office at the most critical moment in the history of the Union, when in the course of the Down Grade controversy Spurgeon withdrew from its fellowship. That the Union was not then shipwrecked was probably due as much to Booth as to any other single individual. Before he resigned, a decade later, in 1898, he had supervised the negotiations which resulted in the complete union of the General Baptist organizations with those of the Baptist Union and the Baptist Missionary Society, thus bringing to completion a process begun in 1832 and actively advocated by many from 1863 onwards. Throughout Booth's secretaryship the Union, like the denomination as a whole, steadily grew in strength and influence.

Booth was a Londoner by birth, brought up in association with the St. Albans church and trained at Stepney College. He had twice held pastorates in Birkenhead and had gained valuable experience as the secretary of the Lancashire and Cheshire

Association and as the organizer of the autumn meetings of the Union in Liverpool in 1866. Shortly after these meetings he moved to London as the first minister of a new church in Holloway Road, sponsored by the recently-formed London Baptist Association. After eight successful years there, he became pastor at Roehampton, Wandsworth, resigning that pastorate in 1877 on his appointment by the Baptist Union and thus becoming at the age of fifty-three the first full-time secretary. Whether or not Booth then envisaged only a short term of office during a transitional period, which might prove difficult, is not clear. At any rate, a little more than two years after his appointment he presented his resignation and it was accepted. The negotiations between the Union and the Home Mission Society had not been proceeding altogether smoothly.

For several months the secretariat of the Union was placed in the hands of a commission consisting of C. M. Birrell, J. P. Chown and Dr. Landels. They had first to find a new treasurer for the Union. John Sands, senior deacon of the Highbury Hill church, who had held this office since 1869, had died in November 1878. Sands had been widely respected for his serenity and generosity, as a simple verse composed by W. Poole Balfern testifies:

> *Always the same to friend or foe*
> *Kind, gentle to the end;*
> *His joy to soften human woe*
> *A true and Christ-like friend.*

In his place S. R. Pattison, who had for some years been legal adviser to the Union, was appointed. Then, as successor to Booth, William Sampson was chosen. "There was required a clear head and conciliatory manner, and much patience and attention to multiplicity of details, and power of exposition of principles, and public spirit."[1] These qualities William Sampson seemed clearly to possess.

A Bristol man, brought up at the historic King Street church, with accountancy experience and College training, he had served

[1] *Handbook*, 1883, p. 275.

for ten years in India and had acquitted himself well when called upon unexpectedly to undertake responsibilities at Serampore College. Ill health prevented Sampson's serving abroad again, but after he had spent a few years as pastor of a new church at Folkestone, he was sent by the Baptist Missionary Society on a special deputation to North India in company with John Aldis. Sampson's appointment to the joint-secretaryship of the Union and the British and Irish Home Mission would have the advantage, it was hoped, of drawing the Missionary Society also into closer contact with the Union. But in little more than twelve months the new secretary had overtaxed his strength and his health gave way. Booth gallantly came to the rescue and resumed the direction of affairs, assisted for a time by the Rev. T. G. Atkinson, who had rendered useful pastoral service in North London. There seemed good prospect that Sampson would recover, but while recuperating in North Wales, he died suddenly on 11th November 1882. At its next meeting the Council of the Union paid tribute to "the zeal, the courtesy and the ability" with which Sampson had begun his duties and without hesitation asked Booth to accept office again. This he agreed to do.

A few months earlier the aged Edward Steane had passed away. His official connection with the Union stretched back over nearly half a century and to the end he had been designated honorary secretary, though long able to take little part in affairs. In October 1883, another influential veteran, Charles Stovel, died and, on the same day, J. H. Millard. E. B. Underhill remained an important figure in the affairs of the Missionary Society, but effective control was passing into the strong hands of Alfred Henry Baynes, a layman, who had received training as a youth in the office of Sir Morton Peto.[2] A new field of missionary work was being opened up in the little-known territory of the Congo. Baptists everywhere were thrilled by the heroism of the pioneers, many of whom laid down their lives, and by the challenge of so vast and needy an area.

[2] Brief biographical sketches of both Underhill and Baynes will be found in E. A. Payne, *The Great Succession*, 1938.

George Gould, of Norwich, was President of the Union in 1879—his election had been proposed by C. H. Spurgeon—and at the autumn session, held in Glasgow, he took occasion to speak on "The Use and Disuse of Confessions of Faith" with an eye to the Presbyterian tradition so powerful in Scotland. Some remarks he made about the Baptist Union indicate how it was generally regarded at the time by one of its most faithful supporters:

"Our Union does not claim or exercise any legislative authority over the churches or individuals who constitute it. We do not pretend to meet, as the Assemblies of our Presbyterian brethren, with any right to control the action of any church, however feeble, or any association of churches. We do not claim the power to adjudicate on any question in dispute between individuals and the churches of which they are, or have been, members. We receive no appeals from the judgment of any church, nor do we confirm or annul any sentence passed by the vote of a church, or of any association. We do not profess to try cases of heresy, nor to have dominion over the faith of our brethren. We meet as a deliberative body of Christians, who, agreeing in the belief of evangelical truth, and desiring to maintain the ordinances of the Gospel as our Lord hath delivered them to us, take counsel together that we may act, as far as possible, in concert for the furtherance of the Gospel of Christ, and in promotion of the efficiency of our body through its various organizations."[3]

Three other addresses delivered to the assembly in the early years of Booth's secretaryship help to give a picture of the general denominational situation at the time. In 1884, Dr. Joseph Angus surveyed the numerical progress of the previous century. Basing himself on the information collected by John Rippon in *The Baptist Register* and on the records of the Union, he presented the following figures:

	England		Wales	
	Churches	Members	Members	Total
1789	400	20,000	5,000	25,000
1833	1,000	60,000		
1863	1,700	150,000	46,000	200,000
1883	1,900	223,000	75,000	300,000

[3] *Handbook*, 1880.

Baptists had increased at a greater rate than the population, but there were certain parts of the country where their progress was far from satisfactory. At the same time, £70,000 a year was being spent on new chapels, and in the twenty years, 1863–83, more than a million and a half had been put into new buildings. William Woods, of Nottingham, had made a careful study of the denominational structure in England and in an address delivered in 1883 pointed out that of the 1,935 churches no fewer than 525—that is, more than a quarter—were not linked with any of the existing Associations. It was, he urged, most important that the Union and the Associations come closer together. "The Union must practically become a federation of the Associations for Christian work." But, a year or so earlier, John Aldis had indicated some of the difficulties facing both the Union and the Associations:

"We all know," he said, "that church authority is at low water-mark. For these last forty years in the wilderness, the forms and meaning of ordination services and church appointments have been dying out. Individualism, independence and liberty are the idols of the day. One cause of this we cannot name without homage and thanks; 'tis the reaction from priestism. . . . But, in resisting evil, have we not overshot the mark? By dashing at tyranny, have we not rushed into anarchy?"

This was the general situation Booth had to face. His resumption of the secretaryship coincided with the successful completion of the complicated negotiations for bringing together the Union and the Home Mission, and in 1882 the Union was provided with a new Constitution. The Declaration of Principle remained in the form adopted in 1873, but to the objects of the Union the additional clause was added from the laws of the British and Irish Home Mission:

"To spread the Gospel of Christ in Great Britain and Ireland: by employing ministers and evangelists, by establishing Christian Churches, by forming Sunday Schools, by distributing the Scriptures and religious tracts, and by adopting and using such other methods as the Council shall deem advisable."

The Union became thereby itself an evangelistic agency. At the same time the former committee of the Union was transformed into a Council of 100 members, seventy of whom were to be elected at the assembly in the spring. The elected members were then to co-opt a further thirty, "having special regard to an equitable representation of the whole country, and of each of the objects of the Union". Each church affiliated to the Union was required to pay a subscription of 5s., each personal member a subscription of 10s. These changes marked an important stage in making the Union more representative of the country as a whole. Dr. Stock, of Huddersfield, tried in 1884 to secure that the election of the Vice-President take place by ballot, but this was not agreed to until some years later. The Union showed its appreciation of the way Booth had piloted all these proposals through rather stormy seas by presenting him with a fine bust of himself, which may now be seen in the library of the Baptist Church House.

II

There was a growing popular interest in public affairs and this was reflected in the resolutions submitted to the new Council and to the spring and autumn assemblies. Not long before Booth first became secretary of the Union, events in eastern Europe began to claim the attention of Britain. Disturbances in Turkey were followed, first, by the massacre of Christians in Bulgaria, and then by war between Turkey and Russia. A wave of sympathy with the oppressed Christian minorities did not prevent the British public from recognizing the unfavourable changes in the balance of power which would follow from a Russian occupation of Constantinople. By the arrangements agreed upon at the Congress of Berlin in 1878—from which Disraeli claimed that he brought back "peace with honour"—over 11,000,000 persons were freed from the Turkish yoke, but the Turk remained in Europe. Britain received Cyprus, but the general settlement left much uneasiness in British minds. In 1879, in the course of a famous journey through Midlothian, Gladstone vigorously

JAMES HENRY MILLARD, B.A.
SECRETARY OF THE UNION
1863–1877

SAMUEL HARRIS BOOTH, D.D.
SECRETARY OF THE UNION
1877–1879
1883–1898

ALEXANDER MCLAREN
B.A., D.D., Litt.D.

CHARLES HADDON SPURGEON

JOHN CLIFFORD
M.A., LL.B., B.SC., D.D.

F. B. MEYER, B.A., D.D.

attacked the foreign as well as the domestic policy of the Conservative government and, when Parliament was dissolved in 1880, the Liberals won a resounding victory.

Almost all Baptists, whether or not they had a vote, were supporters of the Liberal party. Many of the Liberals elected to the House of Commons came of a Nonconformist background. Among them was William (later Judge) Willis, a Baptist lawyer, whose fervour quickly made him a well-known figure. Not a few of the new M.P.s were pledged to press for the disestablishment of the Church of England. The Liberation Society was still active and its annual meeting was still held in the Metropolitan Tabernacle, with the support by presence or letter of C. H. Spurgeon. But in 1881 Edward Miall, for so long the leader of militant political dissenters, passed away. For some years radical politicians had been influential in the affairs of the Society and its records indicate the part played by Joseph Chamberlain, John Morley and Frederic Harrison, as well as by those more closely identified with the life of the Nonconformist churches, like Samuel Morley. The question of the separation of Church and State was not, however, to be one of the main issues of the succeeding years. Gladstone's second ministry was in office from 1880-5. It had to face a series of unexpected and difficult situations.

As soon as the new Parliament met, the long-drawn-out and undignified conflict with Charles Bradlaugh began. Elected for Northampton, he declined to take the customary oath of allegiance on the Bible and demanded the right as a free-thinker to affirm. John Bright, who was a Quaker, and many, though by no means all, Nonconformists were ready to grant Bradlaugh what he asked, but a majority of members refused to let him cithcr affirm or—as he later offered to do—swear. Not until the succeeding Parliament was he allowed to take his seat. More serious and important were the troubles in Ireland, in South Africa, in Egypt and the Sudan, the threat of war with Russia over the frontiers of Afghanistan, the heated discussions over a further extension of the franchise and the internal stresses in the cabinet itself. The star of Joseph Chamberlain was in the ascendant

5

and he began to gather to himself the hopes of the more radically-minded in the constituencies. Chamberlain was of Unitarian stock, but was a close friend of Dr. R. W. Dale, the influential Congregationalist preacher, one of the best-known Nonconformist leaders of the day. When, however, after the General Election of 1886, which again returned the Liberals to power, Gladstone introduced a bill granting Home Rule to Ireland, a substantial group, led by Chamberlain, deserted their leader. In a second General Election, Gladstone was defeated and Lord Salisbury took his place as Prime Minister.

The breach in the Liberal Party was a serious matter for Nonconformity. Writing to Gladstone in September 1877, his colleague Lord Granville had said that a great mass of people "did not care twopence about the Eastern question, country franchise, or anything else, but only Miall and Disestablishment". Disillusion was in store for them. That neither Gladstone nor Disraeli would take up the cause was one reason for the failure of the long agitation that had once or twice seemed on the verge of success; but it was only one of the reasons. The relative strength of Dissenters in Parliament was never equal to their strength in the country, because of the restriction of the franchise. At the same time the Church of England had been considerably reformed and revivified. More important, however, were the diversion of public interest from domestic and ecclesiastical matters to foreign and military affairs, and then the split in the ranks of Nonconformists and Radicals over Home Rule for Ireland.[4]

That many Baptists were closely involved in the discussions over the future of the Liberal Party—and were regarded as an influential element in the situation—is shown by the fact that in February 1887 Joseph Chamberlain, at the very time a Round Table Conference was trying to re-unite the two Liberal groups, chose *The Baptist* as the medium for a famous letter which did much to make the breach permanent. The same journal published

---

[4]Though it was not realized at the time, the formation in 1881 of the Social Democratic Federation, and in 1884 of the Fabian Society, were of great importance for later political and social developments. John Clifford was for a time a member of the Fabian Society.

a lengthy reply by Gladstone! Spurgeon was among those supporting Chamberlain against Gladstone.

Other important changes were taking place in those years, which marked the end of a period in the great Victorian age. In the early eighteen-eighties famous public figures such as George Eliot, Thomas Carlyle, Disraeli, Dean Stanley, Charles Darwin, the poet Rossetti, Dr. Pusey, the Tractarian, and Lord Shaftesbury passed away. Younger men were coming to the front. The intellectual and religious climate was subtly changing. Dr. Willis B. Glover has shown that until the eighteen-eighties the reaction of evangelical Nonconformists to a critical and historical approach to the Bible was almost entirely negative.[5] It was the ten or fifteen years from 1880 that were of major significance in determining their ultimate attitude of acceptance. The transition from older to newer views was not easy, however. The Robertson Smith case, which disturbed the Church of Scotland between 1876 and 1881, was a foreshadowing of stresses and strains within other Churches. The controversies in the Congregational Union in 1877–8 have already been referred to. Baptists avoided serious trouble until the Down Grade controversy of 1887–8. In the early eighteen-eighties storm clouds were beginning to appear on their horizon, but it was not clear when or where the storm would break.

It was in May 1881 that the Revised Version of the New Testament was first published. In its preparation, which occupied more than ten years, Anglicans and scholars of other churches co-operated. Four years later, the revision of the Old Testament appeared. Dr. Angus was one of the New Testament revisers; Dr. Benjamin Davies, of Regent's Park College, and Dr. F. W. Gotch, of Bristol Baptist College, shared in the work of the Old Testament Committee. The Baptist Union Assembly thanked them for their contribution to the new version, but not without a debate in which various views of the work were put forward. When the revisers began their labours in 1870, Dean Stanley had invited the whole company to a Communion Service in Henry

---

[5] *Evangelical Nonconformists and Higher Criticism in the Nineteenth Century*, 1954.

VII's chapel in Westminster Abbey. The presence there of Dr. E. Vance Smith, a Unitarian, caused a storm of protest. This gradually died down and the comradeship built up during the years of work together undoubtedly prepared the way for better ecclesiastical relations.

The Evangelical Alliance, in the founding of which Edward Steane and other Baptists had had so large a share, continued to unite those of whatever Church who were ready to accept its doctrinal basis, and it was in touch with Evangelicals in many other parts of the world. But the Alliance ignored the relations of Churches as such, and by the eighteen-eighties it had passed the peak of its influence, largely because its particular expression of Calvinism was no longer so widely acceptable as it had been. The Anglican Communion was becoming conscious of the need to define its attitude to other Churches, whether the Orthodox Eastern Churches, the Lutheran and Reformed Churches of the Continent, or the Free Churches of England and the United States. At a meeting in Chicago in 1886, the General Convention of the Protestant Episcopal Church drew up a list of the four things it regarded as "essential to the restoration of unity among the divided branches of Christendom". This Chicago Quadrilateral was, with minor modifications, accepted two years later by the 1888 Lambeth Conference Committee on Home Reunion as supplying "a basis on which approach may be, under God's blessing, made towards Home Reunion". It has since been known as the Lambeth Quadrilateral. The part this declaration was to play in subsequent decades was not apparent in 1886 or 1888, but its adoption and publication were significant of a new direction of interest. When in 1889 the declaration was transmitted by the Archbishop of Canterbury to the various Churches in Britain, it drew from the Baptist Union a careful reply, to which reference will be made later. The bishops of the Anglican Communion throughout the world had been meeting since 1868. In 1877 a General Presbyterian Alliance was founded to bring together all the Reformed Churches of the presbyterian order. In 1881 the first Methodist Ecumenical Conference met in London with delegates from twenty countries. The day of world confessional bodies had begun.

III

Baptists were not in the van of these new movements. They were still preoccupied with domestic problems, still on the fringe rather than in the centre of the changing intellectual and religious currents. As, however, under Booth's careful leadership, the amalgamation of the Union and the Home Mission was consolidated, new denominational problems began to emerge.

Dr. Landels was one of those who, in season and out of season, had advocated greater care in the choice and recognition of ministers. At a meeting in Leicester in 1883, the Council appointed a committee to consider whether or not a Board of Reference was desirable and practicable for advice to churches needing pastors and to pastors seeking churches. A plan drawn up by the committee and approved by the Council was submitted to the autumn Assembly in Swansea in 1885 but was referred back. Renewed consideration was given to the matter at the spring Assembly of 1887 and it was then decided to set up a Board of Introduction and Consultation, consisting of twenty members representing ten large "districts", together with the President, Vice-President and Secretary of the Union. The setting-up of this Board, which was to meet quarterly, involved a considerable increase in the correspondence to and from denominational headquarters. The procedure adopted proved somewhat cumbersome and awkward, but it prepared the way for subsequent developments in the field of the settlement, removal and recognition of ministers. If pastors and churches were to be officially introduced to one another, more scrutiny had to be given to the credentials of the former.

In 1886 the Assembly appealed to all the churches to observe a Baptist Union Sunday, when interest could be stimulated in the growing responsibilities of the Union. The most notable event that spring was, however, the joint session held by the Baptist Union and the Congregational Union in the City Temple on

14th May. The addresses delivered are of considerable interest as an indication of the mood and outlook of the time. Charles Williams, of Accrington, who was President of the Baptist Union, began by making clear that they unchurched nobody. "If," he said, " 'a congregation of faithful men', 'the members of Christ', meeting in any one place 'in His name' be a church of God, Presbyterians and Methodists can claim that their denominations are made up of such churches. For myself, I rejoice to believe that Episcopalians, who gather together in obedience to Christ, that they may hold fellowship with Him and keep His commandment, are no less and no more a church than the believers who congregate in this City Temple or in a village Baptist chapel." Both Dr. Clifford and Dr. E. R. Conder, a Congregationalist, noted and rejoiced at the spread of congregational principles and practice in other bodies. Dr. Henry Allon, of Kensington, said he put church organization simply and explicitly on the grounds of expediency. Guinness Rogers declared: "If I had my lot cast in a small place where the Baptists had a flourishing church, I would go and join the Baptist church if they would have me, and would not start a rival Congregational Church in the place." Other speakers were Dr. R. W. Dale, Dr. Culross, Dr. Angus, John Aldis and Dr. Joseph Parker. Some of the utterances were perhaps due to the exhilaration of the occasion, but they showed on the one hand the lack of serious theological and ecclesiological interest on which John Aldis had commented in 1878 and, on the other hand, the growing desire for Christian unity.

In 1887 Queen Victoria's Jubilee was celebrated. Dr. Culross and Samuel Harris Booth visited Windsor to present an Address to the Queen. The Baptist Union decided to mark the occasion with a Jubilee Fund to aid Home Missions. Within twelve months £1,773 was contributed. The condition of the village churches was exciting concern. British agriculture was passing through a period of serious decline. Large numbers were moving from the villages into the towns or were emigrating. Many village causes were in dire straits and needed assistance if a regular ministry was to be maintained. The situation also called for an increase in the number of lay preachers and their more adequate training. These matters received increasing attention from the platform of the Union. The relation of the Union to the churches and evangelistic stations in Ireland also required further consideration. In 1887 John Clifford and Charles Williams visited Ireland and reported in favour of the transfer of direction of the work across the Irish Channel, a step in accord with the sympathy many Baptists felt with the proposals for Irish Home Rule.

Two other contemporary developments deserve mention before an account is given of the crisis of 1887–8. In 1886 Andrew Martin Fairbairn moved from Spring Hill, Birmingham, to Oxford to begin the establishment of Mansfield College, the first Nonconformist theological college at one of the older universities. In the autumn of the same year, Messrs. Hodder & Stoughton launched *The British Weekly* and secured William Robertson Nicoll as editor. Fairbairn and Nicoll were convinced evangelicals of a new type, with a wide range of intellectual interest and learning. Both these developments were welcomed by many Baptists, but caused others concern. Robertson Nicoll had already become editor of the monthly theological magazine, *The Expositor*. This had been started in 1875 and had been for nine years edited by Dr. Samuel Cox, minister of the Mansfield Road Baptist Church, Nottingham. Cox was an able scholar, trained at Stepney College in the early years of Angus's Principalship. "The influence of the magazine upon religious thought in England can hardly be overestimated."[6] In *Salvator Mundi*, published in 1877, and other works, Cox had indicated his rejection of the traditional doctrine of eternal punishment in favour of what was termed the "larger hope". This was to be one of the special points at issue in the Down Grade Controversy. In 1864, in the course of the outcry over *Essays and Reviews*, Archbishop Longley stated that the eternity of the punishment of the wicked was "clearly and decidedly" held by the Church of England. Pusey and Bishop Samuel Wilberforce joined forces in supporting him, but during the succeeding twenty years the general climate of opinion changed greatly. To insist on

[6] *Dictionary of National Biography*, art. "Cox, Samuel".

endless misery as the corollary of endless blessedness seemed to
many an offence to the Christian conscience.[7] But Cox's views on
the inspiration of the Bible were also regarded by many as unsatisfactory. Though on detailed points of criticism he showed himself extremely conservative, he admitted himself impressed by
Robertson Smith's book *The Old Testament in the Jewish Church*,
which provoked widespread controversy in the early eighteen-
eighties. Cox was regarded as unorthodox and somewhat eccen-
tric in his views, though none could question his learning or his
expository skill. Spurgeon welcomed the change in the editorship
of *The Expositor*, chiefly perhaps because Nicoll rejected any idea
of the ultimate salvation of all men and vigorously asserted the
fact of inspiration. But in the succeeding years, as Willis Glover
remarks, "Nicoll certainly did far more to destroy the concept of
the Bible held by Spurgeon than Samuel Cox could ever have
done."[8] There was growing uneasiness in the theological world, in
the pulpit and in the pew. None, however, anticipated the unfortunate form in which trouble arose for the Baptist Union itself
in 1887.

[7] See Geoffrey Faber, *Jowett*, 1957, cc. XI and XII.
[8] Op. cit., p. 148.

CHAPTER 7

THE DOWN GRADE CONTROVERSY, 1887-8[1]

I

PERSONAL and theological issues were inextricably joined in the crisis which suddenly developed in 1887. "To unravel the threads is an almost impossible task," wrote J. C. Carlile in his biography of Spurgeon,[2] and his own attempt cannot be regarded as a very successful one. We possess, besides Carlile's account, one by Fullerton, who as a young man was closely associated with Spurgeon, and one by Sir James Marchant, based on a lengthy statement by John Clifford, which appears now to be lost.[3] There are some discrepancies in the three accounts, all of which suggest that the writers set down only a part of what they knew. The Down Grade controversy was, in the words of T. H. Darlow, a "lacerating dispute".[4] It cast a shadow over the Baptist denomination for more than a generation and there has been a general desire to say as little as possible about it, lest old wounds be re-opened.

Some account of it is, however, essential, for it was an important landmark in the history of the Baptist Union. Indeed, the successful surmounting of the crisis and the fact that so few followed Spurgeon in withdrawing from the Union showed that the great majority of Baptists had come to regard a national organization of their churches as essential to their well-being and the exist-

[1] This chapter is based on a more detailed unpublished account prepared by the writer, a copy of which is deposited at the Baptist Church House.
[2] *C. H. Spurgeon: An Interpretative Biography*, 1933, p. 256.
[3] W. Y. Fullerton, *C. H. Spurgeon*, 1920; James Marchant, *Dr. John Clifford*, 1924.
[4] *William Robertson Nicoll*, 1925, p. 84. Cp. S. Pearce Carey, *The Story of Stockton Baptists*, 1941, p. 49: "It was a torturing time. All our nerves were frayed. We were all partisans, and ranged in contrary camps; none of us really fair to one another: all of us abnormal and unhappy."

ing Union as adequately safeguarding the concern all had for the essentials of the faith. Instead of relying solely upon the accounts provided by Fullerton, Marchant and Carlile, it seems better to follow the course of events from contemporary records, supplemented by a number of other published and unpublished sources.

By the 1880s Spurgeon had been thirty years in London. His fame and influence were at their height and he had built up around himself, the Metropolitan Tabernacle and the Pastors' College Conference a network of evangelistic and charitable agencies. He had not shown himself unfriendly to the Union and at the autumn meetings in various provincial centres had frequently preached one of the special sermons. His closest and most constant connection had been, however, with the London Baptist Association, in the establishment of which he had had a considerable share.

Spurgeon was present at the meetings of the Union in Liverpool in 1882 and moved the vote of thanks to the citizens for their hospitality. He was not at the Leicester meetings the following year, but later alluded more than once to an incident that occurred there. A Unitarian minister, who had formerly been a Baptist, made at a mayoral reception a number of flippant remarks of a semi-jocular character, which gave considerable offence. Spurgeon admitted that the Union officials could not be held responsible for what was said by a visitor, but he used the incident as an excuse for declining the subsequent invitations to preach which Samuel Harris Booth and A. H. Baynes, of the Baptist Missionary Society, more than once conveyed to him. Though barely fifty years of age, he was subject to increasingly frequent bouts of ill-health and was also growingly out of sympathy with the new trends in Biblical and theological thought. "I have declined to take a public part in the meetings because I could not feel sure that I should not be compromised thereby." So he wrote a few months after the outbreak of the Down Grade controversy.[5] Richard Glover had come to the presidency of the Union in 1884 and of him his son later said: "He was frankly interested in Darwin, and it never seemed to occur to him that you could not be friends at

[5] Letter from Mentone, 19th December 1887. See *Freeman*, 30th December 1887.

once with Darwin and St. John."[6] Three years later, John Clifford was elected to the vice-presidency, though his election was opposed by James Douglas, of Kenyon Chapel, Brixton. "I must . . . place in the foreground the faith once delivered to the saints," he said. "I do not look upon Dr. Clifford as a sufficient exponent of that faith for the office of Vice-President."[7]

Attempts have been made to represent the events of 1887–8 as a personal clash between Spurgeon and Clifford. There were no doubt some who at the time thought of it in these terms. But Spurgeon himself explicitly disclaimed this. Fullerton quotes him as saying: "You (i.e. Clifford) are a General Baptist, and you hold your own views: you and I understand one another."[8] In the introduction he wrote to a life of Clifford, published in 1904, Sir William Robertson Nicoll said: "I can testify from conversation with Mr. Spurgeon during the Down Grade controversy that he declined to rank Dr. Clifford among the heretics. He spoke with warm admiration of Dr. Clifford's fine character, and believed that on various points of controversy he was misunderstood."[9] Moreover, Clifford himself, in an account he wrote of the crucial interview in January 1888 between Spurgeon and representatives of the Baptist Union, noted that "Mr. S. did say he was not referring to me or to General Baptists, though he added, 'As you know, we differ, but we hold vital evangelical truth in common: still I do not like your last book!' "[10] These contemporary testimonies are important, since H. G. Wood in his life of T. R. Glover states that there is no doubt that to Spurgeon, Clifford was "the arch-heretic", while Willis B. Glover, Jr. appears in *Evangelical Nonconformists and Higher Criticism in the Nineteenth Century* to charge Clifford with dishonesty.[11]

It was the views of some of the younger men that more seriously troubled Spurgeon, including those of two or three who were

[6] Quoted by H. G. Wood, *Terrot Reaveley Glover*, 1953, p. 5.
[7] *Freeman*, 29th April, 1887.
[8] W. Y. Fullerton, *C. H. Spurgeon*, 1920, p. 315.
[9] C. T. Bateman, *John Clifford*, 1904, p. 15.
[10] Letter to F. A. Jones, February 1888, in the possession of the writer.
[11] Op. cit., 1954, pp. 172–5.

members of the Baptist Union Council. Booth also felt some concern. He and Spurgeon had been on terms of intimacy with one
another. There seems little doubt that in the mid-eighteen-
eighties they more than once discussed together the general denominational situation. Booth himself had been involved in an
unfortunate episode over the young student from Regent's Park
College who had become pastor of the newly-formed church at
Elm Road, Beckenham, W. E. Blomfield by name, later to become Principal of Rawdon College and a President of the Union.
Booth was dissatisfied with Blomfield's preaching, chiefly because of what he regarded as its omissions. When tension developed, it was arranged that J. R. Wood, E. B. Underhill and
J. W. Todd hold an inquiry. They examined some fifty of Blomfield's sermons and exonerated him from the charges made.
Booth and his wife withdrew from membership at Elm Road,
but a few months later, in 1886, Blomfield judged it politic to
accept an invitation to the pastorate of another church. There
were other more prominent ministers, whose sermons were
widely reported in the Press and whose views were likely to dis-
turb both Booth and Spurgeon. Those whose names were most
frequently mentioned as the controversy developed were J. G.
Greenhough and James Thew, ministers of neighbouring churches
in Leicester. Both had been trained at Rawdon College.[12]

Spurgeon was gravely troubled at the growing departure from
the traditional doctrines of Calvinism, particularly those relating
to eternal punishment and the substitutionary nature of the
Atonement. Nor was he ready to countenance any reformulation
of the doctrine of the inspiration of the Bible. He had never been
happy at the change in the constitution of the Union in 1873,
when the phrase regarding "the sentiments usually denominated

---

[11] S. G. Green, Principal of Rawdon College from 1863–76, was a man with broad
interests in the field of Biblical studies. The men trained there sought to

> "Unite the pair so long disjoined
> Knowledge and vital piety."

See J. O. Barrett, *A Short History of Rawdon College*, 1954. Thew was colleague and then
successor of James Phillippo Mursell.

evangelical" was dropped. On the contrary, he wished for an elaborated doctrinal statement similar to that of the Evangelical Alliance. He was in process of drawing the limits of his fellowship more narrowly. Early in 1887, he decisively rebuffed Joseph Parker, of the City Temple, with whom four years earlier he had been willing to exchange pulpits. The issue here seems to have been mainly that Parker did not disapprove of theatre-going. Whether the matters related to conduct or doctrine, Spurgeon was becoming more rigid and exclusive. It should also be noted that in the controversy over Home Rule for Ireland, which at this very time led to the break between Chamberlain and Gladstone, Spurgeon—unlike most Nonconformists—supported Chamberlain.

The Baptist denomination as a whole was, however, clearly taken by surprise at the storm which broke out in the spring of 1887.

II

Public controversy was touched off by two unsigned articles which appeared in Spurgeon's magazine, *The Sword and Trowel*, under the title, "The Down Grade". They dealt mainly with the rationalistic movements of the eighteenth century, but suggested that there was widespread contemporary apostasy from evangelical truth and that the nineteenth century might be about to repeat what had happened a hundred years earlier. The articles came from the pen of Robert Shindler, a Baptist minister then at Addlestone. They were generally regarded as an attack on the General Baptists with the theme—then not uncommon in certain circles—that Arminianism tends towards Arianism and Socinianism, but there is little evidence that they caused serious concern. Indeed, E. B. Underhill later confessed that he had rejoiced when he read the articles, never thinking that they would soon be turned on the Baptist Union.[13]

There is no evidence that Spurgeon inspired the articles, but he appears to have been impressed by them or else to have seized

[13] *Freeman*, 24th February 1888.

upon them as the opportunity for a public statement of his views. In August, September and October 1887 he put his own name to three further articles: "Another Word concerning the Down Grade", "A Reply to Sundry Critics and Inquirers" and "The Case proved". Both Fullerton and Carlile candidly admit that Spurgeon was not "a good controversialist",[14] but he had a gift for forthright, pungent phrases, which, whether intentionally or not, proved provocative and wounding. In the first of his articles he declared:

"The Atonement is scouted, the inspiration of Scripture is derided, the Holy Spirit is degraded into an influence, the punishment of sin is turned into a fiction, and the resurrection into a myth, and yet these enemies of our faith expect us to call them brethren and maintain a confederacy with them."[15]

In the subsequent articles the charges became more pointed. It was alleged that certain unnamed ministers had initiated "a new religion, which was no more Christianity than chalk was cheese" and by so doing were "making infidels". Since Spurgeon had already made clear that he thought the Wesleyan Methodists, although traditionally Arminian, true to the great evangelical doctrines, it seemed clear that he was attacking some of his fellow-Baptists.

The articles began to circulate through the denomination on the eve of the autumn meetings of the Baptist Union. These took place in Sheffield in the first week of October. Spurgeon, says Willis B. Glover, "seems to have expected that the majority of English Baptists and perhaps of other denominations would rally round him in opposition to pernicious influences".[16] No doubt he felt that his reputation and position were such that his articles must be publicly taken note of. His expectations may have been even more specific. Perhaps he believed that Booth was meditating some action of his own or could be forced into it. Whatever the explanation, Spurgeon was clearly upset by the fact that the

[14] Fullerton, op. cit., p. 303; Carlile, op. cit., pp. 243–4.
[15] Sword and Trowel, August 1887.
[16] Op. cit., p. 167.

Sheffield meetings proceeded according to plan and that no formal discussion of his charges took place. On the other hand, as was subsequently pointed out, he had sent no communication to the Council and if the officials of the Union, or anyone else, had desired to raise the matter, longer notice and preparation would have been necessary.

A number of things happened in connection with the Sheffield meetings, however, which exacerbated feelings on both sides and precipitated the subsequent breach. On the eve of the Assembly, *The Scotsman* printed a report from its London correspondent that he had heard "on the most trustworthy authority" that Spurgeon had "intimated his intention of definitely withdrawing from the Union if certain ministers whom he considers heretical— notably Mr. Greenhough of Leicester—are not expelled". *The Freeman* subsequently described this as an "ill-timed and ungenerous *canard*", but admitted that it was "the all-absorbing theme of conversation". On its appearance Spurgeon's secretary had issued an "unqualified contradiction".[17] Unfortunately, *The Freeman* had the previous week published a facetious paragraph which said that in the train on the way to Sheffield "the great joke was the Down Grade question". Though apology was later made for this paragraph, it seriously wounded Spurgeon and some of his friends. They were also distressed by certain passages in a speech by E. G. Gange, of Bristol, who had been trained at Spurgeon's College. *The Scotsman*, on 10th October, said that Spurgeon had "changed his mind", because it was clear at Sheffield that "he would have no considerable support". *The Freeman* evidently felt that nothing serious would now occur and on 21st October stated in a leading article: "The 'Down Grade' storm has, by this time, we trust, somewhat subsided."

In truth, however, the storm had not yet broken. On Friday, 28th October, Spurgeon wrote to Booth withdrawing from the Baptist Union. "The reasons," he said, "are set forth in the *Sword and Trowel* for November." There the Baptist Union was clearly implicated in the general charges already made. "To be

[17] *Freeman*, 14th October 1887.

very plain," said Spurgeon, "we are unable to call these things 'Christian Unions', they begin to look like Confederacies in Evil". In his letter to Booth he said: "It is on the highest ground alone that I take this step, and you know that I have delayed it because I hoped for better things." Booth's acknowledgment, however, bears about it all the marks of genuine surprise and dismay.

> "I cannot express adequately the sense of pain such a step has caused me. Nor can I at present calmly think of the future. I can only leave it as it is for awhile, merely adding that I think you have wounded the hearts of some—of many—who honour and love you more than you have any idea of, and whose counsel would have led to a far different result."

The news of Spurgeon's withdrawal from the Union caused a sensation far beyond the borders of the Baptist denomination. *John Bull* published an article with the title, "The Decomposition of Dissent". *The Pall Mall Gazette*, then being edited by W. T. Stead, published a long reply by Clifford to Spurgeon's *Sword and Trowel* articles. The matter was discussed at considerable length in the columns of *The British Weekly* and *The Christian World*, both papers expressing regret at Spurgeon's action and sympathy with the Union. Public meetings were held in a number of places. John Aldis, Joseph Angus and Alexander McLaren, three of the most distinguished and respected "seniors" of the Baptist denomination, appealed for restraint in a joint letter to *The Freeman*, but it was not easy to stay popular excitement and controversy. A few of Spurgeon's close associates, including his son, Charles, followed his example in withdrawing from the Union, but a meeting of a hundred Pastors' College men, while expressing sympathy with Spurgeon, decided to seek ways of overcoming the crisis.

A specially convened meeting of the Baptist Union Council was called at the Mission House in Furnival Street on 13th December 1887. It was attended by eighty members. To it Angus submitted a Declaration which he and a few others had drawn up. The Declaration was mainly of an historical character, setting out the changes in the basis of the Union since 1832, affirming confidence in the evangelical loyalty of the denomination as a whole, and specifying certain fundamental doctrinal tenets. Spurgeon's brother James, however, proposed that the Union adopt the doctrinal basis of the Evangelical Alliance. Discussion of both motions was deferred. Although in his letter of resignation Spurgeon had said: "I beg you not to send anyone to ask for a reconciliation," the Council decided that a deputation should seek an interview with him, if necessary at Mentone, to which he had gone, to deliberate with him "how the unity of our denomination in truth and love and good works may be maintained".

Unfortunately the Council was not able to avoid the raising of the question whether Spurgeon had or had not "made any private remonstrance to officials of the Baptist Union". Their reply was that "in no conversation or communication they had had with Mr. Spurgeon had he formulated any charge as to laxity of doctrine in the Union such as would have justified an appeal to the Council". Spurgeon clearly believed he had made repeated remonstrances, of which notice should have been taken. The breach between him and his former friends was widened.

III

After some delay and uncertainty, the meeting with Spurgeon took place at the Metropolitan Tabernacle on 13th January 1888. Spurgeon had his brother with him and the Baptist Union representatives were Culross, Clifford and Booth. It was not an easy meeting as the agreed minute showed. Spurgeon refused to withdraw his resignation. He made it clear that he wished the Union to adopt a doctrinal declaration similar to that of the Evangelical Alliance and did not think that that of Angus went far enough. At the same time, even if a statement of "evangelical doctrines" which he could approve were adopted, he would not undertake to rejoin the Union. "He would wait and see how it worked." Moreover he "positively declined to give the names of any brethren since he did not believe that the Union had any authority over them, nor did he know of anyone who had violated our Constitution, because he did not believe there is any power under our Constitution for dealing with the utmost divergence of doctrinal opinion".

Spurgeon's attitude on this last point was strongly resented. He had made, it was felt, a "charge against anonymity" and even if he had not actually described the Union as "a confederacy in evil", he had said that it began to look like it. Many people thought that he should withdraw his charges or name the individuals against whom they were directed. Otherwise all were under suspicion. "Such was the fame and deserved authority of the great preacher," said R. F. Horton, the Congregationalist, "that to lie under his censure was to forfeit the ear of by far the larger proportion of evangelical Christians".[18] Similar testimony is given by C. T. Bateman:

"The pastor of the Metropolitan Tabernacle swayed a public larger than the Baptist denomination. . . . His illimitable powers as a preacher and exponent of the Bible had endeared him to thousands who without question gave credence to his views. As a result bishops quoted them in their charges and Anglicans generally found abundant evidence therein of the decadence of evangelical truth in Free Church communities."[19]

It is against this background that the subsequent action of the Baptist Union Council must be judged. At a meeting on 18th January 1888 two resolutions were passed. The first regretfully accepted Spurgeon's resignation, and no hands were held up against it. The second was more controversial and, when it became known, caused great and long-continuing resentment on the part of Spurgeon and his friends. It was as follows:

"That the Council recognizes the gravity of the charges which Mr. Spurgeon has brought against the Union previous to and since his withdrawal. It considers that the public and general manner in which they have been made reflects on the whole body, and exposes to suspicion brethren who love the truth as dearly as he does. And, as Mr. Spurgeon declined to give the names of those to whom he intended them to apply, and the evidence supporting them, those charges in the judgment of the Council, ought not to have been made."

[18] *An Autobiography*, 1917, p. 88.
[19] *John Clifford*, 1902, p. 71.

This resolution was passed with only five dissentients, one of whom was James Spurgeon. It was moved by William Landels, who during his long ministry at Regent's Park Chapel had been a close friend of Spurgeon. Landels had already made clear that he regarded the sending of the deputation as "a farce". Charles Williams's description of it as "one of love's blunders"[20] was more accurate, though in distant retrospect the meeting with Spurgeon must be regarded as one of the incidents which helped to preserve the Union intact, even if the subsequent "Vote of Censure", as it came to be called, made Spurgeon's return unlikely. In the course of the discussion on the resolution, J. G. Greenhough took occasion to give what *The Freeman* described as "a confession of faith" on behalf of himself and some of his friends. He affirmed their belief in the authority of the Bible, the atoning death of Christ and the inevitable punishment of those rejecting the Gospel, and his speech clearly made a deep impression on all who were present. By the time the resolution was finally agreed, the meeting had lasted many hours and the discussion of Angus's Declaration was again deferred until the next meeting.

Those who supported Spurgeon began to plan for an appeal from the Council to the Assembly. But when at the adjourned meeting of the Council on 21st February Angus moved his Declaration in a somewhat revised form, it was supported by James Spurgeon, who claimed to have had a share in hammering it out. It was not, however, to go through easily. Richard Glover, George Short, S. G. Green and J. G. Greenhough made critical speeches regarding its terms. Many Baptists had become deeply suspicious of doctrinal statements and creeds, if used as tests of orthodoxy or membership. There was considerable diversity of opinion as to the right of the Council to issue such Statements. Agreement was finally reached, by 35 votes to 5 "in a meeting reduced in numbers, many of the brethren having had to leave",[21] by adding a preamble suggested by Clifford:

[20] *Freeman*, 10th February 1888.
[21] *Freeman*, 24th February 1888.

"First—That the doctrinal beliefs of the Union are and must be determined by the doctrinal beliefs of the churches and Associations of which the Union is composed. Secondly, that the Council of the Union therefore disclaims altogether any authority to formulate a new and additional standard of theological belief as a bond of union to which assent shall be required."

This preamble was accepted by James Spurgeon and the members of the Council seem to have assumed that his acceptance carried with it that of his brother. Said *The Baptist Magazine*, in commenting upon the meeting: "There is no reason why, notwithstanding the differences which have been thus far revealed, we should not now be heartily and thoroughly reunited".[22] But Spurgeon thought differently. In a letter to Booth, who had sent him a copy of the Declaration, he said:

"Its form is totally different from that which was agreed upon by Dr. Angus and my brother. The preamble gives it another meaning altogether. It is an historical document but it is not a basis of union such as I recommended."[23]

The situation now became more tense again. The Pastors' College Conference had been re-formed on a narrower basis and sent to the Union a protest against the "Vote of Censure". Controversy had spread to the London Baptist Association and it was clear that many were preparing for a dramatic struggle in the Assembly. James Spurgeon had throughout occupied a key position in the conflict. He had not withdrawn from the Union when his brother did, though he was closely associated with him in all the enterprises which centred at the Metropolitan Tabernacle. In the debates in the Council he was inevitably regarded as his brother's representative. He appeared there to have been filling the role of mediator, since he had co-operated with Angus, under whom he had been trained at Regent's Park College, in the drafting of the revised form of the latter's Declaration. Now, however, he gave notice that at the Assembly he would move an amendment to the Declaratory Statement, and at the same time he and Thomas Greenwood joined Spurgeon in resigning from the London Baptist Association.

[22] *Baptist Magazine*, March 1888, p. 124.
[23] *Freeman*, 2nd March 1888.

Angus, supported by J. R. Wood, of Upper Holloway church, made one more attempt at conciliation. So far as theological issues were concerned, discussion had begun to concentrate on the question of Eternal Punishment and the Last Judgment. The Council met again on 20th April 1888, three days before the opening of the Assembly. It was at once clear that neither side was really anxious for a public trial of strength. After a morning spent in trying to reach agreement regarding the Declaratory Statement, on the basis of Angus's new proposals, there was an adjournment to allow James Spurgeon and William Cuff, of Shoreditch Tabernacle, to consult their friends—including, presumably, Spurgeon himself. On the resumption of the discussion, "it was found that the difference had dwindled down to the wording of a historical note"[24] to the clause dealing with the Resurrection. There were further consultations over the weekend and on the Monday morning Booth received a letter from James Spurgeon saying that he would not press in the Assembly the amendment of which he had given notice, provided that the preamble adopted in February was withdrawn. The Council met again, only half an hour before the session of the Assembly was due to begin, and agreed to this course.

In the morning Clifford had delivered his presidential address. It was a masterly utterance, entitled "The Great Forty Years: The Primitive Christian Faith, its real substance and best defence", and by its argument and eloquence prepared the ground for what happened a few hours later. The afternoon session was held in the City Temple and, in addition to the ministers and delegates, there are said to have been between five and six hundred visitors present, including Joseph Parker, Guinness Rogers and Hugh Price Hughes, though not Spurgeon. "The whole place was crammed and in tumult," wrote a journalist. "The battle at the Temple doors will go down to history in conjunction with the truce inside."[25] The Council's resolutions of 18th January, as part of the Council's Report, were not challenged. The Declaratory

[24] *Freeman*, 27th April 1888.
[25] Quoted by C. T. Bateman, *John Clifford*, 1902, p. 87.

Statement in its final amended form was adopted by special vote on the motion of Charles Williams, seconded by James Spurgeon, with only seven dissentients, who included, however, James Douglas and Hugh D. Brown, of Dublin. The doxology was sung and the session closed with prayer.

IV

The Declaratory Statement,[26] after "expressly disavowing and disallowing any power to control belief or restrict inquiry", stated that in the light of the observance of baptism and the Lord's Supper by the churches, the Union is "an association of churches and ministers, professing not only to believe the facts and doctrines of the Gospel, but to have undergone the spiritual change expressed or implied in them". "This change is the fundamental principle of our church life." It then listed six facts and doctrines "commonly believed by the Churches of the Union", with a brief word of elaboration in regard to certain of them. They were (1) the Divine Inspiration and Authority of the Holy Scriptures; (2) the fallen and sinful state of man; (3) the Person and Work of Jesus Christ; (4) Justification by Faith; (5) the Work of the Holy Spirit; (6) the Resurrection and the Judgment at the Last Day, "according to the words of our Lord in Matthew xxv. 46".

To the last of these clauses there was appended the note:

"It should be stated, as an historical fact, that there have been brethren in the Union, working cordially with it, who, while reverently bowing to the authority of Holy scripture, and rejecting dogmas of Purgatory and Universalism, have not held the common interpretation of these words of our Lord."

Apart from the somewhat strange omission of any reference to the doctrine of the Trinity and the cumbersome wording of the last clause, about which there had been so much discussion, the Declaratory Statement has many similarities with the Doctrinal Basis of the Evangelical Alliance. The latter makes reference to:

[26] See Appendix VI.

"The Immortality of the Soul, the Resurrection of the Body, the Judgment of the World by our Lord Jesus Christ, with the Eternal Blessedness of the Righteous, and the Eternal Punishment of the Wicked."

This clause is said to have been added to the original draft in 1846 at the insistence of delegates from the United States who were troubled by the move towards Universalism in their own country. The Declaratory Statement of 1888 should also be compared with the statement adopted in the Carter Lane vestry in 1813 at the first meeting of the Baptist Union,[27] and with the action taken by the Congregational Union during this troubled period.

In 1878, following the controversies over the views of J. Allanson Picton, the Congregational Union reaffirmed its adherence to "Evangelical Religion" and referred to the Congregational Declaration of Faith and Order of 1833. This was a much more lengthy and elaborate document than anything ever produced by the Baptist Union.[28] In 1887, however, at the autumn session of the Congregational Union, Alexander Mackennal, who was then Chairman, devoted half his address to the general charges which Spurgeon had been making in his articles in *The Sword and Trowel*. Dogma, he said, is a finished product, a final statement. Doctrine is something that is progressing. Congregationalists rejected dogma, but retained doctrine.[29] The discussions in the Congregational Union during the following months turned chiefly on R. F. Horton's book, *Inspiration and the Bible*, published early in 1888. Horton had been invited to preach the Home Missionary Sermon at the autumn assembly of the Baptist Union in 1888, but in view of the controversy over his book and the troubles through which they had been passing the officers accepted his offer to cancel the engagement.

There is little doubt that many of the delegates in the City Temple on 23rd April 1888 voted as they did under the impression that the agreement which had been arrived at would

[27] See page 24 above.
[28] The full text is given by A. Peel, *These Hundred Years*, 1931, pp. 69 f. For a discussion of its significance see R. W. Dale, *History of Congregationalism*, 1907, pp. 699 f.
[29] See Willis B. Glover, op. cit., pp. 175–6.

result in, or at least pave the way for, Spurgeon's return to the Union. Matters had gone too far, however. Words had been uttered, on both sides, that could not easily be recalled. The wounds were too deep. Spurgeon remained outside the Union, a sad, isolated and sick man, and less than four years later passed away at the early age of fifty-seven. In the months following the Assembly of 1888 a few of those who sympathized with him discussed the possibility of together withdrawing from the Union, but even men like Archibald Brown, of the East London Tabernacle, who had already done so, cautioned them against hasty action, while Spurgeon himself made it clear that there was little he would be able to do to help them.

In the early stages of the controversy Spurgeon had perhaps failed to realize the way in which the Union had rooted itself in the life of the churches during the previous twenty years and how essential it had become both to their local and corporate witness. There is a revealing passage in one of his *Sword and Trowel* articles in the autumn of 1887, directed against the Baptist Union.

"The expedient is not needed among Churches which are each one self-governing and self-determining; such churches can find their own affinities without difficulty, and can keep their own coasts clear of invaders. Since each vessel is sea-worthy in herself, let the hampering ropes be cut clean away, and no more lines of communication be thrown out until we know that we are alongside a friend who sails under the same glorious flag. In the isolation of independency, tempered by the love of the Spirit which binds us to all the faithful in Christ Jesus, we think the lovers of the gospel will for the present find their immediate safety."[30]

But, quite apart from the question whether or not such an attitude was theologically satisfactory, social changes had made it practically impossible. The pastor of the Metropolitan Tabernacle might speak like this. For the minister of the average Baptist church the situation was different. The Augmentation and Annuity Funds, Home Missions and the Board of Introduction were drawing together and supplementing the resources of the individual churches, carrying out tasks they could not otherwise

[30] *Sword and Trowel*, 1887, p. 560.

fulfil. The necessity of union had to be balanced against any desire for complete uniformity of doctrine.

On the more personal aspects of the Down Grade controversy, it is unnecessary and unwise to make extended comment. The letters alleged to have passed between Spurgeon and Booth in the months or years prior to the summer of 1887 have never been produced, so that it is impossible, as it would now be unprofitable, to offer judgment on that particular issue. It was in any case subsidiary. So far as the history of the Union is concerned, the significant thing is that, although within living memory there had been secessions over "Fullerism" and "Open Communion", on the main theological issues raised by Spurgeon—and with all the personal prestige he possessed—no schism took place. The churches, as well as the leaders of the Union, showed themselves determined to maintain the structure of corporate life which had been built up. In spite of changing ways of thought and expression, they did not doubt the general loyalty of the denomination to "evangelical religion". Could he have known what was to happen, how surprised J. H. Hinton would have been.

CHAPTER 8

PREPARING FOR FURTHER ADVANCE, 1888–98

I

The Baptist Union emerged from the Down Grade controversy shaken but not shattered. At the spring Assembly in 1888 an increase in church membership of 1,770 had been reported. The total from 2,764 churches was given as 304,385. As a result of the controversy a number of churches had not sent in returns. Had their figures been included, the increase might, it was thought, have been as great as 20,000. The following year the withdrawal of five churches and thirteen personal members was reported, but no fewer than sixty-one churches and 116 personal members had joined the Union. The report submitted at the 1890 Assembly recorded a further increase of 4,600 in the membership of the churches. Some of these churches were not directly affiliated to the Union, but the figures indicated the continued growth of the Baptist community as a whole. The upward trend in the statistics was to continue fairly steadily until the returns submitted in 1906.

There was a widespread desire to let bygones be bygones so far as the unhappy events of 1887–8 were concerned. In the autumn of 1889, on the eve of the Union meetings in Birmingham, there appeared in the columns of *The Baptist* an attack on John Clifford, based on the newspaper report of one of his speeches. F. B. Meyer, who after a notable ministry in Leicester had recently moved to London, intervened on Clifford's behalf and it was clear that the attempt to reopen controversy was widely and deeply resented. When, in January 1892, Spurgeon passed away at Mentone, the tributes to him were general and heartfelt. He was recognized as unquestionably the greatest preacher in an age of great preachers. It was significant of the general feeling in Baptist circles that within five years of Spurgeon's death, his brother felt able to ask Clifford to contribute to a volume of personal recollections.

The Down Grade controversy divided Booth's secretaryship of the Union into two parts of almost equal length. His second decade in office saw several important developments which prepared the way for and foreshadowed the more spectacular changes which came with the appointment of his successor.

At the autumn session of the Union in Birmingham in October 1889, a number of significant decisions were made. One of special interest was the adoption of the official reply to the letter of the Archbishop of Canterbury in regard to the Lambeth Quadrilateral. The Archbishop had indicated the readiness of the Church of England to confer with other churches, on the basis of this declaration, as to "what steps can be taken, either towards corporate reunion, or towards such relations as may prepare the way for fuller organic unity hereafter". Baptists recognized that this invitation marked "a historic moment in the history of English Christianity".[1] The preparation of their reply is said to have occupied the Council the whole of a four hours' sitting. When he read the document in full to the Assembly, presenting it not as an argument but a bare statement of facts in the light of which Baptists must decline to take part in a conference, Dr. Booth was greeted with uproarious cheers. The reply asserted that Baptists were as concerned as Anglicans to promote

"fraternal intercourse, practical co-operation and also organic union amongst societies of Christians, whenever such fellowship can be secured without impairing the sole and absolute authority of the Lord Jesus Christ over His people, and without a departure from His teaching concerning the doctrine, worship and government of His Church, as contained in the New Testament Scriptures."[2]

But Baptists believed that the Christianity of the New Testament was essentially the introduction of a spiritual, personal and

[1] *Freeman*, 11th October, 1889.
[2] For full text see Appendix VII. In their reply to a similar communication from the Archbishop, the Wesleyan Conference, while deploring "needless divisions", contended that the four articles, especially the fourth, "do not in the absence of fuller information and more exact definition, provide a practical basis for the discussion of the subject".

non-sacerdotal religion; their view of baptism required that it be preceded by personal repentance; they believed that the internal government of the Church should be in no way controlled by the State; moreover, they held that their churches possessed "the historic episcopate" as laid down in the New Testament. In seconding the adoption of the reply, T. V. Tymms urged that sacrifice of principle was not permitted even for outward union. He had to answer the question—put forward with the Down Grade controversy in mind and the differences among Baptists about terms of communion—"Have you not done this in your own Union?" Tymms claimed that since freedom of interpretation was conserved, there was no compromise involved. The document prepared by the Council was adopted without further discussion.

The Assembly in Birmingham was more deeply interested in closer unity among Baptists. It had before it a report on "Amalgamation of General and Particular Baptists". This was approved and the Council was instructed to carry the proposals into effect "as far and as speedily as possible". The process of bringing together the churches of the New Connexion and those of the Particular Baptists associated in the Baptist Union had begun, as we have seen, more than fifty years earlier, in 1832. But the General Baptist Association, as it had come to be called, had maintained a separate organization. It had its own annual meetings and its own missionary society. It had its own Building Fund, its own college, and a number of separate trusts. The holding of the meetings of the Baptist Union in Nottingham in 1857 had aided closer relationships. A more complete fusion of the two bodies had been actively advocated since the early eighteen-sixties. The question had been raised in a formal way by Dr. John Haslam at the autumn meetings of the Baptist Union in Huddersfield in 1886. The position which John Clifford had won for himself in the affairs of the Union made easier the formal negotiations which occupied the years 1889–91.

What was at length agreed upon was the dissolution of the General Baptist Association and the redistribution of its member churches among the existing Particular Baptist Associations, if they were not already in fellowship with them, as in fact many of them were; the fusion of the two missionary societies; the uniting of the General Baptist Building Fund with that established by the Particular Baptists in 1824; and special arrangements in regard to the other funds and trusts of the two bodies. The foreign missionary work of the General Baptists, which centred in Orissa, had, like the Midland Baptist College, always been under "the direction, control and management" of the Association itself. The final assembly of the General Baptist Association took place in Enon Chapel, Burnley, on 25th June 1891. After a four-hour session with Clifford in the chair, the resolution in favour of amalgamation with the Baptist Union was carried by 155 votes to 39. With remarkable ease and amity, the older distinctions passed from the mind of the denomination as a whole.

II

Partly in preparation for these notable changes and partly to facilitate the growing financial and trust responsibilities of the Baptist Union, the Baptist Union Corporation, Ltd., was formed in 1890. The scheme was prepared by S. R. Pattison, who had been treasurer of the Union since 1879, and by two distinguished Queen's Counsel, Mr. Richard Booth and Mr. Foulkes Griffiths.

The strain of the Down Grade controversy and the complicated negotiations leading up to the amalgamation of the New Connexion and the Union told on Booth's health, which had never been robust. He was in his late sixties. A prolonged rest and change were necessary. He was therefore sent on holiday to Egypt. During his absence John Clifford and Charles Williams undertook the oversight of the affairs of the Union.

The holiday prepared Booth for the events of 1892. In January of that year, as already noted, Spurgeon died at Mentone. The Union at once reaffirmed the respect and regard in which the great preacher was held by Baptists and Booth set himself to overcome the personal estrangements which had been caused by the events of 1887-8. Within a few months of Spurgeon's death, Booth and many other Baptists had to face serious private misfortune. The Liberator Permanent Building and Investment Society, established in 1868, had gained much of its support from Nonconformists in all parts of the country. S. R. Pattison, the treasurer of the Baptist Union, was chairman of the Society's directors. By 1892 he was an elderly man. For many years the leading figure had been Jabez Spencer Balfour, a well-known Congregationalist. Unfortunately, the Society engaged in highly speculative estate development, of a kind subsequently made illegal. On 2nd September 1892 it announced that it was unable to find the money for the withdrawals that were taking place, and went into bankruptcy. Depositors and shareholders lost the greater part of £3,000,000, then an even more substantial sum than it is today. Booth was among the many Baptist ministers who lost all their savings. He bore this reverse with courage and continued to devote himself with all his strength to the affairs of the Union.

There was much to be done. In 1892, partly in consequence of the union of the General and Particular Baptist organizations, the East Midland Association was formed. Also in 1892—the year of the Liberator crash—the Baptist Missionary Society celebrated its centenary with special meetings all over the country and a Thanksgiving Fund of over £100,000. The Union held both its spring and autumn assemblies in London in order to aid the celebrations. For the spring session a remarkable paper was prepared by J. H. Shakespeare, the young minister of St. Mary's Church, Norwich. It was Shakespeare's first appearance on the platform of the Union. He had made a careful and exhaustive study of the distribution of Baptist churches and the substance of his challenging address, together with the diagrams and tables of statistics he had drawn up, was subsequently published. Shakespeare's address led to the immediate appeal for a Church Extension Fund, which by 1894 was able to give substantial help with the building of a church in Leamington Road, Blackburn. This was followed in 1897 by help to the new cause in Heaton,

Newcastle. The policy of direct building grants from a central fund was, however, a new one and did not universally commend itself. Many felt that the main responsibility for the erection of buildings should rest with the local communities, though loans on advantageous terms could provide useful aid.

Colonel James Theodore Griffin—an American by birth, but long a member of Regent's Park Chapel and President of the Union in 1891—had for some years been treasurer of the Home Mission Fund, which continued to promote church extension by the support of evangelists and itinerant preachers. The resignation of S. R. Pattison from the treasurership of the Union paved the way for a reorganization of the general finances. In addition to the Home Mission Fund, the Union managed an Annuity Fund, an Augmentation Fund and an Education Fund. From the last of these, small grants were made towards the schooling of ministers' children. The income of the Union for general purposes was still not much more than £1,200 a year, a quite inadequate sum for a really effective headquarters. Nearly a tenth of the income was paid to the Baptist Missionary Society for the rooms occupied in the Mission House in Furnival Street. As a step towards a more satisfactory management of the finances, William Wilberforce Baynes, J.P., became in 1894 general treasurer of all the funds directly controlled by the Union. Baynes was a brother of the secretary of the Baptist Missionary Society and was himself secretary of the Star Life Assurance Company. He had been for some years treasurer of the Annuity Fund. At the same time an appeal was made for a general purposes income of at least £2,000.

This was followed by another important development, which brought special satisfaction to Dr. Landels, now an elderly man, living in Scotland. The Board of Introduction and Consultation set up in 1887 to aid ministerial settlement and removal had not functioned as well as had been hoped. The need for a more effective scheme of Ministerial Recognition was increasingly evident. In 1896–7 this was made the concern of a "department" of the Union, of which Charles Williams became chairman. The right of the churches to choose whom they would as pastors was expressly recognized, but it was agreed that the Union had certain inescapable responsibilities for the supervision of the list of ministers which it published in the annual Handbook. The purpose of the list was declared to be:

> "1. To prevent the unworthy or unfit entering the ministry.
> 2. To commend those qualified to the denomination.
> 3. To secure to those recognized eligibility for Funds."

It was also stated that it should be regarded as highly desirable that all intending Baptist ministers receive college training. The new department was to be managed by a committee of twelve appointed by the Council. The committee was to base its decisions upon reports from College Principals and from auxiliary committees for different areas of the country, each consisting of not fewer than five members. These auxiliary committees had to have before them applications in writing from men who desired their names added to the Baptist Union ministerial list.

Yet another interesting development, foreshadowing things to come, had occurred in 1894. The church at Moss Side, Manchester, appointed as one of its delegates to the autumn assembly held in Portsmouth a woman, Mrs. Stockford. Such a thing had never been done before. The Council of the Union felt it necessary to consider whether women were eligible to be delegates. An affirmative decision was given. A year or so earlier the Congregational Union had been faced with the same issue. Its first woman delegate, Miss Harriet Spicer, had difficulty in persuading the police that she had any right on the floor of the assembly. Women had, however, already appeared on the platform of the Baptist Union. At the spring assembly of 1889, Mrs. Edward Medley—a daughter of the manse, the wife of a minister and a sister of Augustine Birrell, Q.C., who that year became M.P. for West Fifeshire—had spoken on Young Women's Guilds, which were becoming a popular feature in the larger churches. At the autumn assembly the same year in Birmingham, Mrs. Dawson Burns—the wife of a minister—gave an address on "Women's

Work in the Church". Two years later, at the autumn assembly in Manchester, two single women were among the speakers: Dr. Ellen Farrer spoke on "Women's Work among the Sick Poor" and Miss Edith Angus—daughter of Dr. Joseph Angus—on "Women's Work in connection with the Social Condition of the Poor". These two addresses were based on the work which had recently been begun in London by a small group of deaconesses, women with some nursing training ready to devote themselves to visiting and social work. Mrs. Hugh Price Hughes was leading a movement of this kind in Methodism, and as part of a London Baptist Association Forward Movement, F. B. Meyer was engaged in establishing a Baptist Deaconesses' Home and Mission. This new avenue of service for women was not universally approved, and in 1893 the London Baptist Association decided that the work had better be independently managed.[3] Fifteen years elapsed after the addresses of Dr. Farrer and Miss Angus before another woman speaker appeared on the platform of the Union, though the number of women delegates to the Assembly slowly but steadily increased. The Churches generally showed no inclination to welcome or even take seriously the claim for women's suffrage which John Stuart Mill had put forward as early as 1867.

III

All the Free Churches were subject to the same influences. They were facing similar problems. They were being drawn together in a new way. It was in the eighteen-nineties that the National Free Church Council was formed.

The lead in urging Nonconformists to associate more closely was taken by Hugh Price Hughes, a Methodist, and Guinness Rogers, a Congregationalist. Their pleas were supported from the Baptist ranks by Dr. Clifford and F. B. Meyer, then minister at Regent's Park Chapel, and a rising power in the denomination. The matter of Free Church unity was taken further by Dr. Henry Lunn, a Methodist who had recently started *The Review of the*

[3] See D. M. Rose, *Baptist Deaconesses*, 1954.

Churches and was engaged in promoting informal gatherings of church leaders—Anglican and Free Church—at Grindelwald. With his friend Mr. Percy Bunting, Lunn called a meeting in Manchester in January, 1892. At this meeting Alexander McLaren moved a resolution in favour of the convening of a Free Church Congress. It was held in Manchester the following November. At least thirty Baptists attended and McLaren and Clifford took prominent parts in the proceedings, which ended with a Communion Service. At a second Congress, held in Leeds in 1894, Dr. Richard Glover, of Bristol, was one of the speakers. A third Congress met in Birmingham in 1895 and it was then that the Quakers, George and Richard Cadbury, promised generous financial support so that the whole country might be covered with local councils of Free Churchmen. In consequence, at the fourth Congress, held in 1896 in Nottingham, a National Council of the Evangelical Free Churches was established, with a formal constitution and a full-time organizing secretary. Offices were secured in the Memorial Hall, London. There were by then over 200 local councils and federations. Hugh Price Hughes and Charles Berry, of Wolverhampton, saw the movement as a step towards a United Free Church and as an agency for evangelism. In 1897 Gipsy Smith became the special full-time missioner of the new Council and a number of other well-known Nonconformists undertook united evangelistic campaigns. F. B. Meyer, who had crossed the Thames to be minister at Christ Church, Westminster, undertook the editing of a monthly magazine, *The Free Churchman*. The report of the Baptist Union Council for 1896 welcomed the formation of the National Free Church Council and its branches as "an answer to the revival of sacerdotalism by the priests of the Anglican Church". This was presumably Booth's judgment and represented a backward look rather than an understanding of what was in the mind of younger men like Hugh Price Hughes and Charles Berry. Baptists had, however, already shared officially in a first conference on "overlapping" held under the auspices of the Free Church Congress.

Evangelism and Church Extension were receiving increasing

attention in Baptist circles. At the 1895 Assembly in London, Charles Brown, the minister of Ferme Park church, had called attention to the approaching centenary of the Home Mission and had pleaded for a larger income in order to extend its work. He was commissioned to prepare a book outlining the history of what had been accomplished since the formation of the Home Mission Society in 1797,[4] and in April 1897 a great bazaar was held in the Holborn Restaurant and realized £1,785. In the same year George Plumb, of Norwich, was appointed Deputation Secretary of the Union on behalf of Church Extension.

A London Baptist Association Forward Movement had already been in progress for some years, with F. B. Meyer as its Honorary Director, and John Clifford and William Cuff, of Shoreditch, among its leading supporters. F. C. Spurr had been brought from Cardiff to become L.B.A. Evangelist, and in 1894 the Union agreed to make a contribution towards his support. The following year Spurr was appointed the full-time evangelist of the Union, a position he held until 1904, engaging in missions in all parts of the country. F. B. Meyer was responsible for yet another new development when he formed the Baptist Ministers' and Missionaries' Prayer Union.

All these activities indicated a quickened denominational life. More was being expected of the Baptist Union, and its officers did their best to respond. It was felt that a serious attempt should be made to stimulate interest in Baptist history. Accordingly, encouraged by a resolution passed at the autumn assembly in Cardiff in 1890, George Pearce Gould, then a tutor at Regent's Park College, edited three historical and biographical manuals. They appeared in 1895, one on the Anabaptists by Richard Heath, one on Vavasor Powell by David Davies, and one on Hanserd Knollys by James Culross. The series was intended for a wide public, though based on sound scholarship. Unfortunately, the response did not enable it to be continued.

There were other proposals which fell for a time on deaf ears. As early as 1891 the suggestion of a new weekly denominational

---

[4] See Charles Brown, *The Story of Baptist Home Missions*, 1897.

paper was mooted, one more closely in touch with headquarters than the privately owned *Freeman* or the *Baptist*. Soon afterwards an attempt was again made to draw together the theological colleges. It was suggested that an Arts College be established under denominational auspices and that all students should go there before being sent on for theological and directly ministerial training. The founding of a scholarship for advanced study was also urged. These proposals were in large measure a revival of what Edward Steane had suggested sixty years earlier and of the scheme put forward by Dr. Green in 1871, but in 1895 they were withdrawn. The colleges still felt that they were doing and were able to do all that was necessary.[5] Yet another subject that began to be talked about was the need for a larger and separate head-quarters for the Union. Negotiations were already in progress for a new Baptist hymnbook.

Booth's strength was failing, however. The century to which he belonged was drawing to a close. Public events must have deepened his feeling that an epoch was ending and that new forces were at work which required the guidance of a younger man. At the General Election of 1892 the Liberals had again been re-turned to power. The new House of Commons contained over one hundred Nonconformist M.P.s, of whom at least eleven were Baptists. Gladstone, at the age of eighty-two, formed his fourth administration. But within two years he had to retire, emerging again into public life only to denounce the atrocities committed by the Turks against the Christian communities in Armenia. These atrocities drew a strong protest from the Baptist Union Council in December 1894. The great majority of Noncon-formists were once more united in their political allegiance. They had not followed Joseph Chamberlain as he moved to closer association with the Conservatives. They regarded his colonial policy as dangerous imperialism.

The Nonconformist Conscience was an active force in public

---

[5] In 1893 the College at Pontypool had moved to Cardiff and was in 1899 joined by that which had been at Haverfordwest from 1839–94 and then for five years at Aberystwyth. The proposal for a united institution had first been made by Dr. Thomas Thomas in 1872.

affairs. Its power had been strikingly demonstrated a few years earlier when the Irish leader, Parnell, had been involved in divorce proceedings and, as John Morley put it, "platform-men united with pulpit-men in swelling the whirlwind".[6] But the Free Churches seemed more interested in campaigning against the remaining privileges of the Anglican Church and against intemperance, than in supporting demands for better working conditions. An ominous gulf had developed between organized religion and much of the industrial population. John Clifford was not afraid to associate with those who called themselves Socialists, while younger ministers, like J. C. Carlile, made a name for themselves by supporting the dockers in their strike for more satisfactory terms of employment. But many Baptists looked askance at such actions.

The diamond jubilee of Queen Victoria was celebrated in 1897. At the spring assembly the following year Booth submitted his resignation of the secretaryship of the Union. In accepting it, the Council placed on record "the rare dignity and courtesy, unfailing graciousness and patience, and singular ability and devotion" which he had shown. It was a well-deserved tribute. The twenty-one years of his secretaryship had seen many changes. Instead of suffering complete shipwreck, as it might well have done in the stormy days of the Down Grade controversy, the Union had been kept afloat, strengthened and prepared for voyaging in wider seas than any it had ventured upon before.

[6] *Life of Gladstone, III*, 1903, p. 433.

CHAPTER 9

WIDER HORIZONS, 1898–1914

I

DURING the eighteen-nineties, as the health of Samuel Harris Booth began to fail, the minister of St. Mary's Church, Norwich, had slowly but steadily come to be regarded as the next secretary of the Baptist Union.

John Howard Shakespeare was the son of a Baptist minister.[1] Though born in Yorkshire, he had spent his boyhood in the Midlands. During some of the most formative years of his youth, he had sat under James Thew, of Leicester. After a brief, but useful, experience in a London office, he had entered Regent's Park College, distinguishing himself there and at University College, London, as a student. Though only twenty-six years of age when he undertook the Norwich pastorate, he had quickly made a place for himself in the life of the city and had added fresh lustre to a pulpit made famous by the ministries of Joseph Kinghorn, William Brock and George Gould. Joseph Parker and Hugh Price Hughes were, Shakespeare once confessed, the contemporary leaders by whom he had been most deeply stirred. He had been a member of the Baptist Union Council throughout the painful Down Grade controversy. He knew the chief personalities in the denomination and the strong cross-currents that flowed beneath its surface. He had spent much time analysing the distribution of Baptist churches throughout the country and his address to the assembly in 1892 had been an impressive plea for church extension.

When the invitation to succeed Booth reached him, Shake-

[1] See Sir Geoffrey Shakespeare, *Let Candles be Brought In*, 1949, ch. XVII, and *Baptists Who Made History* (edited by A. S. Clement), 1955, ch. XIII.

speare asked for time to consider the matter. Acceptance would involve his turning aside from pastoral service in which he had been notably successful. While he reflected on the issue, he was taken seriously ill and it seemed at one time likely that he would have to decline on health grounds. As he recovered, however, he became convinced that he must accept the call that had come to him. Samuel Vincent, Charles Williams and J. R. Wood[2] had temporarily taken over secretarial responsibilities from the failing hands of Booth. Shakespeare was at length installed in office at the Autumn Assembly of the Union held in Nottingham in October 1898.

The following spring, William Wilberforce Baynes resigned the treasurership of the Union, an office he had held during a transition period of considerable difficulty. Baynes was replaced by Mr. Henry Wood, a man of striking appearance and fine character, who seemed ideally fitted for the post. His death a few months later was an unexpected and serious blow, but Mr. Herbert Marnham, a young stockbroker, had already shown unusual personal and professional qualities. He was appointed to the vacant treasurership and for the next thirty-four years proved a most able, kindly and generous leader in the rapidly-developing work of the Union. For some fifteen years Booth had been assisted in the office by W. J. Avery. Soon after Shakespeare's advent, Avery retired, though continuing until 1910 to edit *The Baptist Handbook*. That control had passed into more vigorous hands was soon apparent.

At the Nottingham meetings at which Shakespeare was formally appointed, the President of the Union, Samuel Vincent, put forward bold proposals for the raising of a large fund to mark the opening of a new century and to provide resources for advance in several directions. Under the leadership of the new secretary, the scheme quickly took shape and in 1899 an appeal was launched for a Twentieth Century Fund of £250,000. Of the

---

[2] J. R. Wood, who became President of the Union in 1902, was an influential figure in all its affairs at this time. For an attractive account of him by one of his sons, see H. G. Wood, *Christianity and the Nature of History*, 1934, pp. x ff.

sum asked for half was for church extension, particularly in urban areas where Baptists were inadequately represented. Thirty thousand pounds was to be devoted to raising and maintaining the stipends of village ministers, £30,000 to the Annuity Fund, £25,000 to various educational and propaganda purposes. It was suggested that £6,000 should be used to provide scholarships for advanced theological study, which might later be transferred to a denominational college in Oxford or Cambridge. The remaining £34,000 was to be used for a denominational headquarters. The day had passed when the Union could be content with or adequately served from a few rooms in the Mission House in Furnival Street. The projected construction of Kingsway gave a new importance to the property of the old Eagle Street Church, Holborn. It was there that the Union had met in 1815 for its third annual meeting. After long and delicate negotiations it appeared that the church could be provided with new premises, while at the same time a fine site would be available on Southampton Row for a Baptist Church House.

The raising of the Twentieth Century Fund was taken up with enthusiasm.[3] The election of Dr. Alexander McLaren as President of the Union for a second term helped the success of the appeal. Sir John Barran, of Leeds, and Mr. Herbert Marnham became joint-treasurers. A. Fitzgibbon Riley, minister of the Highgate church, assisted by Mr. H. H. Collier and Mr. W. W. Parkinson, were responsible for a special young people's effort. Wales was asked for £50,000, Scotland for £20,000 and Ireland for £7,000. The names of subscribers of more than 10s. could be set down in either the "Historic Roll" or the "In Memoriam Roll", a series of large volumes now preserved in the Baptist Union Library. Special simultaneous collections were asked for in 1899 and 1900.

Unexpected distractions made it necessary to prolong the campaign somewhat. The National Free Church Council was engaged in a nation-wide "mission", and in this John Clifford

---

[3] See *The Story of the Baptist Union Twentieth Century Fund*, 1904. The contributions from Lancashire and Cheshire, where Mr. Harold Knott was organizer, amounted to £1 0s. 8d. per member.

and F. B. Meyer were taking leading parts. The Boer War was in progress and had excited a good deal of public controversy. Clifford, Meyer and Shakespeare were among those called in to help in expressing the mind of the Free Churches on the right terms of peace. These and other factors somewhat delayed the completion of the Twentieth Century Fund. At the Annual Assembly in 1902, however—held on the eve of the final surrender of the Boers—Shakespeare had the satisfaction of announcing that the target, high as it was and unprecedented for Baptists, had been passed. The final amounts had come in unexpectedly and somewhat dramatically. "The top stone has been laid by the hand of death—by the hand of God", Shakespeare told the Assembly. The death of Mr. William Chivers, of Histon, had led his family to give a further £5,000 as a memorial to him, and the small balance still needed had been promised by both Mr. John Marnham, of Torquay, and Mr. Edward Robinson, of Bristol.

Large individual gifts had been a feature of the giving to the Fund. The wealthier members of the denomination had come forward generously, particularly in England. Ireland had raised its quota very speedily. The Welsh churches responded well, though the wealthier individuals there are said to have been more hesitant. Only Scotland proved a somewhat disappointing field for the appeal. The division and distribution of the money was speedily put in hand, a special committee undertaking the allocation of the large sum available for church extension projects. By 1902 it was possible to have a stone-laying ceremony in Southampton Row and the following year the new Baptist Church House was opened. The substantial increase in the capital funds of the Union was accompanied by another change that marked the end of an epoch. For twenty-six years Mr. B. Worsley Chandler, F.C.A., had voluntarily audited the accounts. In 1903 he retired and the first professional auditors were appointed.

II

The success of the Twentieth Century Fund provided a fine

6*

beginning to Shakespeare's secretaryship. There were other reasons for growing confidence. The denominational statistics continued to show a steady increase. The Union had acquired a number of new assets.

As early as 1891 the Council had agreed that it would be a good thing to have an official weekly paper. Within a few months of moving from Norwich to London, Shakespeare carried to a successful issue negotiations for the purchase by the Union of the privately owned *Freeman*, which had been appearing since 1855 and had a considerable circulation and influence. The secretary himself took a large share in the editorial direction of *The Baptist Times and Freeman*, the new official paper, and secured the competent and loyal assistance of his brother, Mr. Alfred W. Shakespeare, in this and other of the denominational enterprises. A few years later, in 1910, the Union acquired *The Baptist*, a journal started in 1872,[4] and amalgamated it with *The Baptist Times*.

The Union had also gained a Home of Rest for Ministers and their Wives. Early in 1899, not long before he would have assumed office as President, Dr. James A. Spurgeon died suddenly. As a memorial to him, his widow presented Arundel House, Brighton, to the Union. To fill the vacancy caused by Dr. Spurgeon's death, Dr. Clifford, who had been President in the difficult year 1888-9, was again called to the chair. This brought to Shakespeare's side one of the most popular and effective of the denominational leaders. Clifford played an important part in bringing the Twentieth Century Fund appeal to a successful conclusion and in the subsequent unification and reorganization of the Home Mission, Augmentation and Church Extension Funds under the general title, "Baptist Union Home Work".

A new century, a new leader, a new paper, new resources— and with these a revised constitution, a new hymnbook, new departments and new responsibilities.

Changes in the Constitution were not easily agreed upon. They

[4] Its first editor was G. A. Hutchinson, of the *Boys' Own Paper*. From 1886-1910, T. H. Stockwell was editor.

were first publicly discussed at the autumn assembly held in Derby in October 1903. The Council proposed that the attenuated Declaration of Principle of 1873 be enlarged so as to read:

"The Basis of this Union is:
1. The sole and absolute authority of our Lord Jesus Christ in all matters pertaining to faith and practice.
2. The recognition of the liberty of every Church to interpret and administer the laws of Christ as contained in the Holy Scriptures, and
3. That Christian Baptism is the immersion in water of those who have professed repentance toward God and faith in our Lord Jesus Christ, into the Name of the Father, the Son and the Holy Ghost."

To the sevenfold objects of the Union as set out in 1894 it was proposed to add the clause:

"To afford opportunities for the declaration of opinion upon such public questions as the Council may from time to time determine."

This, however, merely expanded the phrase "the public declaration of opinion", which had formerly had a place in one of the other clauses. At the same time it was proposed to remove from the Constitution the detailed description of how the Council should be composed. There it was simply to be stated that the business of the Union should be conducted by a Council of not more than one hundred members, including both the co-opted and *ex officio* members.

In the by-laws, submitted to the Assembly at the same time, it was proposed that England be divided into ten districts, each with a stated number of representatives totalling in all sixty-eight persons. There were to be two representatives from Scotland and as many from Wales as there were Associations in the Welsh Baptist Union in membership with the Baptist Union of Great Britain and Ireland. Each member of the Assembly was to have as many votes as the number of places allotted to his district and was only to vote for his own district representatives. Those elected in this fashion were to bring the number of members representing England up to one hundred.

The procedure proposed would have been difficult to operate satisfactorily. The proposed changes were outlined to the Assembly by the Secretary in what was described as "an exhaustive speech". Several notices of amendment had been received, and after four or five speeches of a critical character Shakespeare withdrew the recommendations for further consideration by the Council. At the same time, Dr. Richard Glover and Dr. Charles Brown moved and seconded a resolution that was carried, instructing the Council to confer with the Committee of the Baptist Missionary Society with a view to the revision of the existing arrangements for the Spring Assembly so that the Union might secure "a more sufficient opportunity for presenting its claims and for conference on matters requiring denominational action".

The Constitution again came before the Assembly at an autumn session held in Broadmead Church, Bristol, in October 1904. This time the proposals were unanimously adopted. The Declaration of Principle had been re-phrased as follows:

"The Basis of this Union is:
  1. That our Lord Jesus Christ is the sole and absolute authority in all matters pertaining to faith and practice, as revealed in the Holy Scriptures, and that each Church has liberty to interpret and administer His laws.
  2. That Christian Baptism is the immersion in water, into the Name of the Father, the Son and Holy Ghost, of those who have professed repentance toward God and faith in our Lord Jesus Christ, Who 'died for our sins according to the Scriptures; was buried, and rose again the third day'.
  3. That it is the duty of every disciple to bear personal witness to the Gospel of Jesus Christ, and to take part in the evangelization of the world."

The addition to the objects of the Union was adopted in the form suggested in 1903. The proposals for the election of the Council were abandoned. Instead, as part of the Constitution of the Union, it was agreed that the Council consist of representatives of affiliated Associations, certain *ex officio* and Honorary Members, forty-five members elected by the Assembly on an unrestricted vote, and fifteen co-opted members.

Three years later, in 1906, it was unanimously agreed that the phrase, "our God and Saviour", be added after "our Lord Jesus

Christ" in the first clause of the Declaration of Principle. Though recognized a generation later to be unsatisfactory theologically and replaced by the words, "God manifest in the flesh", the new phrase clearly excluded a Unitarian interpretation of the Person of Christ.

So much for the Constitution. The new hymnbook was produced jointly by the Psalms and Hymns Trust and the Baptist Union. In return for the handing over of its property in the *Baptist Hymnal*, the *School Hymnal*, the *Union Hymnal*, with tune books, etc. and the *Union Mission Hymnal*, together with an agreement by the Baptist Union not to produce hymnbooks of its own in future, the Trustees agreed that, while continuing to distribute most of their profits to the widows and orphans of Baptist ministers, one-third should be paid directly to the Union and be at its absolute disposal, provided that not less than £1,000 had in any one year been available for widows and orphans. On this basis a new trust was created, of which the Union appointed one-third of the trustees.[5] The *Baptist Church Hymnal* appeared in 1900. It had been prepared by a committee presided over by the aged Dr. S. G. Green, who after twenty-four years on the staff of Rawdon College—first as tutor, then as President—had been editorial secretary of the Religious Tract Society and adviser to Mrs. John Rylands in the establishment of the Rylands Library in Manchester. The new hymnbook was quickly adopted in all parts of the British Isles, in the Dominions and in those fields of the Baptist Missionary Society where the English language was used.

The first of the new departments of the Union was a Publication Department. In January 1902 the Baptist Tract and Book Society was taken over. Before long a bookshop was opened in the new Baptist Church House, and under the direction of Mr. Charles Courtier, plans were made for the publication of books and pamphlets. Side by side with these developments went the

---

[5] By 1956 the total paid out to widows and orphans by the Psalms and Hymns Trust had exceeded £100,000 and the amount accruing to the Baptist Union since 1900 was more than £30,000.

organization of special activities for young people. A Young People's Union was formed in 1904,[6] to which the youth societies of the local churches could affiliate. Examinations in Biblical and historical subjects were arranged, and, in 1907, under the energetic leadership of J. Brown Morgan, a touring-club was started, offering young Baptists holidays at centres in Britain and tours on the continent of Europe.

Shakespeare had already co-operated with the officials of the Congregational Union in securing from the authorities of the Army and Navy the right of young men joining the forces to attest as Baptists and Congregationalists. He next pressed for the right to appoint chaplains to minister to them. Full opportunity to do this had to wait until the First World War, but preliminary steps were taken at the beginning of the century and were a further evidence of Shakespeare's determination and skill as a negotiator.

There was an almost breathless quality about the developments during the first ten years of Shakespeare's secretaryship. New means of granting denominational recognition to lay preachers were devised and a scheme prepared for helping them with training. The Union became officially associated with the management of Bloomsbury Central Church. In 1905, a Baptist Insurance Company was formed. In 1908, encouraged by a resolution adopted by the Assembly, a Baptist Historical Society came into being, with a journal of its own and Dr. W. T. Whitley as secretary. Nine years earlier, A. S. Langley and Mr. H. J. Cowell had advocated in the columns of *The Baptist Times* the formation of such a society in order to carry on the work begun fifty years earlier by the Hanserd Knollys Society. Also in 1908, the Baptist Ministers' and Missionaries' Prayer Union, in the formation of which F. B. Meyer had taken the lead twenty years earlier, was amalgamated with the more recently established Baptist Ministers' Fraternal Union.

---

[6] A Baptist Young People's Union of America had been formed in 1891. In 1910 it was linked with the American Baptist Publication Society and the Board of Education of the recently formed Northern Baptist Convention.

Of even greater significance was the formation in 1908 of the Baptist Women's Home Work Auxiliary, which became in 1910 the Baptist Women's League. The first branch meeting in London was held in the drawing-room of Mrs. Russell James, the daughter of Shakespeare's friend, A. Fitzgibbon Riley. With Mrs. C. S. Rose, the wife of a Baptist minister, as secretary and Mrs. Herbert Marnham as chairman, the League soon became an important and valued adjunct of the work of the Union.

The Baptist Total Abstinence Association had become a vigorous organization, with two travelling secretaries. In 1904 alone, ninety-five new Bands of Hope were formed, making the total in the denomination 2,037. During the same year 115 churches abandoned the use of fermented wine at the Lord's Table, making the total of those that had done so, 2,077.

In 1910, yet another auxiliary to the work of the Union appeared. A small society which had been aiding Baptist work in South Africa was, with the encouragement of the Assembly, turned into the Baptist Colonial Society. In the opening years of the century, one scheme alone came to grief, namely, the plan for a Northern Baptist College, put forward in 1902-3. The existing colleges in Manchester and Rawdon would have been its nucleus. Local sentiment and the loyalty of former students to the colleges where they had been trained proved too strong and the plan had to be abandoned.

III

These many new developments were in large measure the product of Shakespeare's fertile brain, his organizing skill and his power to gather around him able men and women. The enthusiasm called forth by the growing activities of the Union was fed by a rising tide of denominational confidence following the first Baptist World Congress. In 1790 John Rippon had dreamed of a gathering in London representative of the Baptists of different continents. When he collected material for his *Baptist Annual Register* relating to the churches of Britain and America and the Mennonite communities on the continent of Europe, it was

> "in serious expectation
> that before many years elapse
> (in imitation of other wise men)
> a deputation from all these climes
> will meet probably in London
> to consult
> the ecclesiastical good of the whole."

Like Carey's project of a world missionary conference, Rippon's scheme had to wait a century before it was seriously revived. In 1904, however, the idea of a gathering of the Baptists of the world was advocated and pressed in the columns of *The Baptist Argus,* an American publication, edited by Dr. J. N. Prestridge. Shakespeare took the matter up energetically and the Baptist Union Council issued an invitation for the holding of a congress in London.

It met in July 1905, and was attended by representatives from twenty-three countries. The main sessions were held in the Exeter Hall, in the Strand. For over seventy years this had been the centre for great religious gatherings in the metropolis, but a few months after the Congress the lease was sold and it ceased to be one of London's famous buildings. The veteran Dr. Alexander McLaren presided over the Congress. The Baptists of the United States were strongly represented. Interest focused, however, on the small delegations which came from the continent of Europe, particularly those from Russia and south-eastern Europe. The Mennonite communities were not represented, direct contact with them having been lost in the second half of the nineteenth century. It was the new Baptist movement which stemmed from J. G. Oncken which sent delegates to London in 1905. Many came from groups suffering severe persecution from both civil and religious authorities. At the Congress Baptists discovered with joyful surprise the extent and variety of their fellowship, it being estimated that the total number of Baptist church members was over six and a quarter millions. If, as some desired, the

Churches of Christ were included, then the number was at least seven and a half million. On 17th July 1905 it was unanimously agreed that a Baptist World Alliance be formed. Dr. Clifford was appointed as the first President. Dr. Shakespeare and Dr. Prestridge became joint-secretaries. One of the first concerns of the new organization was the encouragement of the little groups in Europe. With this in view a Continental Congress was held in Berlin in 1908, two gifted young ministers, Newton Marshall and J. H. Rushbrooke, both of whom had studied in Germany, giving much time to making contacts in different central European lands, while C. T. Byford travelled among the Slav-speaking peoples.

Within ten years of Shakespeare's appointment as secretary, the Baptist Union had clearly become vigorous and influential in a quite new way. Developments of a somewhat similar character, though on a smaller scale, had also been taking place in Wales. Around the Baptist Union of Wales and Monmouthshire, formed in 1866, there had grown up a group of independent societies and funds—a Building Fund, a Ministers' Provident Society (1871), a Temperance Society (1879), a Literature Society (1887), a Sunday School Union (1888), a Home Mission (1895). In 1899–1900 these were united more closely with the Union itself and its Council became a more important body. Edwyn Edmunds became the first full-time secretary of the Union and, a few years later, Ilston House, Swansea, was erected as a denominational headquarters.

The Baptist Missionary Society was also considerably extending its work. The new schemes of Shakespeare had been viewed with some concern by Alfred Henry Baynes, who had presided for so long over the activities which centred in the Mission House in Furnival Street. When Baynes retired in 1905, the Union joined in honouring him and in welcoming his successor, Charles Edward Wilson, who had spent some years as a missionary in India. It was hoped that there might at once develop new and closer collaboration between the Union and the Missionary Society. It was even arranged that the *Missionary Herald* and its juvenile counterpart (later known as *Wonderlands*) should be published by the new Baptist Union Publication Department. The rapid growth of the Union under Shakespeare's leadership caused, however, some reaction on the part of those who were accustomed to regard the Missionary Society as the senior and stronger body. The Baptist Zenana Missionary Society had since 1867 been a separately organized body, responsible for women's work overseas. There was now a Baptist Medical Mission, with Dr. R. Fletcher Moorshead as its energetic secretary, busily engaged in gathering funds to send doctors and nurses to India, China and Africa, and to build mission hospitals.[7] Moreover, the B.M.S. and the London Missionary Society had received a munificent bequest from a Leeds recluse, Robert Arthington. This made possible extensive new enterprises in all the mission-fields and the Society began to expand its home organization in more vigorous fashion, setting up a publication department of its own and, later, a young people's department. In 1907 a young layman, H. L. Hemmens, was invited to join the staff at Furnival Street, one of his chief tasks being the organizing of study circles and summer schools.[8] Five years later, when John Brown Myers retired, after more than thirty years at the Society's headquarters as Deputation Secretary, he was succeeded by William Young Fullerton, of Leicester, one of Spurgeon's students and a man of outstanding personality and power. He was appointed Home Secretary, with a standing and authority equal to that of C. E. Wilson, who became known thereafter as Foreign Secretary.

IV

Almost all of these important denominational developments took place during the brief reign of Edward VII. Queen Victoria had died in January 1901, and within a few months four of the outstanding Baptist leaders of the Victorian epoch passed away—

[7] See R. F. Moorshead, *Heal the Sick*, 1929, and H. V. Larcombe, *First the Kingdom*, 1936.
[8] See H. L. Hemmens, *Such has been My Life*, 1953.

first, E. B. Underhill, then the handsome and beloved Colonel Griffin, then Samuel Harris Booth, then Joseph Angus. Charles Williams and John Aldis lived until 1907, Alexander McLaren and George Short until 1910, Judge Willis until 1911 and Sir George White until 1912. The two last had sat in Parliament as Liberal M.P.s and were well-known public as well as denominational figures. With the passing of these familiar leaders a new age seemed to have dawned. The general mood was still one of confidence and expectation. Dr. John Wilson, of Woolwich, in his Presidential Address to the Union in 1904, noted that three hundred years earlier Nonconformists were probably only one in thirty of the population; early in the nineteenth century they had been one in eight; they had grown to be one in two. He then committed himself to the prophecy that

"in fifty years we shall be two to one—or rather, by that time our witness to liberty will be crowned with success, and the Anglican Church, freed from the bondage of the State, will unite with the Free Churches in every conflict for righteousness and truth."

There were many utterances of this kind. They proved to be strangely wide of the mark. The Edwardian period was, in fact, but a brief Indian summer following the rich harvest of the second half of the nineteenth century. In the early years of Shakespeare's secretaryship, the denominational statistics rose steadily. In the one year 1905, largely as a result of the revival in Wales associated with the name of Evan Roberts, an increase of nearly 32,000 was recorded. On the eve of this revival, F. C. Spurr, who had been Baptist Union missioner since 1895, gave up his work to take up the pastorate of the historic Maze Pond church in the Old Kent Road. He was succeeded as missioner by A. Weaver Evans, and he in turn, in 1910, by H. C. Wagnell. C. S. Rose, the husband of the secretary of the Baptist Women's League, organized a number of caravan missions. There were other special evangelistic efforts. F. B. Meyer was among Shakespeare's closest friends and collaborators. As President of the Union in 1906–7, he undertook an extensive campaign of visitation and evangelism in country districts, usually accompanied by the Secretary. At the close of his year of office, Meyer resigned his Christ Church pastorate and undertook a long tour in the East. When he returned in 1909, Shakespeare had a considerable share in persuading him to settle for a second time as minister of Regent's Park Church.[9]

By then it was clear that all was not well with the general religious situation in Britain. The Baptist Union figures for 1907 had shown a decrease of 5,000. This was repeated the following year. By 1909 the Baptist Union Council felt impelled to set up a special committee on Baptist Arrested Progress (later known as the Spiritual Welfare Committee). It was realized that something was wrong, though not that a downward trend had set in which was to continue steadily, with only one brief interlude, for several decades.[10]

The reasons for this are not easy to analyse. Nor are they yet all apparent. Political, social and economic factors played their part, as well as more specifically religious ones. Writing of the decade 1895–1905, Halévy points out that "as a result of the increasing indifference to religion of the general public, the social position of the Nonconformists was improving every year, and this indifference and tolerance endangered the old Puritan tradition of Dissent".[11] His comment on the movement for the federation of the Free Churches is also to be noted: "The 'Protestant' emphasis on independence and individuality was yielding to the 'catholic' emphasis on unity and organization."[12] But it was not Nonconformity alone which, in Edwardian times, began to lose ground. All the Churches were subject to the same influences and tendencies.

[9] See W. Y. Fullerton, *F. B. Meyer*, 1930.

[10] The separate figures for the Baptist Union of Scotland showed a slightly different movement. Between 1900 and 1906 there was a relatively rapid increase from 15,400 to 19,000. Thereafter the rise continued at a somewhat slower rate until 1935 when the total reached 23,310. This was followed by a slow but uninterrupted decline for twenty years, bringing the total down to under 20,000 again. In 1955 a gain was once more registered and the total became 20,122.

[11] *History of the English People*, Epilogue, Bk. II, ch. 1 (Penguin edition, p. 71).

[12] Ibid., p. 76.

A religious census conducted by the *Daily News* in 1902–3 and the more careful and systematic investigation of conditions in London carried out by Charles Booth between 1897 and 1900—the results of which were published in 1903[13]—had shown the growing gap between the Churches and the working-classes. The Victorian Sunday had been undermined for the wealthy by the growing habit of spending weekends in country-houses and for other sections of the population by the Sunday opening of museums and art-galleries. Nonconformists appeared to be holding their own better than Anglicans. Their institutional churches with secular as well as religious interests were meeting with considerable success in some of the larger cities. "Pleasant Sunday Afternoons" and "Brotherhoods" attempted to meet half-way those concerned with political and social issues.

These efforts, however, whatever judgment may be passed on their merits, had come too late. The Labour Movement was capturing the enthusiasm of an increasing number of those who had formerly been attached to the Free Churches. The methods by which the branches of the Independent Labour Party were run and financed were in large measure borrowed by the members from their experience in religious organizations.[14] Early Methodism is said to have saved England from an outbreak similar to the French Revolution. Its close connection with the Nonconformity of the closing decades of the nineteenth century was probably the main reason why British Socialism never acquired the anti-religious bias of its continental counterpart. But by 1909 it was apparent that the new political forces were moving away from the Churches.

The public controversies of the time played their part in distracting and confusing men's minds. Most Nonconformists were extremely unhappy about the Boer War. Some were strongly opposed to it. Before it was concluded, bitter controversy had

---

[13] *Life and Labour of the People of London*. In *Church and People in an Industrial City*, 1957, E. R. Wickham has provided evidence of "the persistent alienation of the urban industrial masses from the time of their very emergence in the new towns." His study is based on a detailed examination of the situation in Sheffield.

[14] See R. C. K. Ensor, *England, 1870–1914*, 1936, pp. 528–9.

broken out over the Education Bill introduced in March 1902 by Mr. Balfour's Conservative Government. Though it provided much-needed aid to Secondary Schools, the bill gave great offence to Nonconformists by its provisions in regard to denominational schools. This was made plain to the Prime Minister in June by a strong deputation led by Dr. Fairbairn, of Mansfield College, and of which Shakespeare, Clifford and Mr. Lloyd George were members.

Dr. Clifford became the popular leader of a Passive Resistance Movement, once the bill became law. This movement, whose real author is said to have been Alderman (later Sir) George White, M.P. for Norwich and President of the Baptist Union in 1903,[15] aimed at persuading householders to refuse to pay that proportion of their rates which was to be devoted to church schools. From the spring of 1903 onwards, many "resisters" had their goods distrained on. A number, including several Baptist ministers, at least one of whom was subsequently President of the Union, received sentences of imprisonment. By 1910, P. T. Thomson, of Leicester, had indeed been in prison on eight occasions. Not all Nonconformists approved of the militant attitude adopted by Clifford, though it had the energetic support of most of those associated with the National Free Church Council, including Shakespeare. The Passive Resistance Movement quickly gained momentum throughout 1904 and 1905 and continued with little diminution until the outbreak of the First World War.

It seemed for a time that the protest might be successful. That the Nonconformist Conscience was still a political force was shown at the time of public excitement over atrocities in the Congo rubber-plantations, when Clifford and the Baptist Union Council were outspoken in their denunciations. The importation of Chinese labour into the Transvaal also awakened sustained protests. Vigorous disapproval of what was regarded as the weak and vacillating conduct of the Balfour government in regard to these matters joined with a wave of radical enthusiasm to carry the Liberal Party to victory at the polls in January 1906. Clifford

[15] T. H. Darlow, *William Robertson Nicoll*, pp. 378–9.

and Meyer were among the many Free Church leaders who worked strenuously for the return of Liberal candidates. In the new House of Commons there were no fewer than 157 members with Nonconformist affiliations, a larger number than at any time since the Commonwealth. Many of the Liberal leaders, including Mr. Asquith, the Prime Minister, were of Dissenting parentage. Mr. Lloyd George had been brought up among the Churches of Christ, but he associated himself closely with the Baptists and frequently appeared on their platforms, including that of the World Congress of 1905. Mr. Augustine Birrell, C. M. Birrell's son, was a member of the government. The Chief Whip of the Liberal Party, Mr. Percy Illingworth, was a Baptist. Mr. George Hay Morgan, who had been minister of Woodberry Down Church, was among the newly-elected M.P.s.

The Liberal triumph was, however, quickly followed by a sense of frustration. Though Thomas Law, John Clifford and the Passive Resisters had made a considerable contribution to the result of the election, no agreement on a new Education Act could be secured, repeated attempts ending in failure.[16] Political controversy became more bitter, centring finally in the question of the powers of the House of Lords over money bills and resulting, in 1910, in a serious constitutional crisis. At the same time, the disestablishment of the Welsh Church, women's suffrage, and Home Rule for Ireland were bitterly contested issues, while on the horizon appeared a dark cloud of uncertainty as to the intentions of Germany, which was rapidly increasing its armaments. Baptists shared the general excitement on all these issues and were to be found solidly supporting the Liberal Party.

V

But the spiritual malaise that was becoming apparent could not be accounted for simply in terms of the political preoccupations of the time. The Welsh Revival had been of brief duration. It did not spread to other parts of the country. The missions of

[16] See E. K. H. Jordan, *Free Church Unity*, 1956, and G. K. A. Bell, *Randall Davidson*, ch. xxix, "The Education Controversy, 1906–1908."

Torrey and Alexander, and of Gipsy Smith, held under the auspices of the National Free Church Council, did not achieve the results that were hoped for. At the very time these and similar special evangelistic efforts were in progress, sharp controversy broke out over the views of Dr. R. J. Campbell, the successor of Dr. Joseph Parker at the City Temple. Campbell's sermons caused lively discussion and the republication of some of them in *The New Theology* (1907) and other volumes provoked widespread concern.[17]

Campbell's emphasis on the immanence of God and his assertion that "every man is a potential Christ, or rather, a manifestation of the Eternal Christ" found few echoes in Baptist circles, but his association with various Labour and Socialist groups and his proclamation of a "social gospel", which placed man in society under religious judgment, were paralleled within the denomination, even if not to the same extent as within Congregationalism.[18] There was everywhere a slow but growing awareness of the gulf between most of the Churches and an industrial population which was becoming increasingly restive. At the Autumn Assembly of the Baptist Union in October 1911, J. E. Roberts, McLaren's successor in Manchester, proposed a resolution on "Social Unrest", which referred to inadequate wages. A committee was appointed "to consider the attitude which the Denomination should take up towards such a serious economic condition, and report". No report was in fact presented in 1912, because by then a large-scale strike of miners had begun in an effort to secure recognition of the principle of a legal minimum wage.

[17] The criticisms of Campbell within the Congregational Union culminated in his making a personal statement to the May Assembly in 1910. A few years later he resigned his pastorate, repudiated his earlier views and in 1916 entered the Anglican Church. See J. W. Grant, *Free Churchmanship in England, 1870–1940*, 1955, pp. 131–42.

[18] John Clifford in particular was outspoken. See a speech at Forest Hill Baptist Church in June, 1908: "Socialism in the soul of it is divine. It is of God. The Churches ought . . . to take full share in the gradual reformation and rebuilding of society, to welcome every practical extension of the Socialist principle." In the United States the writings of the Baptist Professor Walter Rauschenbusch "spearheaded what came to be called the Social Gospel Movement". *Christianity and the Social Crisis*, his best-known work, appeared in 1907.

It is against the background of all these public events and controversies that Shakespeare's second great appeal to the Baptist denomination must be judged. He asked for a capital fund of £250,000 for the purpose of supplementing the stipends of the more poorly paid ministers, and accompanied the appeal with an elaborate and carefully worked-out scheme for ministerial settlement and removal, and the appointment of ten General Superintendents. As originally conceived, the scheme was also to involve the reorganization of collegiate training under the supervision of the Union. The Colleges still cherished their independence, however, and preferred to set up an Inter-Collegiate Board of their own, to which they invited the Union to appoint representatives. This part of the scheme therefore lapsed, and it cannot be said that the Inter-Collegiate Board ever functioned very successfully, or had any substantial achievements to its credit. So far as the main proposals of Shakespeare were concerned, they were, after much committee work, submitted to the Associations and churches, while special conferences took place with representatives of the Baptist Unions of Wales, Scotland and Ireland. The response was satisfactory and at the Assembly in London in April 1912 the appeal for the Sustentation Fund was launched.

Shakespeare had, as usual, carefully prepared the ground and before the Assembly met had secured promises of £51,685, over £4,000 of it from ministers. The main plea for the fund was made by F. B. Meyer, who hit on the happy idea of linking the target with the building of a "Nehemiah's Wall" of 250 stones, each representing £1,000. The carrying of the appeal to the country owed even more than had been anticipated to Meyer and to certain younger men such as F. G. Benskin, of Bristol, for soon after the 1912 Assembly Shakespeare suffered a serious breakdown in health and had to be away from the Church House for nearly eight months. J. R. Wood, of the Upper Holloway Church, once more undertook much of the general secretarial work of the Union, while Meyer and his helpers, including five treasurers, began their campaign. By the Assembly of 1913 no less than £138,511 was in sight and, a year later, Shakespeare was able to announce in Westminster Chapel the completion of the fund. A special Thanksgiving Meeting was held in the Royal Albert Hall and plans were put in hand for implementing the ministerial settlement scheme.

During the years 1911–14, full as they were of political excitement, there had been other developments in the work of the Baptist Union. The Baptist Young People's Union had drawn attention to the need for more care of the Sunday Schools of the denomination and, in 1911, Miss Annie E. Skemp was appointed Organizing Secretary and Educational Director. The following year the Y.P.U. was formally turned into a department of the Union. The promotion of "study circles" in the churches became one of its main aims, and Edward Hayward, one of Dr. Clifford's "boys" from Westbourne Park, became Honorary Organizing Secretary of a Social Service Section. At the same time, a serious effort was made to bring together the work being done among young people by the Baptist Union and the Baptist Missionary Society by setting up a United Board, consisting of four representatives from each side. In 1912 this Board produced a useful report. Among the things it recommended was that the B.M.S. Young People's Meeting in the spring and the Baptist Union Young People's meeting in the autumn "should both be utilized as opportunities for exhibiting the real unity of the denominational spirit". This was first put into effect in 1913. A few months later the increasingly successful Touring Club associated with the Baptist Young People's Union was turned into a limited liability company under the name the British and Continental Touring Club, Ltd. J. Brown Morgan, J. E. Roberts and Hector V. Thomas became the first directors.

During the same period the Baptist Women's League had continued to grow under the devoted leadership of Mrs. C. S. Rose and in 1912, under its auspices, a Hostel for Business Girls was opened in Mecklenburgh Square.[19] In all the new enterprises which were being embarked upon from the Baptist headquarters,

[19] The Hostel was transferred in 1934 to Amhurst Park, Stamford Hill, and in 1939 to St. Andrews, Green Lanes.

Shakespeare was greatly aided by the efficient service of his chief assistant, Mr. W. H. Ball, who had joined the staff of the Union in the days of S. H. Booth and was to continue there until 1947. The growing work of the finance department was in the hands of Mr. E. Blake, who also had an important part in the growth of the Baptist Insurance Company.

The second Baptist World Congress was held in Philadelphia in June 1911, under the presidency of Dr. Clifford. The previous year Shakespeare had visited the United States to share in the preparations. The coronation of George V prevented some from Britain who would otherwise have done so from attending the Congress, but there were between four and five hundred delegates from this country. The meetings resulted in an increased interest in Baptist world fellowship. Clifford's Presidential Address was one of the most impressive utterances of his career. A second European Congress, held in Stockholm in 1913, quickened concern for Baptist groups on the continent and, early in 1914, it was decided to set up a British Continental Committee, consisting of ten representatives of the Union and ten representatives of the Missionary Society, to consider what help could be rendered from this country.

The Peace Movement, the plans for a World Alliance for Promoting International Friendship through the Churches, and the beginnings of the Faith and Order Movement attracted the attention of a number of Baptists. Clifford and Rushbrooke were already prominently associated with the efforts to link the Churches of the world in the cause of peace. At a meeting of the Baptist Union Council in January 1914, Dr. Newman Smyth, of New Haven, Dr. Peter Ainslie, of Baltimore, and Dr. W. H. Roberts, of Philadelphia, spoke of the plans for a World Conference on Faith and Order. "After protracted discussion", it was unanimously resolved to appoint a Baptist Commission of fourteen persons "to represent the Baptist Union of Great Britain and Ireland with a view to co-operating with the other Commissions with regard to the arrangements". The Southern Baptist Convention of the United States, as well as the Northern Convention, had already returned similarly sympathetic answers to the invitation to join in Faith and Order discussions.

It is not without significance that Dr. W. W. Barnes in his history of the Southern Convention entitles the chapter covering the years 1899–1919 "Expanding Horizons". Developments in the United States were in many ways parallel to those in Britain. Extreme "Landmarkism" had failed to secure control of the Convention after half a century of effort. In 1906 a number of "Landmarkers" withdrew altogether. Thereafter the Convention showed a new sense of unity and aggressiveness in all fields of activity. What Dr. Barnes calls "corollary interests" increased, almost all of them becoming, in due course, absorbed into the Convention itself. A Standing Committee, set up in 1913 to co-ordinate the activities of the various boards, developed a few years later into a strong Executive Committee, which became the directing agency of the largest and most powerful Baptist organization in the world. For the time being there was readiness to co-operate with those of other denominations.

In Britain the disturbing decline in church statistics continued. The political scene became increasingly troubled. But as Baptists looked back on the previous ten or a dozen years, they could not but marvel at the rapid growth in the strength and importance of the Union and at the many new opportunities of service which were presenting themselves. Suddenly—and, as it seemed, almost without warning—in August 1914, Britain learned that Germany had invaded Luxembourg and Belgium and found herself at war.

CHAPTER 10

THE FIRST WORLD WAR AND ITS AFTERMATH,
1914–25

I

THE outbreak of the First World War on 4th August 1914, came as a profound shock to the whole nation, and not least to the Churches. Even those who had been concerned at the international rivalries and tensions of the preceding decade were unprepared for the outbreak of open conflict involving Britain. Clifford and Rushbrooke had journeyed to Constance at the end of July to share in the establishment of the World Alliance for Promoting International Friendship through the Churches. The meeting had to be abandoned, though certain effective decisions were taken which became fully operative when hostilities came to an end. Rushbrooke had to make his way from Constance into Germany, as his wife and daughter were on holiday there. For a time he and they were under arrest, then under close surveillance. Not until October, when there was an exchange between England and Germany of churchmen and medical personnel, was it possible for them to return home.

What attitude Baptists and other Nonconformists of radical sympathies would take towards the war was at first uncertain. Their initial hesitation was similar to that of a number of members of the Liberal government, including Mr. Lloyd George. The invasion of Luxembourg and Belgium, however, so shocked Christian sentiment that it was soon evident that there would be little holding back, even by those who had been most ardent in their work for peace. Shakespeare, Clifford, F. B. Meyer and T. R. Glover were among the Baptists who, on 23rd September 1914, signed a reply by British Church leaders to an appeal sent to Evangelical Christians abroad by a group of German theologians, who claimed that their country had been the victim of "a web of conspiracy".

"We have taken our stand," said the British leaders, "for international good faith, for the safeguarding of smaller nationalities, and for the upholding of the essential conditions of brotherhood among the nations of the world."[1]

The following month Clifford and Shakespeare were present at Lambeth at a conference of Christian ministers and laymen, called by the Archbishop of Canterbury, "to study the deeper bearings upon our own country, Europe, and the world of this great war and convulsion of the nations". On 10th November they both supported Mr. Lloyd George at a great meeting in the City Temple, which further rallied Free Church opinion in support of the cause of the Allied Nations against Germany. When the Baptist Union Council met, it addressed a Message to the Baptists of the Empire calling on them to join in "a war to end war". Thereafter, there was no serious division of opinion until the struggle was over, though, when conscription became necessary, alertness on behalf of the rights of conscientious objectors was shown.

The general Baptist attitude again found formal expression in the spring of 1917, when the United States entered the war on the side of the Allies. Dr. W. Y. Fullerton, then the President of the Union, Dr. Clifford and Dr. Shakespeare addressed a message to American Baptists in the name of the Baptist Union. It was a lengthy and reasoned statement on behalf of a denomination which had long strenuously advocated international peace.

"We are fighting," it was said, "for Christianity against paganism, for right against cruel might, for liberty against cruel tyranny; for humanity against the works of the devil."

The entrance into the war of America was regarded as "a guarantee for a real and abiding peace, and for the abolition of war once and for all from the category of human crimes". Mr. Richard H.

[1] See G. K. A. Bell, *Randall Davidson*, pp. 740–4.

Edmonds, of Baltimore, undertook the distribution of the message in the United States, and was able later to send to London evidence of the widespread interest and response it aroused not only among Baptists. A rather briefer message with the same main purport was addressed in the name of the Baptist Union to the Baptists of Sweden, a country which remained neutral throughout the war.

With few exceptions, the young men of the churches volunteered for the citizen army. Many ministers sought service as chaplains or undertook work with the Y.M.C.A. When Mr. Lloyd George replaced Mr. Asquith at the head of the government, Shakespeare became one of the new Prime Minister's most trusted Free Church advisers and a frequent visitor to Downing Street. As secretary of the Baptist Union, he had taken the lead in insisting that Free Churchmen must be appointed as chaplains. Before the end of 1914, E. L. Watson and T. N. Tattersall found themselves the first Baptist ministers on active service with the troops in France. The Baptist Union undertook the provision of huts and institutes for recreational and religious purposes, and through the Women's League arranged for the collection and despatch of comforts for the troops, as well as giving help to Belgian and French refugees. In 1916 an institute was built on land belonging to the War Office at Aldershot as a memorial to the Rt. Hon. Percy Illingworth, a Baptist who had been Chief Liberal Whip. The same year Shakespeare paid a visit to France and was decorated with the Protestant Cross of the Belgian Army for services rendered to Belgian refugees, many of whom had been received into Baptist homes in England.

The autumn assembly of the Union was to have been held in Halifax in 1914. This had to be cancelled and autumn assemblies were not thereafter resumed. The pace of life had quickened and two series of meetings had been proving difficult to organize and maintain. A number of promising developments had to be put on one side because of war conditions. J. Owen Clover began his work as Travelling Organizer for the United Board of the Baptist Union's and Baptist Missionary Society's Young People's

Departments in September 1914, but after only a few weeks left
to undertake service with the Y.M.C.A. At the same time, Miss
Skemp resigned owing to ill-health from her work in the Sunday
Schools and was not replaced. It did, however, prove possible in
the early months of the war to conclude negotiations which had
been in progress for some time between the Baptist Union and
the British and Foreign Unitarian Association. These concerned
certain properties and trusts which had originally belonged to the
General Baptists, but which had passed into Unitarian hands. By
an agreement signed in 1915 and approved by the Assembly in
1916, the old Pierce John and Joseph Davis Trusts were regulated;
all trusts belonging to, or under the control of, the General Baptist
Assembly were left undisturbed, so far as the Baptist Union was
concerned; four chapels were recognized as belonging to the
Baptist Union and all other chapels listed in the Essex Hall Year-
Book for 1915 were recognized as belonging to the Unitarian
denomination.[2] The two bodies agreed that, whether or not the
scheme was ratified by Parliament, they would "use to the utmost their influence at all times to prevent anything from being
done or any local action being taken which would in any way
break in upon this Agreement and Settlement". In the same year
John C. Foster completed a catalogue of the Baptist Union
library, which was subsequently published. A scholarly minister
with a wide knowledge of Puritan literature, he had had to retire
from the pastorate at Sydenham owing to throat weakness.

The most pressing issue facing the Baptist Union was the question whether in war-time the Sustentation and Ministerial
Settlement scheme should be put into operation. Since the
necessary funds were available, it was decided to proceed and the
arrangements were put into effect from January 1916. The
country had been divided into ten areas, over each of which a
General Superintendent was appointed. What seemed to some a

[2] The Pierce John Trust was set up in 1698 by Captain Pierce John, a member of
White's Alley church, the Joseph Davis Trust in 1692 by Joseph Davis, who built and
endowed a meeting-house in Mill Yard for the London Seventh Day Baptist Church. The
four chapels recognized as belonging to the Baptist Union were Bethnal Green, Headcorn,
Long Sutton and Saffron Walden.

J. H. SHAKESPEARE
M.A., D.D., LL.D.

M. E. AUBREY
C.H., M.A., D.C.L., LL.D.

J. H. RUSHBROOKE, M.A., D.D.

B. GREY GRIFFITH, B.D.

THE MISSION HOUSE
FURNIVAL STREET
1870–1940

THE BAPTIST CHURCH HOUSE
SOUTHAMPTON ROW

radical departure in Baptist polity was, in certain respects, a return to the "Messenger" system, which had been a feature of the life of the General Baptists in the seventeenth century.[3] The General Superintendent of the North-Western area was to combine with his duties the secretaryship of the Lancashire and Cheshire Association. His area included Cumberland and a number of churches in North Wales, Anglesey and the Isle of Man. Similarly, the General Superintendency of the Metropolitan Area was combined with the secretaryship of the London Baptist Association. The other English areas were the North-Eastern, the East Midland, the West Midland, the Western, the Eastern, the Central and the Southern, the last of these including the few Baptist churches in the Channel Islands. The Superintendent for South Wales worked in association with a South Wales Joint-Board which united three Associations of English-speaking churches affiliated to the Baptist Union: the Monmouthshire English Association and those of East Glamorganshire and West Wales. The secretary of the Baptist Union of Scotland acted as a kind of General Superintendent for the Scottish churches. It was agreed that £350 a year be paid over for the purpose of Ministerial Sustentation in Ireland. Shakespeare and the Council chose the first group of Superintendents with great care, for there was a measure of prejudice to be overcome. Among them were J. W. Ewing, who had already been President of the Union, and C. T. Byford, who had acted as Baptist Commissioner for Europe. Dr. George Pearce Gould, of Regent's Park College, undertook the chairmanship of the monthly meetings of Superintendents in London, as well as of the Sustentation Fund Committee.

The minimum stipend for a married minister was fixed initially at £120 per annum, towards which a local church had to raise at least £70. But prices had already begun to rise and in 1917, when 462 grants were made, the figure was raised to £130 (£150 for those living in London); in addition an allowance of £5 was given for each dependent child. By 1920 the number of ministers receiving grants had increased to 540 and the minimum stipend was

[3] See A. C. Underwood, *A History of the English Baptists*, 1947, pp. 119 f.

7

fixed at £135 per annum, plus a bonus of £20. The financial position of many ministers had by then become extremely difficult and an appeal for an additional central fund was in view. This had become the more necessary because the annual amount secured by a Simultaneous Collection in March had never reached the sum hoped for by Shakespeare and Meyer when the capital of the Sustentation Fund was raised.

The Sustentation Scheme involved considerable changes in Baptist polity and marked an important stage in the abandonment of nineteenth century independency. The making or withholding of a grant was at the absolute discretion of the Union. To qualify for a grant a church must be affiliated to the Union and must comply with other conditions imposed by the Union. Its application for help had to be accompanied by the favourable recommendation of an Association, following a visit of duly appointed representatives and the examination of the church accounts. It was optional for a church to seek aid, but if it did, it subjected itself to a measure of inspection and control both by the county Association and the Union. The scheme also committed the Union to a measure of responsibility for ministers temporarily out of pastorate. For a time the Union agreed to meet the running expenses of the Associations out of the amount received from the Simultaneous Collection in March. This arrangement was later varied, but the principle behind it—namely, that the finances of the Associations were notionally subject to the control of the Union and integrated with its own finance—remained. Thirty years later, the Home Work Scheme involved further developments towards something like a connexional system.

II

As the war dragged on, Shakespeare and the leaders of other Churches became increasingly concerned at the religious situation in Britain. Workers among the troops were shocked by their ignorance and apathy, and it was realized that sustained efforts would be needed to get them back into the churches, when hostilities ceased. Shakespeare was dissatisfied with the leadership of the National Free Church Council, which had no authority over the denominations as such and seemed to have dabbled too much in politics since the controversy over the Balfour Education Act. As far back as 1910, he had appealed for a closer Union of the Free Churches. A joint committee of Baptists and Congregationalists had met the following year to try to avoid or reduce "overlapping" between their two denominations. Many had come to favour for new areas "Union Churches" of the kind established in the Garden Suburbs of Letchworth and Hampstead, that is, churches directly affiliated to more than one denomination.

During 1916–17, when he was President of the National Free Church Council, Shakespeare boldly put out proposals for the federation of the Free Churches. The only way to get action appeared to be to start a new organization. Largely through Shakespeare's energy and persistence, a Federal Council of the Evangelical Free Churches was formed in 1919.[4] To it the co-operating denominations appointed official representatives. Shakespeare became himself the first Moderator. The previous year he had received an honorary D.D. from Glasgow University and a fine portrait of him by the Hon. John Collier was placed in the Library of the Baptist Church House. The portrait had been subscribed for by a large company of friends who included the Prime Minister, four Archbishops and thirty-one bishops, as well as many Free Church leaders. A few months earlier, Shakespeare had issued a book entitled *The Churches at the Crossroads*, which, while primarily an exposition of the Federal Council idea, went a good deal further, envisaging a new United Church of England.

There had been many unofficial consultations between church leaders during the war years. Shakespeare stated that, for the sake of a wider unity and a new religious settlement in England, he would himself be prepared for some kind of conditional

---

[4] For the Declaratory Statement of Common Faith and Practice see Appendix VIII. A Federal Council of Churches of Christ in America had been formed in 1908 with four Baptists on its first Executive Committee.

reordination at the hands of an Anglican bishop. At once a storm of controversy broke out within and outside the Baptist denomination. Robertson Nicoll of *The British Weekly* was extremely critical of Shakespeare's proposals for union with the Anglicans, and it was soon clear that on the matter of church relations Shakespeare had begun to forfeit the confidence of his fellow Baptists. The older generation of Shakespeare's advisers was passing away. J. R. Wood, Charles Joseph and Dr. John Haslam had died in 1917. Richard Glover died in the spring of 1919, but his brilliant son, T. R. Glover, of Cambridge, came forward as an outspoken critic of Shakespeare's views. Clifford at first remained silent, largely for the sake of old friendship and a sense of all that the denomination owed to its secretary, but it soon became known that he also was against any compromise with episcopacy.[5]

The discussion of these matters became more involved when it was learned that the bishops of the Anglican Church were ready for official conversations about new and more comprehensive church relations. Important changes had been taking place in the Church of England, many of them made effective by the Enabling Act of 1919. The "Appeal to All Christian People", issued by the Lambeth Conference in the summer of 1920, caused a considerable stir and led to a series of conversations between representatives of the Federal Council and a group of Anglicans nominated by the Archbishop of Canterbury. History was made for Baptists in April 1921, when Dr. Cosmo Lang, then Archbishop of York, addressed the Baptist Union Assembly on the "Appeal". He was cordially received and his address made a deep impression, though Shakespeare was probably indulging in wishful thinking when he wrote afterwards to the Archbishop: "Your address was so persuasive that I said afterwards that if someone had risen and moved that we accept episcopal ordination, it could have been carried. I think perhaps this is an exaggeration, but some-

[5] See T. H. Darlow, *William Robertson Nicoll*, pp. 384 f. and H. G. Wood, *Terrot Reaveley Glover*, pp. 153–4. Five letters Glover wrote to the *British Weekly* were reprinted under the title *The Free Churches and Reunion*, 1921, with a commendatory word from Clifford.

thing very near it would have been reached."[6] The official conversations, which followed the Appeal, continued for some five years, in the course of which a number of important memoranda were prepared, making plain the main points at issue between the episcopal and non-episcopal churches. Shakespeare shared in some of the earlier meetings, but before they were concluded, his health had completely broken down. Charles Brown, W. Y. Fullerton, J. C. Carlile and Herbert Marnham were the other Baptists who represented the Federal Council in the talks.

Suspicion of where they were being led caused many members of the Baptist Union Council to revise their attitude to some of the wider ecumenical developments which were taking place. As already noted, the Council had in 1914 agreed to co-operate in the preparation for the first World Conference on Faith and Order. Dr. Shakespeare and Dr. Gould had been appointed to the Executive Committee. In 1920 J. E. Roberts represented the Baptist Union at a preliminary committee meeting in Switzerland. In 1923, however, when the Federal Council suggested that the work of the various denominational commissions which had been set up should be placed in its hands, the proposal was declined and it became clear that Baptists were determined to retain full freedom of action.

III

Shakespeare's failure to carry his brethren with him in a cause which had come to mean so much to him contributed to a series of physical and nervous breakdowns, which brought his active life to an end. Before the final collapse, however, there were a number of further developments in the work of the Baptist Union.

It had been decided in 1915 that there should in future be only one Assembly each year, but that if possible it should meet in the provinces in alternate years. The Constitution was altered

[6] J. G. Lockhart, *Cosmo Gordon Lang*, 1949, p. 274. The Bishop of Norwich had preached at St. Mary's Baptist Church, Norwich, in 1919 on the occasion of the 250th anniversary.

accordingly. The Vice-President continued to be elected by ballot at the Assembly. In 1915 the total number of votes cast was under 400. There were four candidates. In a second ballot, it was the candidate who had come third in the first ballot who was elected.

At this same Assembly, an echo of the Down Grade controversy was heard. J. Moffat Logan, of Accrington, moved:

"That without seeking to re-interpret the past, but simply in the interests of spiritual unity and denominational effectiveness, this Assembly thinks that the time has come to delete from its records the Minute of 23rd April 1888, which has reference to the late C. H. Spurgeon."

As an amendment, Dr. Clifford moved, and D. J. Hiley seconded that, after the introductory clause, the motion should run:

"this Assembly of the Baptist Union of Great Britain and Ireland declines to re-open the question of the Minute of 23rd April 1888, referred to by the mover of the resolution."

After a lively discussion, the amendment was carried by a large majority and there were afterwards added to it, on the motion of J. C. Carlile, the words:

"But the Assembly earnestly hopes that the Council will seek some means by which English Baptists now separated may be united in one organization."

In 1917, Alderman Daniel Clarke, J.P., of High Wycombe, resigned from the position of Honorary Legal Adviser to the Union, a post he had held since 1893. In his place Mr. Cecil B. Rooke, LL.B., was appointed and a connection thus began which lasted until 1934. Shakespeare's attitude to Christian unity—and a perhaps inevitable reaction against his long tenure of office and on occasion somewhat autocratic manner—had led to some unrest among the ministers. It was accentuated by the financial difficulties which many were facing. At the time of the 1918 Assembly, some of the ministers held a private meeting and decided to send a deputation to the officials of the Union, consisting of Herbert Morgan, T. N. Tattersall and Arthur Dakin, with the request that there should be an annual pastoral session for the discussion of matters relating to the ministry. The Council agreed to this and the first session was held in 1919.

By then the war was over. The conclusion of the Armistice on 11th November 1918 had been celebrated five days later by a remarkable united Free Church service, held in the Royal Albert Hall and attended by King George V, Queen Mary and the Princess Royal. At the 1919 Assembly of the Union it was reported that Edward Hayward and J. Owen Clover were back at work in the Young People's Department and engaged in promoting a new Sunday School and Young People's programme worked out by a committee presided over by J. H. Rushbrooke. The programme included the formation of Young People's Fellowships in local churches. The Baptist Women's League started a Nurses' Guild to help some of the hundreds of nurses of many nationalities in London hospitals. Plans had also been drawn up for a Baptist Sisterhood to take over and develop the deaconess organization started twenty years earlier by F. B. Meyer. Many young women were seeking new avenues of social and religious service. Preparations were put in hand for a Women's Training College. This was opened with high hopes in 1920 in Hampstead, under the name Havelock Hall. The nucleus of its library consisted of a thousand volumes from the Midland Baptist College, which it had been decided to close. The Baptist Union Library was once more recatalogued by Professor A. J. D. Farrer, of Regent's Park College. It was no doubt a sign of the times that the Assembly of 1919, which adopted a cautionary resolution on Christian unity moved by T. R. Glover, also went on record in favour of "the fuller expression of individual freedom" in the columns of *The Baptist Times*.

New rules for Ministerial Recognition were drawn up. These were based upon the report of a special committee on the ministry presided over by J. E. Roberts. The article regarding the ministry in the Declaratory Statement of the Federal Council was approved and the committee urged the importance of college training, recommending the Council "to tighten up all conditions in respect of non-collegiate candidates". The new scheme was debated by the Assembly in Leicester in 1922, and again in 1923 in London, when general regulations for the recognition of collegiate candidates and for the testing of non-collegiate candidates by examinations were adopted. It was recommended that the commencement of a man's ministry should be marked by an ordination service held with the concurrence and approval of the county association, and that both ordination and induction services should include the observance of the Lord's Supper.

It had been hoped that as soon as the war was over another Baptist World Congress might be held. The Hague was suggested as a suitable rendezvous, but hesitant replies from the Baptists of the United States, together with the confused situation in central and south-eastern Europe, soon caused the plan to be abandoned. Instead, C. A. Brooks, of the United States, and J. H. Rushbrooke were asked to undertake an extensive visitation of European Baptists, and a small but representative conference followed in London. This conference, which met at the Baptist Church House in July 1920, proved of historic significance. It restored contacts broken by the war. It initiated a large programme of relief, assigning different European lands and areas to the Southern Baptist Convention, the Northern Convention, the British Baptist Union and such other unions and conventions as were able to send aid. Not the least important of its decisions was the appointment of J. H. Rushbrooke as Baptist Commissioner for Europe. Rushbrooke had already made an important place for himself in the life of the denomination in this country. He now stepped out on to a wider stage, becoming during the next quarter of a century the incarnation of Baptist world fellowship in and through the Baptist World Alliance. Relief efforts extended into Russia, and Rushbrooke paid several visits to the Soviet Union. Western Europe was deeply disturbed by the attacks of the Bolsheviks on the Orthodox Church, and Clifford and F. C. Spurr were among those who in 1923 signed a weighty protest prepared by the Archbishop of Canterbury.[7]

[7] Bell, *Randall Davidson*, pp. 1079 f.

Soon after its formation, the Federal Council of the Evangelical Free Churches had issued a declaration that no minister could properly discharge his functions if his stipend was less than £250 per annum. The minimum under the Baptist Union Sustentation Fund was far below this figure. There seemed no chance of reaching £250, but clearly something had to be done. The finances of the Baptist Missionary Society were also in a serious condition, as the result of a series of large annual deficits. In these circumstances, encouraged by a munificent offer of £12,000 by Mr. and Mrs. Edward Robinson, of Bristol, it was decided to appeal for a Baptist United Fund of £250,000, half for the Union and half for the Missionary Society. Of the Union's share, £100,000 was to be used for Sustentation purposes, £20,000 for the new Women's Training College and Sisterhood, and £5,000 for relief and the establishment of seminaries in Europe. Sir Alfred Pearce Gould and Mr. Herbert Marnham were the joint-treasurers of the Baptist United Fund; Shakespeare, W. Y. Fullerton and C. E. Wilson the secretaries; and Mr. John Chown the chief commissioner.[8] The appeal met with a speedy and generous response. Within little more than a year £270,000 was in hand or promised. The minimum stipend was at once raised to £160 per annum with a sliding scale reaching up to higher figures and children's allowances of £10. But it was significant that by 1922 grants were being made to close on 600 ministers.

IV

The success of the Baptist United Fund gave the denomination new confidence, but a number of serious personal losses occurred. An outstanding figure, the great China missionary, Timothy Richard, died in 1919. In April 1920 Sir George Macalpine passed away, and eleven months later Dr. George Pearce Gould; both had rendered outstanding service to the Union. A few months later, Vincent Tymms and E. G. Gange, among the last of the nineteenth-century leaders, died. Then Shakespeare himself had another serious breakdown and had to consider resignation.

[8] Mr. Chown died in August 1922, after four months as President of the Union.

The method of electing the Vice-President of the Union had recently been changed and the system of the alternative vote by postal ballot introduced. As a sign of their confidence and affection—in spite of disagreement over Christian unity—members of the Council nominated Shakespeare for the vice-presidency. He was not able to contemplate this additional burden. Indeed, for some months J. C. Carlile, of Folkestone, had to undertake many of the secretarial duties, in addition to the presidency of the Union. Then there came a temporary improvement in Shakespeare's health. A revised scheme for the Lay Preachers' Federation was approved, with Mr. Alfred Ellis, J.P. as its leader. Miss Cecily M. Bird was appointed to the Young People's Department in place of Mr. J. Owen Clover, who had been invited to the staff of the Westhill Training College. With the active assistance of the Baptist Women's League, the Union helped in the raising of a considerable sum for the new buildings of the West Ham Central Mission.[9] The treasurer and two secretaries of the Baptist Missionary Society were made *ex officio* members of the Baptist Union Council. In the ensuing months, Shakespeare was well enough to undertake, with Mr. T. S. Penny as his companion, a series of ministerial conferences in different parts of the country. A new evangelistic campaign was planned. Shakespeare shared eagerly in plans, which proved abortive, to transfer Regent's Park College from London to Cambridge.

His recovery was, however, shortlived. He was able to be present at the third Baptist World Congress, held at last in Stockholm in 1923, and preached in Uppsala Cathedral. During the service the Bible fell from the pulpit and this greatly distressed him. A few months later, he suffered another severe nervous and physical collapse. Again J. C. Carlile came forward to act in his absence. It was apparent that the time was ripe for a thorough review of the Settlement and Sustentation Scheme and a strong committee was set up with T. R. Glover as chairman and Henry Townsend as secretary. There began to be talk of the need for a

[9] See P. Rowntree Clifford, *Venture in Faith—The Story of the West Ham Central Mission*, 1950.

comprehensive Superannuation scheme for ministers. In its annual report for 1923, the Council stated that it had been "faced by peculiar difficulties and grave anxieties". It had also to report the sudden but peaceful death during its November meeting of the veteran, John Clifford, the last active link with the era of Millard, Harris Booth and Spurgeon, always a notable public figure and in his last years the eager advocate of "personal evangelism". Of its secretary, and the work he had done for the Union, the Council said: "He found the organization brick and made it marble," with which may be compared the later tribute of J. C. Carlile: "He was the man for the time and brought to the scattered ranks of the Baptists a generalship that turned a crowd into an army."[10]

Now it was clear that his active life was over. At the Assembly held in Cardiff in 1924, with T. R. Glover as President and B. Grey Griffith as the energetic local secretary, Shakespeare's resignation was accepted and arrangements were made for an annuity for him and for his wife. A special committee was appointed to consider the organization of the Baptist Union and the search began for a new secretary. During the year Douglas Brown was appointed Baptist Union Commissioner for Evangelism and P. T. Thomson Commissioner for Education. These appointments followed the report of a committee on Evangelism and Education, which had issued "an earnest appeal for co-operation" to the Baptist Missionary Society. When the Assembly met in London in the spring of 1925, it approved certain minor changes in the Constitution and unanimously and cordially appointed Melbourn Evans Aubrey, of Cambridge, as the new General Secretary.

[10] *My Life's Little Day*, 1935, p. 152.

CHAPTER 11

ALTERNATING HOPES AND FEARS, 1925–39

I

AT the time of his appointment the new secretary of the Union was forty years of age. The son of a Welsh Baptist minister, he had received training at Cardiff Baptist College and then, after winning a Baptist Union Scholarship, at Mansfield College, Oxford. A short but valuable term as co-pastor with P. T. Thomson at Victoria Road, Leicester, had been followed by a very successful ministry of twelve years at St. Andrew's Street Church, Cambridge. There was a ready welcome for new leadership at the Church House after the difficulties caused by Shakespeare's breakdown in health. The slight upward trend in the membership figures during the early nineteen-twenties seemed to justify confidence in a brighter future. Many still believed that the conflict of 1914–18 had been "a war to end war" and that the League of Nations would secure perpetual peace.

M. E. Aubrey was destined to remain at the helm at the Baptist Church House for twenty-six years. It proved a period of recurring crises in international and public affairs and one of grave difficulty for the Churches. The membership of almost all the main denominations suffered a steady and serious decline, and this was to be accentuated by the Second World War. Between 1925 and 1939, the churches listed in the *Baptist Handbook* lost over 30,000 members and more than 148,000 Sunday School scholars, and these losses were not exceptional compared with those of other bodies. By 1951, when Dr. Aubrey retired, the Baptist churches had lost nearly another 50,000 members and 57,000 scholars. Baptists had also had to face a number of awkward ecclesiastical and domestic issues. In these circumstances courage, wisdom and inspirational power of a high order were required in those in positions of leadership. These qualities Aubrey possessed. He maintained and developed many of the lines of denominational activity which Shakespeare had initiated. He successfully rode out not a few storms. He became widely known and respected in the country at large.

During almost the whole of his secretaryship, Aubrey had the loyal and efficient help in the office of W. H. Ball, who had been at the Church House throughout Shakespeare's term. For the first ten years, much time was given to the affairs of the Union by Mr. Cecil Rooke, the honorary legal adviser. J. C. Carlile continued to be an influential figure. He had rendered great service in the closing years of Shakespeare's secretaryship. When Aubrey was appointed, Carlile was asked to undertake for three years the editorship of *The Baptist Times*. His control of the denominational paper lasted in fact until his death sixteen years later. For the first five years, Alfred Shakespeare continued to assist with the production of the paper, being succeeded in 1930 by H. J. Cowell. Carlile was a man with many journalistic and social contacts and, though never a popular figure, played a considerable part in all the affairs of the Union for more than a quarter of a century. Another important personality was J. H. Rushbrooke, first European Commissioner, then Eastern Secretary, then General Secretary, and finally President of the Baptist World Alliance. Rushbrooke also was a man of great ability, whose influence was felt in the concerns of the Baptist Union and of the Free Churches generally.

The first fourteen years of Aubrey's secretaryship, the period from his appointment in 1925 to the outbreak of the Second World War in 1939, were marked by alternating hopes and fears in both denominational and public affairs. The immediate denominational enterprise which faced the new secretary was the raising of a capital sum of £300,000 for a re-organized and comprehensive Superannuation Fund. The main proposals for this had already been agreed upon before he took office. They were laid before the Annual Assembly which met in Leeds in 1926. It proved necessary to re-present them the following year when, for the first time, on account of the larger number of persons attending, the Assembly met, not in Bloomsbury Central Church, but in the City Temple. The advocacy of the new fund by Aubrey himself, the organizing ability of Mr. Arthur Newton, a London layman greatly trusted and beloved, and the support of a devoted band of ministers and laymen in all parts of the country, secured its success. The appeal closed—somewhat surprisingly and perhaps a little incongruously—at a dinner party at the Savoy Hotel, given by Mr. H. O. Serpell, with Mr. Stanley Baldwin, then Prime Minister, as the chief guest and Sir Philip Sassoon and Lord Shaw among the other speakers.

The successful establishment of the Superannuation Fund was a notable illustration of the growing sense of brotherhood within the ministry. It was agreed that premiums should be a fixed percentage of a man's salary—at least half of this paid voluntarily, it was hoped, by the church he served—and that the benefit when a man retired be the same in every case, the amount depending on the regular actuarial valuation of the assets of the fund. To qualify for membership a minister must be on the accredited list and must be pastor of a church affiliated to the Union. As ministers naturally desired to take advantage of the new scheme, their influence was directed towards getting churches into the Union and keeping them there. The scheme was also an added inducement to ministers to become accredited by the Union.

II

The Leeds Assembly of 1926 had proved a memorable one, though not of the kind that had been hoped for. Its opening coincided with the declaration of a General Strike in support of the miners' demands for the nationalization of the mines, following seven years of almost continuous unrest in the coal industry. Many delegates decided not to make the journey to Yorkshire. Some who did, returned home immediately. The meetings were, however, important. The President for the year was J. H. Rushbrooke and the programme included a carefully planned series of addresses on Baptist belief and polity, subsequently published under the title *The Faith of the Baptists*. These addresses were linked with the Baptist reply to the Lambeth Appeal of 1920, a document of considerable importance. It had been drawn up with great care by a small committee, of which Rushbrooke himself had been chairman and F. Townley Lord, then a rising young London minister, convener. It registered the Baptist reactions to the inter-church "Conversations" of the preceding years. "Union of such a kind as the Bishops have contemplated is not possible for us" was its categorical conclusion.[1] Rushbrooke's presidential address with the title "Protestant of the Protestants" elaborated a number of points in the reply. The address was described as "an undisguised beating of the Baptist drum" and expressed the general mood of the hour.

The reaction from the ecumenical interests of Shakespeare was shown in the decision that the Baptist Union should not be officially represented at the Lausanne Conference on Faith and Order, which met in August 1927, in spite of the earlier decision to co-operate in the preparations. The 1926 Reply to the Lambeth Appeal was sent to Lausanne, but not unnaturally the committee felt unable to treat it as a paper which should be circulated to the delegates. The action of the Baptist Union Council in regard to the Lausanne Conference separated the Baptists from the other British Churches, for Anglicans, Presbyterians, Congregationalists, Methodists and Churches of Christ were all represented. There were also present at Lausanne official delegates of the Northern Convention of the United States, the Seventh Day Baptist General Conference, the Baptist Union of Ontario and Quebec, and the Baptist churches of Germany. Many British Baptists were deeply disappointed at the decision of the Union. Two, at least, travelled to Lausanne at their own expense. One of them, Dr. W. T. Whitley, already known as the outstanding Baptist historian of his time, became closely associated with the joint studies initiated at the Faith and Order Conference. The

[1] For the full statement see Appendix IX.

other, Dr. J. E. Roberts, who had been President of the Union in 1918, accepted membership of the Continuation Committee. The Council soon saw that some, at least, of its fears about the movement had been groundless and that, even though the Baptists of the Southern Convention of the United States were turning away from ecumenical contacts, British Baptists need not, and should not, do likewise. On Dr. Roberts's death in 1929, Mr. Aubrey took his place on the Faith and Order Continuation Committee and played an important part in the discussions of the subsequent two decades.

The Southern Convention, as already noted, had originally declared in favour of participation in Faith and Order discussions. A complete reversal of denominational sentiment had taken place between 1911 and 1919. According to Dr. W. W. Barnes, this was due to two causes: first, the Inter-churchWorld Movement of North America, organized during the First World War. This embarked on an over-ambitious programme of foreign missions and "collapsed under its own weight". The second cause was the policy of the American War Department on religious work in the armies: this appeared to Baptists to favour Roman Catholics in an unconstitutional way.[2] Neither of these causes was directly related to what Bishop Brent and his colleagues were seeking to do, but the result was that Southern Baptists turned their energies into purely denominational channels and became increasingly suspicious of all united activities. In Britain, on the other hand, circumstances made Baptists feel that they could not afford to be cut off from their fellow Christians and that they had nothing to fear from theological discussion with them.

Tension on the question of Christian Unity continued, however, among British Baptists. Most, though not all, Baptists welcomed the rejection of the Revised Book of Common Prayer, when it was presented to the House of Commons in December 1927 and again in June 1928. They also disapproved of the subsequent licensing of the Book by the Anglican bishops in July 1929. The declarations of the Lambeth Conference of 1930 in

[2] W. W. Barnes, *The Southern Baptist Convention*, 1845–1953, pp. 280–83.

regard to the Free Churches and their ministers proved disappointing. They led, nevertheless, to a further series of "conversations" and in these Baptists again shared. The eighteen representatives of the Federal Council of Evangelical Free Churches included three of their number: Mr. Aubrey, the Rev. Gilbert Laws and the Rev. Hugh Martin. These renewed "conversations" continued somewhat desultorily throughout the nineteen-thirties. In 1938 an *Outline of a Reunion Scheme* and other documents were issued. The authority behind them was at once questioned. Criticism fastened on the use of the names of representatives who had ceased regular attendance at the meetings. Controversy over the documents continued even after the outbreak of the Second World War. In 1941 a group of Merseyside Baptist ministers issued a somewhat intransigent declaration regarding union with other Christian bodies, declaring in particular their objection to episcopacy. This document was given wide publicity by Mr. R. Wilson Black, who had a few years earlier left the Churches of Christ and become a Baptist.[3]

The Merseyside declaration had also in view the discussions which had gone on during the previous decade regarding the possibility of closer relations between the Free Churches. Challenged by this suggestion, the Baptist Union Council set up an influential committee to consider the issue of union between Baptists, Congregationalists and Presbyterians. Appointed in 1932, under the chairmanship of Mr. C. T. Le Quesne, K.C., its report was adopted by the Council in March 1937. This report concentrated almost exclusively on the rite of believers' baptism. The discussions in the committee had drawn attention once more to the fact that, though a very large number of Baptist churches in England had adopted "open membership", in the north, in Wales and in a number of other places the practice of "closed membership" was still strictly adhered to. The general tone of the report was negative and made clear that the Baptist Union could not, as a united body, support any of the proposals for closer union which were being canvassed.

[3] See H. Townsend, *Robert Wilson Black*, 1954, pp. 111 ff.

Baptists had no difficulty in sharing in the Birmingham Conference on Politics, Economics and Citizenship (COPEC). They collaborated in the Universal Council for Life and Work, which had grown out of the Stockholm Conference of 1925. Mr. Aubrey and the Rev. P. T. Thomson were appointed delegates of the Baptist Union to the Oxford Conference on Church, Community and State, held in July 1937, and found there delegates from the Baptist Union of Wales and the National (Negro) Convention, the Northern Convention and the Southern Convention of the United States.

British Baptists also decided to send a strong delegation to the Second World Conference on Faith and Order, which met in Edinburgh the following month. Mr. Aubrey, Dr. Rushbrooke, the Rev. Gilbert Laws and Mr. C. T. Le Quesne played there an active part in representing Baptist views on the ministry and sacraments. The personal influence gained by Mr. Aubrey was shown by his appointment to the important "Committee of Thirty-Five", charged to review the inter-church co-operation which had developed since the Stockholm and Lausanne Conferences. This committee reported to both the Oxford and Edinburgh Conferences of 1937 and from it came the first proposal for a World Council of Churches, which in due course the Baptist Union decided to join.

On the ground that it had no authority in such matters, the Southern Convention had in 1932 declined to appoint delegates to the Second World Conference on Faith and Order. In 1937, however, the Executive Committee elected Dr. J. R. Sampey, President of Louisville Seminary, as "the official representative and spokesman of the Southern Baptist Convention" to both the Oxford and Edinburgh Conferences. Three years later the Convention returned to its earlier attitude and, on the ground that it had "no ecclesiological authority", declined the invitation to join the proposed World Council of Churches.[4]

[4] See W. W. Barnes, op. cit., 286.

Meantime, under Aubrey's leadership, a number of important developments had been taking place in denominational organization in Britain, though not without many distractions and difficulties.

From the time of his appointment, the secretary of the Union was responsible for a greatly enlarged and more comprehensive annual report. There was much to record. In 1926 the work of the formerly independent Baptist Total Abstinence Association became an integral part of the Union's activities. The following year the Rev. Edward Hayward resigned from the leadership of the Young People's Department and, after a few months during which P. T. Thomson gave oversight, Dr. T. G. Dunning was appointed to the staff at the Baptist Church House with responsibility for Temperance, Social Service and Youth matters. This appointment proved a fillip to the work in several directions, not least in the development of international contacts, as a result of Dr. Dunning's interest in the Youth Committee of the Baptist World Alliance. The work of the Women's Department also continued to expand. In 1934 Mrs. C. S. Rose was succeeded by Miss Doris M. Rose, who had had valuable experience at the headquarters of the Girls' Life Brigade. Women were taking an increasingly prominent part in public life and it was agreed by the Council that they were eligible for admission to the ministry. There were many Baptists who would have liked to see Mrs. Rowntree Clifford (Sister Hettie), of the West Ham Central Mission, elected President of the Baptist Union, either on her own or jointly with her husband.

In 1934, Mr. Herbert Marnham resigned the treasurership of the Baptist Union. He had played a vital part in the notable growth in the activities and responsibilities of the Union during the previous thirty years, and his graciousness and generosity had made him a much-loved and respected figure. Mr. Arnold S. Clark was appointed as Mr. Marnham's successor. Well-known in London as a lay-preacher and for his interest in the Baptist

Missionary Society, Mr. Clark was also closely identified with the work of Spurgeon's Orphanage, the National Sunday School Union and the British and Foreign Bible Society. The lay preachers of the denomination had long looked to Mr. Alfred Ellis, J.P., of Amersham, as their leader. He, in 1934, became the Honorary Legal Adviser to the Union in succession to Mr. Cecil Rooke, but his service in this capacity was brief, as he died suddenly in 1936. His partner, Mr. Gordon G. Fairbairn, the son of a minister, was able to take his place and had indeed already been undertaking much of the work. To Mr. Clark and Mr. Fairbairn the Union became deeply indebted in the ensuing years.

The general pattern of the Ministerial Settlement and Sustentation Scheme was reviewed and re-adopted during these years, but it continued to be necessary, because of the inadequacy of the annual Simultaneous Collection, to draw on the capital of the Supplemental Fund raised after the First World War. In 1926 the Pastoral Session had set up a Commission of its own on "Matters affecting the Efficiency of the Ministry", with F. J. H. Humphrey as chairman and W. H. Matthew as secretary. Its report was issued in 1928, but did not result in any notable proposals. Three years later, the ministers set up another committee to consider the "time limit" attached to invitations under the ministerial settlement scheme. Its report, though critical of the arrangement, did not put forward any effective alternative. Church life generally was passing through a difficult period. In 1936 the Baptist Union Council itself set up a Committee on Baptist Polity at the request of the Pastoral Session. It consisted of fifteen ministerial and seventeen lay members. Major W. N. Town, of Leeds, was elected chairman and the Rev. J. O. Barrett became associate secretary with Dr. Aubrey. The review on which it embarked was a comprehensive one and had not been completed at the outbreak of the Second World War.

The unrest in the ministry, of which these frequent committees are evidence, came from a variety of causes. Many churches and ministers were facing increasing financial difficulties. The Missionary Society had year after year to declare a deficit. The steady decline in church membership caused concern and depression. In these circumstances the Union took the lead in a number of attempts at more aggressive evangelism. The first effort was a two-year Discipleship Campaign, launched in 1932, with the object of securing that every church member lead at least one person into the direct service of Christ and the Church. Though widely taken up by the Associations and churches, the campaign did not achieve any spectacular results.

In 1931 the Union had been joined by the Twynholm Church, formerly in membership with the Annual Conference of the Churches of Christ, and by its leading personality, Mr. Robert Wilson Black, J.P., a man of great wealth and energy. Mr. Black came swiftly to a position of influence in the Baptist denomination and began to call attention to the urgent need for evangelism and church extension. A general shift of population was already in process and little had been done to meet the changing situation. Mr. Black's first move was to provide the money for the appointment of the Rev. J. N. Britton as Baptist Union Evangelist and Commissioner for Evangelism, the appointment lasting from 1935 to 1938. In 1936, again at the call of Mr. Black, the Union undertook a Forward Movement. Launched at a meeting held in the Royal Albert Hall, it was to have a double purpose, first evangelistic and secondly financial. Between 1931 and 1936, some £426,000 had, it was estimated, been spent on, or promised to, new building schemes. A national appeal was issued with the object of raising this figure to £1,000,000 by 1941. The drive and generosity of Mr. Black carried this campaign to a successful issue, in spite of the outbreak of the Second World War. The evangelistic efforts, which accompanied the Forward Movement, did no more, however, to stay the continued decline in membership than did similar efforts undertaken by other denominations.

The impetus given to the establishment of new causes was, however, accompanied by an important revision of the Model Trust Deed recommended by the Union. The change made involved a fundamental departure from past tradition, the full effects of which are only likely to be apparent to future generations.

In the eighteenth and nineteenth centuries the trust deeds of Baptist properties took many forms. They were often inadequate to secure a property to the Baptist denomination. The doctrines set out in many of them were not peculiar to Baptists. The important question as to what was to happen in the event of the named church or society of Baptists coming to an end—that is to say, the ultimate trust—was frequently, though by no means universally, solved by naming the Particular Baptist Fund or the Baptist Building Fund as beneficiaries. The trustees, who were often a group of individuals who lived, or had at one time lived, in the locality, were given little or no say in the management of the property. Local trustees were becoming increasingly difficult to find and the Union had long had a model trust deed which placed the trusteeship in the hands of the Baptist Union Corporation and the ultimate trust with the Union itself, but this did not remedy all the defects of earlier deeds. In particular it gave no help in the sometimes difficult matter of proving that those who were in a particular church and claimed to be Baptists might in fact not be Baptists in the commonly understood sense. Where churches became redundant or the number of members became very few, it often proved impossible to sell the property and use the proceeds for church extension elsewhere because of the resistance of a small group, or for other technical reasons. Accordingly, a clause was included in the Model Deed which made it possible for the Association and the Union acting together to close the church, sell the property and dispose of the proceeds as they thought fit. It was also required that churches adopting the deed be in membership with both an Association and the Union and that the minister be on the accredited list. The adoption of the new Model Deed could not, of course, be compulsory on any particular church, nor could it affect cases other than those where trusts were being declared for the first time. In the ensuing years, however, the deed has in fact been adopted by almost all the newly-formed churches.[5]

In 1927, the Home Counties Association became affiliated to

[5] For further developments in the matter of trusts see pp. 253 f.

the Baptist Union. Formed in 1877 and originally known as the Surrey and Middlesex Baptist Association, this was the Association which had in 1890 been joined by the Metropolitan Tabernacle and a number of other churches sympathetic to Spurgeon. The step taken in 1927 marked the healing of one of the wounds left by the Down Grade controversy. But the Union was not entirely free from internal theological tensions in the nineteen-twenties and nineteen-thirties, It had in its membership some who continued to look askance at Biblical scholarship and whose Calvinism was of a conservative kind. Dr. James Mountain had opposed Shakespeare's plan for a Federal Council of the Free Churches on the ground that its Declaratory Statement of Faith was inadequate. The Baptist Missionary Society had been involved in controversy in 1922-3, the attack being led by the Rev. R. Wright Hay and concentrating attention on *The Soul of India*, a volume of lectures by Dr. George Howells, of Serampore College. In 1929 there was public criticism of Dr. A. C. Underwood and the teaching given at Rawdon College and about the views of Dr. H. Wheeler Robinson, of Regent's Park College.

More serious controversy developed—somewhat unexpectedly —during the preparations for the Discipleship Campaign. T. R. Glover, at the invitation of the Baptist Union Council, drafted a study pamphlet with the title, *Fundamentals*. One of the sections was devoted to the doctrine of the Atonement. Its adequacy was challenged by the Rev. H. Tydeman Chilvers, who, after service among the Strict Baptists, had been since 1919 pastor of the Metropolitan Tabernacle, and by the Rev. Thomas Greenwood, then minister in Liverpool. It was suggested that Glover's notes were, in effect, an attack on the substitutionary view of the death of Christ held by Spurgeon, Moody, Wesley and Whitefield. As a result of controversy in the pages of *The Baptist Times* and *The Sword and Trowel*, as well as of a number of private letters, "the officers of the Union and some of the older statesmen began to fear that they were in for a second down-grade controversy, before the earlier breach was fully healed".[6]

[6] H. G. Wood, *T. R. Glover*, p. 161.

Glover had had no intention to offend. He was, however, sensible of the dangers involved for himself and the Council if the pamphlet were withdrawn. In the end, largely through the skilful mediation of Dr. Percy W. Evans, of Spurgeon's College, it was agreed by both parties to the dispute, and by the Council in March 1932, that another pamphlet should be prepared setting out the substitutionary view of the Atonement, and that this should be distributed by the Union together with that by Glover. A crisis was avoided, as was a minor one that immediately threatened as a result of the publication of an article by Glover in the London *Times* on "The Free Churches these last fifty years". It was a characteristically brilliant article, but the somewhat critical references to Spurgeon again gave offence and Aubrey felt it necessary to send to *The Times* a letter dissociating the Union from what Glover had written.

These episodes provided evidence of the diverse elements still to be found within the Baptist denomination and of the nervous suspicions not far below the surface. They were a reminder of how difficult remained the task of leadership. As a result of similar controversies in the United States, there were substantial secessions from the Northern Baptist Convention, and divisions also occurred among Canadian Baptists.[7]

IV

The public affairs of the time were characterized by growing uneasiness, both at home and abroad. The General Strike left a legacy of bitterness in industry. Economic and financial crises were accompanied by unemployment on an unparalleled scale. The high hopes that had been placed in the League of Nations were discovered to be insecurely based. First Mussolini, then Hitler, climbed to power. Communism emerged as a world

[7] The General Association of Regular Baptist Churches (North) was formed in 1933, the Conservative Baptist Association of America in 1947. The Baptist General Association, formed in 1905 as a split from the Southern Convention, became in 1924 the American Baptist Association. These bodies are not in membership with the Baptist World Alliance. The controversies in which Dr. H. E. Fosdick was involved, and which led to the building of Riverside Church, New York, occurred in 1922-4. A number of churches seceded from the Baptist Convention of Ontario and Quebec in 1927.

movement, revolutionary in aim. The shadow of war again crept over the international scene.

Many Baptist churches had become corporate members of the League of Nations Union. A number of ministers and laymen had declared themselves pacifists. But a series of anxious debates—similar to those taking place in other denominations—revealed Baptists to be perplexed and divided. In March 1933 the Baptist Union Council received a resolution from the Baptist Union of Wales demanding a clear lead against any future participation in war. A draft answer had to be withdrawn the following November and there was set up a strong committee under the chairmanship of the Rt. Hon. Ernest Brown, M.P. (later succeeded by Dr. J. H. Rushbrooke), to consider "The Attitude of the Baptist Denomination to War". Its report, adopted by the Council in November 1936, urged the surrender of a measure of national sovereignty in order to secure the establishment of a really effective World Organization, but admitted hesitation in connection with "the contention—endorsed by the majority of the committee—that a peaceful world cannot be ensured apart from force organized in such form and on such a scale as to be equal to the task of restraining disloyal and aggressive States".

In 1935 Mr. Lloyd George, who was hoping for a restoration of his political influence and still retained the rather nostalgic loyalty of many Free Churchmen, took the lead in the establishment of a Council of Action for Peace and Reconstruction. This was joined by Dr. S. W. Hughes, who was at the time secretary of the National Free Church Council, by Mr. Wilson Black, Dr. Charles Brown and a number of other Baptists. Mr. Black became treasurer of the Council of Action. Following the break-up of the Liberal Party, however, Free Churchmen had become divided in their political judgments, some moving to the right, some to the left. Dr. Aubrey and Dr. Carlile held aloof from Mr. Lloyd George's schemes, and there was controversy on the matter in the columns of the *Baptist Times*. The Council of Action petered out, and within a few months other questions occupied the mind of the nation. King George V died in January 1936, and before the year was out the secretary of the Baptist Union was summoned with Dr. Sidney Berry, of the Congregational Union, to discuss with Archbishop Lang the affairs of Edward VIII. In the subsequent abdication crisis, Free Churchmen and Anglicans were in substantial agreement with the line taken by the Prime Minister. On the accession of George VI it fell to Dr. Aubrey as Moderator of the Free Church Federal Council to present the Loyal Address to the new King on behalf of the Free Churches. Dr. Aubrey and Dr. Berry put forward a request that the Free Churches be granted some official part in the Coronation Service, but this was not acceptable to the Anglican authorities. In May 1937 Dr. Aubrey was created a Companion of Honour.

It was in the midst of these preoccupations that Baptists found themselves facing a complicated situation which involved the whole structure of denominational organization. Previous chapters have told the story of the slow growth of the Union and its changing relationships to the many societies formed in the early years of the nineteenth century. The Baptist Missionary Society remained not only the oldest but the largest of the denominational societies. Its work in Asia, the West Indies and Africa had steadily grown in volume, and the society itself had become deeply rooted in the confidence and affection of the denomination. Support was forthcoming from a number of Baptist churches not directly affiliated to the Union. When the Baptist Union of Wales and Monmouthshire and the Baptist Union of Scotland were formed, no attempt was made to organize separate missionary societies. The rapid development of the Union's strength and activities in the early years of the twentieth century, the building of the Baptist Church House as a denominational headquarters, and the appeals for increased financial support, which had to be made, created a number of new problems. The working out of fresh and closer relationships between the Union and the Missionary Society seemed necessary for many different reasons. The occasion seemed to be provided by the fact that the Society's headquarters in Furnival Street were understood to be sought after as the site for new government offices.

The leaders of the Missionary Society came, almost unanimously, to the view that, instead of seeking fresh premises of their own, they should press for the erection of new denominational headquarters, capable of housing once more both the Union and the Society. Discussions were therefore initiated between the two bodies. Mr. Wilson Black, who had already considerable experience in promoting schemes for new headquarters for religious and philanthropic organizations, began negotiations for a site in Russell Square belonging to the Bedford Estate. Most of the leaders of the Union, while reluctant to leave the Church House in Southampton Row, were not averse to new headquarters. They felt, however, that if the two bodies were to be housed together, there must be a closer integration of their life and that some scheme for unified control should be decided upon before any move was made. It was agreed without much difficulty that the two Publication Departments (Kingsgate Press and Carey Press) and the two Young People's Departments could be brought together and that the two Women's Departments could with advantage co-operate much more closly than they had done. To anything beyond that there was resistance on the part of the Society. The Baptist Laymen's Missionary Movement had since 1933 interested itself in the formation of Contact Clubs and similar groups in local churches, but it was not until 1944 that it became the Baptist Men's Movement aiming "to intensify Christian effort at home and abroad".

After many months of discussion, the Baptist Union Council accepted the view of the General Committee of the Missionary Society that there should be joint headquarters, with certain departments unified and with council chamber and committee-rooms for common use, but with the two bodies still separate and the question of ultimate fusion left in abeyance. A resolution passed in November 1936 stated:

"That the members of the Council of the Baptist Union consider it desirable that the work of the Baptist Missionary Society and of the Baptist Union should, if possible, be carried on in the same building."

The subsequent negotiations occupied some seventeen months. The detailed scheme for a new headquarters in Russell Square was submitted by Mr. Wilson Black to the first session of the Assembly in April 1938. Though the site was leasehold, the lease was for 200 years and adequate safeguards had been secured. The scheme had already been approved by the Council and the General Committee of the Missionary Society. A number of respected leaders—including the treasurers of both bodies—had, however, reserved their right to oppose it, though their reasons for doing so varied and were in some cases contradictory. The session in the City Temple was an unhappy one. The speeches against the scheme were far more effective and forceful than those in favour, and in the end it was defeated, an amendment being passed which gave the Council authority to seek joint-head-quarters, but only if a freehold site was secured.

In effect the whole proposal was thus killed. In the closing stages of the negotiations and in the arrangements for the Assembly debate, a number of personal misunderstandings had arisen. It appeared likely for a time that Mr. Wilson Black would resign his office of Chief Commissioner for the Forward Movement and leave the Council. This dénouement was happily averted, but the whole episode aroused feelings that were not easily forgotten and banished for at least a generation any hope of bringing the Union and the Missionary Society closer together.

Within seventeen months of the rejection of the Russell Square scheme, the Second World War began. Was the denomination saved from a project which could not have succeeded in the changed financial situation? Was it saved from a plan which would have caused continuous embarrassment, because the vital matter of unified control was left on one side? Or was a great opportunity lost, and the cause of denominational unity and progress set back many years? It is perhaps still too early to answer these questions, though they have often been debated. In any case, the session of the Assembly on 25th April 1938 must always remain one that is remembered with a sense of uneasiness, if not shame, for the delegates were given no real opportunity of considering the proposals on their merits.

Within a few months of this episode, the Rev. C. E. Wilson retired from the Foreign Secretaryship of the Missionary Society and was succeeded by Dr. H. R. Williamson, from China.

V

A number of other significant matters occurred during the years under review, of which not the least important was the transfer of Regent's Park College from London to Oxford. Baptists were thereby provided for the first time with a theological college in one of the older university centres. The possibility of such a move had first been mooted by Joseph Angus in the eighteen-eighties, soon after the abolition of religious tests at Oxford and Cambridge. That part of the Twentieth Century Fund devoted to advanced ministerial training had envisaged such a scheme. In 1922 Shakespeare shared in the shaping of plans—which proved abortive—for the moving of Regent's Park College to Cambridge. The successful carrying through of the Oxford project was due to the persistence and standing of Dr. H. Wheeler Robinson, Principal of Regent's Park College from 1920. For some years the Baptist students were closely associated with Mansfield College, but in July 1938 the foundation stones of new premises were laid on a fine site just off St. Giles. The Intercollegiate Board, formed by the Union, had never functioned effectively, but during these years the Principals of the Baptist Colleges began to co-operate much more closely and Dr. Percy W. Evans drew Spurgeon's College into closer association with the Union.

In 1933, the denomination was provided with a new hymn-book, a committee of the Psalms and Hymns Trust, under the chairmanship of the Rev. Carey Bonner, preparing a revised edition of the *Baptist Church Hymnal* which quickly secured acceptance in the churches. Shortly after the successful launching of the new book, Mr. H. W. Pewtress, the secretary of the Psalms and Hymns Trust, resigned, his place being taken by Mr. C. H. Parsons. The Trust had maintained offices and stockrooms of its own in Cursitor Street, in premises belonging to the Missionary Society. In 1935 an agreement was negotiated by which the Baptist Union Publication Department (Kingsgate Press) became the distributing agents of the hymnbook. At the same time Mr. Parsons became manager at Southampton Row in succession to Mr. Courtier, as well as secretary of the Psalms and Hymns Trust.

In 1938, the Assembly which debated the question of joint-headquarters, adopted a revision of the Declaration of Principle of the Union. Two changes were made, which improved the Declaration theologically. The phrase "our Lord and Saviour Jesus Christ, God manifest in the flesh" replaced "the Lord Jesus Christ, our God and Saviour", and the liberty of each Church to interpret and administer His laws was declared to be "under the guidance of the Holy Spirit". In 1939, when the Assembly met in Birmingham, for what proved to be the last time in the pro-vinces, the Baptist Ministers' Fraternal Union was formally united with the Pastoral Session under the name, "The Baptist Minis-ters' Fellowship". Under the devoted and enthusiastic leadership of S. G. Morris, who, after a pastorate of thirty years at Upper Holloway, served for eight years as a General Superintendent and in 1943 became President of the Union, this organization rapidly grew in strength and usefulness. The Pastoral Session ceased to be an occasion for the airing of grievances. A new sense of ministerial brotherhood showed itself and was fostered—after the close of the Second World War—by an annual Summer School for ministers, subsidized by the Union, and by a quarterly magazine, *The Fraternal*.

The failure of the scheme for joint-headquarters was followed by a substantial reconstruction of Kingsgate Chapel, its gallery being taken into the Church House so as to provide a new and commodious Council Chamber. The former one, which had be-come too small, was renamed the Shakespeare Room, in memory of the former General Secretary.

During these crowded and troubled years Baptists became

growingly conscious of widening horizons. This was partly due to the inter-church conferences and conversations to which reference has already been made. They were also made more aware of their own size and diversity as a world community. In this first period of Mr. Aubrey's secretaryship of the Union, three World Congresses were held under the auspices of the Baptist World Alliance, the first in Toronto in 1928, the second in Berlin in 1934, the third in Atlanta in 1939. Each of them registered considerable increases in world membership. The Atlanta Congress in particular revealed the size and vitality of the Southern Baptist Convention. But the Baptists of the rest of the world were cut off from their brethren in the Soviet Union. They were concerned for their brethren in Rumania, so long denied proper civil rights. They were troubled about the failure of those in Germany to protest against the excesses of Hitler's régime.

Nor had the times been propitious for the Baptists of Britain. The number of church members continued to decline. The losses from the leadership of the denomination in the nineteen-thirties were heavy. Among the ministers who had been President of the Union, W. Y. Fullerton, W. E. Blomfield and Carey Bonner passed away. Among the lay Presidents, A. R. Doggart and Alfred Ellis died and *primus inter pares* Herbert Marnham. The Second World War came upon a denomination troubled in mood and somewhat uncertain itself.

CHAPTER 12

THE SECOND WORLD WAR AND ITS AFTERMATH, 1939–51

I

THE dislocation caused to church life by the Second World War was much more extensive than that which resulted from the war of 1914–18 and was different in character. The spiritual impact was probably not so great. Then, the chief effects came through the general unpreparedness, followed by the volunteering or conscripting of all the young and middle-aged men. The air-raids, whether by zeppelins or aeroplanes, were sporadic and affected only certain parts of the country. More poignant and distressing were the heavy casualties suffered in the fighting on the Western Front.

The war of 1939–45, on the other hand, was not unexpected. Women as well as men served with the armed forces, but many men were in "reserved occupations". The whole population, however, was more or less directly involved in the conflict. Women and children in large numbers were evacuated from the main urban centres and from the coast, because of constant air-raids and the threat of invasion. Church buildings were subject to requisition by the authorities. Property was extensively damaged. The total number of casualties—both those suffered by the armed forces and by civilians—though losses were serious on particular occasions and at particular places, was in fact relatively small. Where there had been a large town congregation, only a handful of people might be found worshipping in a damaged schoolroom or vestry, while a tiny village chapel might experience an un-wonted prosperity. Owing to the "black-out" regulations, few evening services or meetings were possible anywhere.

The carrying on of denominational activities was consequently far more difficult than in the First World War. Many religious organizations followed the example of commercial concerns and transferred their headquarters to the provinces. Within a few days of the outbreak of war in September 1939 the Baptist Missionary Society moved its offices from Furnival Street to the premises of Union Church, High Wycombe, returning after a few months as there were no immediate air-raids on London. In the autumn of 1940, however, the Mission House was severely damaged and the Society compelled to undertake a second evacuation, this time to Kettering, the scene of its formation in 1792. Thus, by a strange turn of events, the Society's ter-jubilee celebrations were organized and directed in war-time from the small Northamptonshire town in which it was formed during the early stages of the struggle against Napoleon.[1]

The Baptist Union officials had made plans to move either to the new buildings of Regent's Park College, Oxford, or to the premises of Salem Chapel, Cheltenham, but determined to remain in London as long as possible. In October 1940, the top floor of the Church House was completely destroyed by incendiary bombs and considerable damage was caused to other parts of the building. In spite of the discomforts and dangers, Mr. Aubrey and the staff of the Union decided to carry on where they were. The maintenance of the headquarters in London proved of value in many different ways. Though the work of some departments was reduced, that of the United Navy, Army and Air Force Board was greatly increased, for large numbers of Baptist and Congregational ministers were appointed as chaplains.

During the early months of the war, at the request of the Council, P. T. Thomson, P. W. Evans, J. H. Rushbrooke and the General Secretary prepared a statement on "Baptist Action and the Present Crisis". This was sent to the churches in the spring of 1940. It expressed the view that, after the invasion of Poland by Germany, the British Government could have avoided war only

[1] See *Ter-Jubilee Celebrations*, 1942–4, Baptist Missionary Society, 1945, and F. Townley Lord, *Achievement, A Short History of the Baptist Missionary Society*, 1942.

8

by a disastrous moral surrender. The struggle was interpreted as a conflict between respect for human personality, the freedom of peoples, the common law and the pledged word, on the one hand, and the acknowledgment of violence as sole arbiter, on the other. As was not so surprising at the time as it would have been a few months later, when the German forces moved westwards, much of the statement concerned possible terms of peace. Emphasis was placed on the setting-up of an international organization, based on justice, good faith and an explicit limitation of national sovereignty, and on the principle of trusteeship for all non-self-governing colonies. In a supplementary note on Baptist work for peace, it was claimed that a resolution of the Baptist World Congress in Berlin in 1934 urging some surrender of national sovereignty for the sake of world peace, was the first clear assertion of this need by a world-wide communion of evangelical Christians. Baptists were exhorted to study again the report of the "Special Committee on the Attitude of the Denomination to War", which had been adopted by the Council in 1937 and which took the same line as the Berlin resolution.[2]

Throughout the war, Mr. Aubrey and Dr. Rushbrooke took a prominent part in the discussions of Church leaders about peace terms and a new social order. To five "Peace Points" formulated by Pope Pius XII, British churchmen, in a letter issued in December 1940, added the five standards by which economic situations and proposals should be tested, as suggested by the Oxford Conference of 1937. A few months later President Franklin D. Roosevelt, of the United States, spoke of four essential human freedoms—freedom of speech and expression, freedom of worship, freedom from want, and freedom from fear. These declarations won the warm approval of Baptists.

That Christians found themselves in substantial agreement on these matters, that they suffered together in the dislocation of church life caused by the war, and that in the lands occupied by

[2] At the Oxford Conference on Church, Community and State in 1937 "the abrogation of absolute national sovereignty was judged a duty the Church should urge upon the nations".

Germany the Churches—Roman Catholic as well as Protestant—became the final centres of spiritual resistance to tyranny, resulted in closer and more friendly ecclesiastical relations in Britain. Under the auspices of the "Sword of the Spirit,"a Roman Catholic movement which had the approval of Cardinal Hinsley, Archbishop of Westminster, there developed for a time a hitherto unfamiliar co-operation of Catholics and Protestants in public meetings. Of more enduring importance were the services rendered by *The Spiritual Issues of the War* (the bulletin of the Religious Division of the Ministry of Information, of which the Baptist, Dr. Hugh Martin, was for a while director) and *The Christian News Letter*, edited by Dr. J. H. Oldham. These publications made church people aware of what was going on in different parts of the world. Even during the years when the ultimate issue of the struggle hung in the balance, there was a far more restrained and "Christian" temper evident in the churches than during the 1914–18 war.

II

The new spirit that was abroad in Britain found its first notable expression in a concordat between Anglicans and Free Churchmen on the vexed question of education. The attitude to religion in the totalitarian régimes in Russia and Germany, and the discovery of the mental and spiritual condition of many of the evacuees from the industrial areas of Britain, contributed to agreement between the Churches. On 15th August 1941 the Archbishop of Canterbury (Dr. Lang) led a remarkable joint deputation to the new President of the Board of Education (the Rt. Hon. R. A. Butler). The members were able to state that they were all in favour of

1. Religious teaching in *all* schools, primary and secondary.
2. The daily opening of school by an act of corporate worship.
3. The giving of religious teaching at any hour of the school day.
4. The inclusion of Religious Knowledge in the curriculum of Training Colleges.
5. The inspection of religious teaching by H.M. Inspectors.

That, at the end of the interview, the Archbishop was asked by

Mr. Butler to offer prayer was an unprecedented conclusion to a unique occasion, which was in every way in striking contrast to the controversies over the Balfour and Birrell education proposals a generation earlier.[3]

The five points found embodiment in the Education Bill of 1944, by which time a compromise had also been arrived at on the thorny question of building grants for denominational schools, whether Roman, Anglican or Free Church. Somewhat reluctantly Free Churchmen agreed that 50 per cent of the cost of new buildings might be claimed from public funds.

The Free Church leader in these negotiations was the veteran, Dr. J. Scott Lidgett, a Methodist. The discussions among themselves which Nonconformists had had to engage in were helped by the amalgamation of the National Free Church Council and the Federal Council. The existence of these two organizations had caused increasing confusion and embarrassment during the nineteen-thirties. Mr. Wilson Black and Dr. J. W. Ewing were among those who had taken prominent parts in the somewhat difficult negotiations which occupied the years 1937–40. A Free Church Federal Council, uniting the two bodies, was formally constituted at a meeting held in the Baptist Church House during an air-raid on 16th September 1940. The Declaratory Statement of the Federal Council was adopted.[4] The offices of the Free Church Council in Tavistock Square, provided through a scheme prepared by Mr. Wilson Black, became the headquarters of the new organization and Dr. S. W. Hughes remained there as Secretary.

Two years later, in September 1942, an even more notable gathering took place in the Council Chamber of the Baptist Church House. A British Council of Churches was formed with the new Archbishop of Canterbury, Dr. William Temple, as President. The Council consisted of official representatives of all the main non-Roman Churches of England, Scotland, Wales and Northern Ireland. It quickly established itself as an agency for dis-

[3] See J. G. Lockhart, *Cosmo Gordon Lang*, pp. 368–9, and F. Iremonger, *William Temple*, 1948, pp. 569–78.

[4] See Appendix VIII.

cussion and co-operation on public issues, with special departments dealing with international affairs, social questions and
youth work.

The creation of a British Council of Churches was in part a
product of the movement for a World Council of Churches. This
was described at the time as "in process of formation". It had been
hoped that it could be formally constituted in 1941, but the outbreak of war made this impossible. The provisional committee
continued active, however, and was able during the war years,
through Dr. Visser 't Hooft in Geneva, to maintain contact with
Christians in most lands. A Department of Reconstruction and
Inter-Church Aid laid plans and collected funds for the immediate relief of the grave distress on the Continent. At length, in
August 1948, at an Assembly in Amsterdam, attended by the
official representatives of 147 churches from forty-four different
countries, the World Council of Churches was formed. The
Baptist Union had accepted the invitation to join in 1939. Its
delegates to Amsterdam were Dr. Aubrey, Dr. P. W. Evans,
Mr. C. T. Le Quesne and the writer, with Dr. T. G. Dunning,
the Rt. Hon. Ernest Brown and Dr. Hugh Martin as alternates.
By being asked to represent the Baptist Union of New Zealand,
Mr. Brown secured full delegate status. Dr. Aubrey and Mr.
Brown were appointed members of the Central Committee of
Ninety set up to direct the affairs of the Council between meetings
of the Assembly.

While these "conciliar" developments were taking place, there
were also renewed "conversations" in Britain between the
Church of England and the Free Churches. In 1946, while making
plans for the Lambeth Conference, which was to take place two
years later, Dr. Geoffrey Fisher, who had succeeded Dr. Temple as
Archbishop of Canterbury, preached before Cambridge University a sermon on "Church Relations in England". He suggested
that, instead of again attempting to find a way to organic union,
there might be a measure of "intercommunion", if the Free
Churches would "take episcopacy into their systems", adapting it
to their own traditions and needs.

The sermon aroused widespread interest and the Free Churches declared their readiness to discuss its meaning and implications with Church of England representatives. The Archbishop made clear that, though he had no objection to representatives of the Free Church Federal Council being present, the conversations should be conducted by official representatives of the various church authorities, since any further agreement would have to be between Churches as such and it might be that the Free Churches would not all take exactly the same line. The resulting discussions occupied the years 1947–50. Those appointed to share in them by the Baptist Union Council were Dr. Percy Evans, the Rev. H. Ingli James and the writer. A report entitled *Church Relations in England* was issued in 1950. It made clear that the suggestion of "parallel episcopates" would be as new and difficult a one for the Church of England as for the Free Churches, and that there would be many subsidiary issues to be discussed, if the idea was pursued. At the same time, all those who took part in the conversations agreed that the suggestion ought not to be rejected out of hand and expressed their conviction that new and closer relations between the Churches were desirable.

When the report came before the Baptist Union Council, a special committee was set up under the chairmanship of Dr. Arthur Dakin, of Bristol College. Its findings were that:

"the report *Church Relations in England* does not, as it stands, offer a plan of development which Baptists would consider it either right or practicable to try to implement. Nevertheless, we are glad that the conversations took place . . . We hope that conversations between the Churches will continue."[5]

The report of this special committee did not come before the Council until November 1952. It was discussed again in November 1953, its terms approved and its publication authorized.

The various decisions regarding relationships with other Churches were arrived at in most cases without the tension and division among Baptists which had accompanied the "conversations" a quarter of a century earlier. Both the Baptist Union of

[5] Report of Committee of the Baptist Union Council, p. 10. For the full text see Appendix XI.

Wales and the Baptist Union of Scotland accepted the invitation to join the World Council of Churches, though in the case of Scotland the decision was arrived at by only the barest of majorities and the churches were clearly more divided in their judgment on the Ecumenical Movement as a whole than those in England. Throughout the denomination there were some who took a more negative attitude than did others to any suggestion of organic union with other Christian bodies. In general, however, closer relationships and collaboration were welcomed, even if a way forward which would not involve a surrender of convictions could not be discerned.

Mr. Wilson Black, a resolute opponent of any surrender of Baptist independence, was a strong supporter of the Free Church Federal Council. He was also eager to draw the Baptists and the Churches of Christ closer together. At his instigation and expense, "unofficial conversations" were begun in 1941 and continued intermittently until his death ten years later. Among those who shared in them on the Baptist side were Dr. Wheeler Robinson, Dr. Percy Evans, Dr. Henry Townsend and Dr. Gilbert Laws. One of the products of the discussions was a useful pamphlet, *Infant Baptism Today* (1948). This drew attention to the disquietude regarding the theology and practice of paedobaptism, which was becoming evident in both Reformed and Anglican Churches. Apart from the cordial exchange of messages between the annual Conference of the Churches of Christ and the Assembly of the Baptist Union, little else of practical consequence resulted from the conversations and in 1952 they were brought to an end by mutual agreement.

In most of the Free Church denominations during the war years, a changing theological interest and temper were noticeable. J. W. Grant, in his study of *Free Churchmanship in England, 1870–1940*, regards the controversy which broke out in Congregational circles in 1933 over a "Restatement of Christian Thought", issued by a group of ministers led by the Rev. Thomas Wigley, of Blackheath, as "the end of the liberal epoch". The group had been influenced by *Jesus—Lord or Leader?*, a book published in

1930 by Frank Lenwood, in which the Christological and trini-
tarian statements in the creeds were repudiated, as well as much
else associated with evangelical theology. But Lenwood's book
and the statement issued by the Blackheath group provoked a
sharp reaction. Slowly but surely—and with gathering momentum after 1939—there was "a widespread revival of Reformed
ideals of churchmanship". "As they sought to give expression to
what they felt were the needs of their churches", says Dr. Grant,
"Nonconformists found within their own traditions much of the
light they needed".[6] He draws attention to the writings of
Nathaniel Micklem, J. S. Whale, Bernard Manning and Daniel
Jenkins, among the Congregationalists, and notes that, among the
older generation of scholars, the Presbyterian, Dr. Carnegie
Simpson, and the Baptists, Dr. Wheeler Robinson and Dr. A. C.
Underwood, had constantly protested against the more rationalis-
tic expressions of liberal churchmanship.

Among Baptists, however, a more significant date than 1933
was 1944, when two books on the ministry appeared. In *The
Baptist View of the Church and Ministry*, Dr. Arthur Dakin defined
a Baptist minister as one doing full-time pastoral service. "There
is," he said, "no sense in which a man can claim to be a Baptist
minister when he is not the head of a Baptist church".[7] In *The
Fellowship of Believers*, issued later the same year, the present
writer offered a study of Baptist thought and practice throughout
the past three hundred years on Church, ministry and sacraments.
One of its aims was to show that the mutual relations of Baptist
churches are not a matter for voluntary decision. "The local
congregation is not truly a church if it lives an entirely separate
life".[8] Two years later, in 1946, there appeared *The Gathered
Community*, written by the Rev. R. C. Walton on the basis of
discussions by a group of younger Baptist ministers. The Church,
it was maintained, is not a voluntary society; it is "called into
existence and its life is maintained, not by the decision of men,

[6] Op. cit., pp. 325, 385.
[7] Op. cit., pp. 44 f.
[8] Op. cit., p. 27. Revised and enlarged edition, 1952, p. 31.

but by the will of God". "The glory of the Church is a phrase without meaning unless we are thinking of the World Church".[9] A Christian minister is

"a minister of Christ's Word and sacraments. He is, therefore, more than the pastor of a local congregation. He is a minister of the whole Baptist community. It follows, also, that those who are called to a different kind of ministry as Missionaries, College Principals, Army Chaplains, Denominational Secretaries or Secretaries of interdenominational organizations, are as truly Christian ministers and Baptist ministers as their brethren who serve the local churches."[10]

Such views did not find universal acceptance. But they helped to focus attention on issues which were to demand more and more thought in the years that followed. They showed that Baptists were to share in the general revival of interest in theology.

III

Meantime a number of internal developments were taking place within the Union and the denomination. The Committee on Baptist Polity, set up in 1936, presented its final report to the Council in November 1942. The report urged that the office of General Superintendent should be made primarily one of spiritual leadership; that the United Collegiate Board should attempt the joint planning of theological education and the better use and supervision of the ministers' probationary period; that the minimum stipend under the Sustentation Fund should be raised from £160 to at least £208 per annum; that churches and ministers frame their procedure in matters connected with settlement upon a new agreed basis, abandoning the compulsory time-limit and substituting for it a Settlement Covenant; and that the many pastorless churches be helped by grouping schemes and the encouragement of lay oversight.

The Baptist Union of Scotland had been much concerned at the loss to other denominations of a number of its ministers. A Commission of Inquiry was set up and, after two years of study, issued in 1943 a report which advocated a closer fellowship within the

[9] Op. cit., p. 179.
[10] Op. cit., p. 147.

denomination and a voluntary limitation of independency at several points. There was also a plea for more effective denominational teaching.

Both reports appeared in war-time. The opposition to the time-limit by the committee on Baptist Polity proved decisive. Their other proposals were neither revolutionary nor easy of accomplishment. During the following years, however, progress was made at several points in the carrying out of the recommendations. The financial situation of many ministers was becoming extremely difficult. The resources of the Union were, however, limited. Expenditure exceeded income year after year and the gap had to be made up from the rapidly diminishing balance of the United Fund raised after the First World War. It was clear that before long a serious financial situation would occur. In the early months of the war an Emergency Fund had been raised and by grants from this fund the minimum stipend was increased to £200 per annum. At the same time, the Finance Committee of the Union began a thorough review of the finances. A "short-term" policy was adopted in 1944 and discussions began on a "long-term" policy, which resulted in 1947, when the war was over, in a complete reorganization and the establishment of the Home Work Fund.

A Victory Thanksgiving Fund of £150,000, raised in 1945-6, cleared the way for the new plan. Of this fund, £100,000 was for the rebuilding and repair of damaged churches. The government had not asked for premiums from churches as part of its own War Damage Insurance scheme, but had promised to make good damage done to the churches and to replace those destroyed by plain substitute buildings, either on the same sites or on new ones chosen by the denominational authorities. This generous promise could not be implemented, however, until after the immediate need for houses, factories and schools had been met. The Victory Thanksgiving Fund, which was apportioned to the Associations in proportion to the damage in their areas, helped churches to make good what was not covered by government payments. The official scheme gave the central denominational committee an authority unfamiliar in Baptist circles and one which, however wise, it proved difficult to exercise. The whole process of rebuilding and "porting" was subject to many frustrating delays.

The remaining £50,000 of the Victory Thanksgiving Fund was allocated to relief on the Continent. Of this 10 per cent was paid over to the Christian Reconstruction in Europe Fund of the World Council of Churches, the remainder being placed at the disposal of the Continental Committee of the Baptist Union for the help of Baptists in European lands.

The aim of the new Home Work Fund Scheme, which secured the approval of the Assembly, was to unify the appeals which had been made by the Union for the Sustentation Fund and the various departments, and by the Associations for their own administration. It was agreed that, apart from the affiliation fees of churches and Associations, and the subscriptions of personal members, all monies received at the Church House should be credited to one fund, and that from this fund should be met not only the grants to aided churches but also the administrative costs of the Union. From the total raised within each Association, an agreed percentage would be returned, so that the Association need not make a separate appeal for its own purposes. The "ear-marking" of gifts for special objects was allowed, but not encouraged. It proved necessary to exclude Church Extension from the objects of the Home Work Fund, largely because Mr. Wilson Black felt unable to agree to the merging in it of the monies remaining in the Forward Movement account.

The first authors of the scheme were Dr. Aubrey and Mr. Gordon Fairbairn. It represented a considerable advance on earlier arrangements. Previously, ministerial grants had been a charge only on the income of the capital of the Sustentation Fund raised by Dr. Shakespeare, supplemented by the annual simultaneous collection. Now the whole resources of the Union were pledged to the maintenance of minimum stipends at what might from time to time be considered an adequate or practicable level and this became the continual concern of the Council. At the same time special provision was made for the support of initial pastorates in

new causes, while the supply and maintenance of deaconesses—
hitherto matters of special arrangement between the Union and
any church employing a deaconess—were woven into the
general denominational pattern. The unification of appeals and
the fact that the whole of the expenses of the Union, except so far
as they could be met out of specially designated funds, became
chargeable to the annual Home Work Fund total, involved a
substantial reorganization from the administrative point of view.
A General Purposes and Finance Executive was set up. Previously
very little could be done between the six-monthly meetings of
the Council except routine administrative work. The new executive committee met monthly and became a body which not only
controlled finance but dealt with all important matters arising
between the meetings of the Council. The Rt. Hon. Ernest
Brown, M.C., became the first chairman and his firm and experienced leadership proved of great value.

The successful carrying through of this substantial reorganization of the Union's finances owed much to the skill and persistence
of the Rev. B. Grey Griffith. In 1942, on his retirement from the
Home Secretaryship of the Baptist Missionary Society and at the
time of the Society's ter-jubilee, he had been elected President of
the Union. Thereafter, he gave his time and energy to work at the
Church House in an honorary capacity, serving as chairman of
the Grants Executive and assisting the Union in many other ways.
He had the satisfaction of seeing the appeal for the Home Work
Fund meet with an increasing response, though in the first years
the increase failed to match the declining value of the pound. In
the years under review the totals received were:

1944	Sustentation Fund	£20,382
1945	,,	,,	£19,156
1946	,,	,,	£19,234
1947	Home Work Fund	£22,436
1948	,,	,,	£27,096
1949	,,	,,	£27,932
1950	,,	,,	£30,612
1951	,,	,,	£32,620

The general situation was not an easy one, however. In 1944 the "State of the Churches" was anxiously debated by the Baptist Union Council and a special group was set up, with the Rev. Henry Cook as convener, to discuss matters further. Statistics could not be satisfactorily obtained during the war years. The returns published in 1946 showed a decline of 20,000 in church membership since 1939, and of over 70,000 in Sunday School scholars. That this was partly due to the shift of population, and that other denominations had to record similar or even greater losses, was no satisfaction.

The report on the spiritual welfare of the churches, prepared by Mr. Henry Cook's group, was discussed by the Council and later published under the title, *Speak—that they go forward*. It dealt with the Christian message and with the life and witness of the churches, many of which appeared to have become tired and dispirited, and issued in a call to more aggressive evangelism. Under the leadership of Mr. Cook, the General Superintendents and others conducted a number of short campaigns in some of the districts where the churches seemed most in need of encouragement. The decline in membership was not halted, but slowly the mood of the churches began to change and a greater readiness for more adventurous witness-bearing became apparent.

Other more hopeful signs were evident. After the First World War there had been a dearth of candidates for the ministry. During the Second World War, on the other hand, a considerable number of men, while serving with the forces, indicated their desire to offer for training. Dr. Percy Evans rendered important service on an inter-denominational committee dealing with candidates from the services and Dr. Aubrey interviewed a number during a visit to the chaplains in the Middle East. From 1946 onwards the theological colleges were full of very promising recruits and, as the Universities filled again, the general body of students showed a keener religious interest than for many a day. Denominational societies were soon in existence in almost every university centre. In 1947 a Baptist Students' Federation was formed, and a few years later an older Baptist Theological Students' Union was amalgamated with it. The Federation's annual conference came to be an important and largely attended gathering and teams of students spontaneously undertook evangelistic campaigns during vacations.

In many local churches also, the younger generation showed a renewed keenness. During the war, the Co-ordination Committee of the Youth Departments of the Union and the Missionary Society had become responsible for the Young People's Rally held in connection with the Annual Assembly. The same committee began to plan for a Baptist Youth Movement, the centre of which became a council representative of the young people of all parts of the country and of the various organizations at work among them. Dr. A. B. Crabtree had for some years assisted Dr. T. G. Dunning at the Baptist Church House. When he resigned in 1949, the Rev. W. T. Cowlan, who had been Youth Secretary of the Free Church Federal Council, was appointed Director of a reconstituted Youth Department of the Baptist Union.

The women likewise were embarking on enlarged programmes. In 1946, Miss E. Lois Chapple, formerly a missionary in China, had been appointed as a colleague of Miss Doris Rose in the leadership of the Women's Department of the Union. Three years later, the work of the department was reorganized and Miss Rose began to give the whole of her time to the Baptist deaconesses. Since 1936, deaconess candidates had received training at a small college housed in Carlton Drive, Putney.[11] When Sister Gertrude Kendall retired from the post of Warden, Miss E. Webb Samuel was appointed Principal. In 1945, Mr. Wilson Black provided the money for the purchase of "Struan", a substantial property in Wimbledon Park, and plans were made for a more systematic and thorough training of deaconesses. The Rev. H. H. Sutton, who had been General Superintendent of the Southern Area, became Principal. The financial difficulties

[11] Havelock Hall, of which Miss Jean Arthur had become Principal in 1923, had had to close in 1929 for lack of support. From 1929–36 deaconesses were trained at Hillside, Camden Town.

through which the denomination was passing and a general uncertainty as to the functions and status of deaconesses hindered the
developments which were hoped for. Slowly, however, the
churches came to recognize the importance of the devoted service
the deaconesses were rendering, often in spheres of special difficulty.[12]

Meanwhile, the Women's Department extended its service
beyond the branches of the Baptist Women's League. Many hundreds of women's meetings were linked with headquarters and
new fields of activity were opened up among Young Wives'
Clubs and Business Women's groups. At the annual women's
meeting in the spring of 1949 not far short of 10,000 Baptist
women gathered in the Empress Hall. The Girls' Hostel in Stoke
Newington continued its useful service, while at Yateley a Home
for Unmarried Mothers was opened, in connection with which
in 1948 a Baptist Union Adoption Society was registered. The
Women's Departments of the Union and the Missionary Society
continued to co-ordinate their activities through a joint standing-
committee and arranged regular residential conferences for
women.

A further important step towards the unification of parallel
agencies took place when the Carey Press and the Kingsgate
Press were amalgamated as the Carey Kingsgate Press, Ltd.
Though the assets placed in the new company by the Union were
considerably in excess of those available to the Missionary Society,
the Union agreed that an equal number of directors should be
appointed by each of the two bodies. The new company undertook the sale and distribution of the denominational hymnbook
and *The Baptist Times*, formerly in the hands of the Kingsgate
Press.

Apart from the bringing together of the two presses and the
joint committees which loosely linked the youth departments and
the women's departments, the Union and the Missionary Society
moved somewhat farther apart than they had been in the years
immediately preceding the Second World War. This was due to

[12] See D. M. Rose, *Baptist Deaconesses*, 1954.

several causes. There was inevitably some reaction after the failure of the plan for joint headquarters. The evacuation of the Missionary Society headquarters to Kettering made close daily contacts between the secretariats more difficult. When the Society returned to London, it was to Gloucester Place, near Baker Street, and not to Furnival Street. In 1938 Dr. H. R. Williamson had come back from China to succeed Dr. C. E. Wilson as Foreign Secretary. In 1942 the Rev. J. B. Middlebrook, of Huddersfield, was appointed Home Secretary in place of Mr. Grey Griffith.

The work of the Society in China—one of its major fields—had been dislocated by the Japanese invasion in 1937. Then, after a brief resumption of activities, came the more serious interruption caused by the World War. Many missionaries suffered internment at the hands of the Japanese. Within a few years of their release, China passed under the control of a Communist government and all Western missionaries were compelled to withdraw from the country. Though there was some extension of the work in Belgian Congo and Angola, and Trinidad again became a field of missionary activity, the number of missionaries sent out by the Society declined. The celebration of the ter-jubilee gave a fillip to missionary interest throughout the churches, and rapidly-rising costs made it necessary to appeal for a larger income. This was achieved, though the contributions did not keep pace with the declining value of the pound. The marriage in 1947 of Miss M. Eleanor Bowser took from the Society's headquarters one of the ablest and most experienced of its leaders and was followed by a considerable reorganization of the secretariat. When, two or three years later, Dr. Williamson retired, another former China missionary, the Rev. V. E. W. Hayward, became General Foreign Secretary. The churches showed their appreciation of Dr. Williamson's services during a difficult period by electing him President of the Baptist Union.

IV

Dr. J. C. Carlile and Dr. T. R. Glover were among the well-known Baptists who had passed away during the war years. Within a few days of the close of the conflict, in May 1945, Dr. H. Wheeler Robinson died. These were severe losses. Though he had, unfortunately, never become President of the Union, Dr. Wheeler Robinson had exercised a considerable influence on the life and thought of the denomination. An Old Testament scholar and theologian of world-wide repute, his views had not always been acceptable to all his fellow Baptists, but his monograph, *Baptist Principles*, prepared for the Yorkshire Association in 1911, remained the most important piece of Baptist apologetic for two generations, while his book *The Life and Faith of the Baptists* was a widely-read study of the denomination's traditional convictions and emphases. By effecting the transfer of Regent's Park College from London to Oxford, Dr. Robinson gave the denomination a new and wider opportunity of making its witness known and accomplished a project to which Dr. Joseph Angus and Dr. Shakespeare had looked forward many years earlier.[13]

Dr. Carlile was succeeded in the editorship of *The Baptist Times* by Dr. F. Townley Lord, the popular and versatile minister of Bloomsbury Central Church. Printing difficulties and paper restrictions were not easy to overcome, but the new editor succeeded in increasing the circulation of the denominational journal, making it in a new way a medium of news about Baptists in all parts of the world. In this he was helped by the renewed activity of the Baptist World Alliance.

Dr. Rushbrooke had been elected President of the Alliance at the Atlanta Congress on the eve of the outbreak of war. Throughout the succeeding years he strove to maintain Baptist world fellowship. The new Secretary of the Alliance, Dr. W. O. Lewis, spent most of the war years in America, but was able to be in England for the ter-jubilee celebrations of the Baptist Missionary Society in 1942. As soon as hostilities were over, Rushbrooke

[13] See E. A. Payne, *Henry Wheeler Robinson: A Memoir*, 1946.

and Lewis set themselves to renew contacts with the Baptists of
the continent of Europe. Large-scale relief activities were put in
hand and preparations made for a seventh World Congress in
Copenhagen. There was widespread grief when, suddenly, at the
end of January 1947, Dr. Rushbrooke was taken ill and a few
days later passed away. Honoured in all parts of the world, he
had come to be regarded as the embodiment of Baptist brotherhood and of the claim for religious freedom.[14]

In spite of Rushbrooke's death, the Copenhagen Congress was
held and was attended by over 5,000 Baptists. The largest groups
were those from the Scandinavian countries, Great Britain and
the United States, but Belgium, Bulgaria, Czechoslovakia,
France, Germany, Holland, Italy, Jugoslavia, Poland, Portugal,
Rumania, Spain and Switzerland were represented, as well as
countries in South America, Africa, Asia and Australasia. There
were no delegates from the Soviet Union. An attempt was made
by delegates of the Southern Baptist Convention to get the Executive to consider whether the unions and conventions ought to
be in membership with the World Council of Churches. The
chairman of the session ruled, however, that, in the light of the
constitution of the Alliance, as well as that of the World Council,
a motion of this kind was out of order. What was learned of conditions in Europe stimulated the relief work of the Alliance and it
was decided to hold another Congress at an interval of only three
years.

One of the immediate results of the war was the emergence of
the United States into a position of world leadership and great
economic strength. It was there that the great majority of Baptists were to be found and the number was rapidly increasing.
The new President of the Alliance, Dr. C. Oscar Johnson, set
himself to collect funds for an Alliance headquarters in Washing-
ton. Though the London office in the Baptist Church House was
continued and Dr. W. O. Lewis moved there as Associate Secretary, when succeeded as General Secretary by Dr. Arnold T.
Ohrn, there was an inevitable shift from Britain to America in

[14] See E. A. Payne, *James Henry Rushbrooke: a Baptist Greatheart*, 1954.

the leadership of the Alliance. At the same time, however, plans began to take shape for a European Baptist Federation, which would promote closer relations between the Baptist groups in Europe and, when Dr. Joel Sorenson was appointed Youth Secretary of the Alliance, he opened an office in Stockholm.

The eighth Baptist World Congress met in Cleveland, Ohio, in July 1950. There were 20,000 fully registered delegates and over 40,000 persons attended one of the public demonstrations. Most of them came from the United States and Canada, but it was not an unrepresentative Baptist gathering, save for the absence of delegations from the countries behind the "iron" and the "bamboo" curtains. The British delegates numbered only forty-six, as a result of the hindrances to transatlantic travel, but at the close of the Congress, Dr. F. Townley Lord was elected President of the Alliance and it was decided that plans be made for a Golden Jubilee Congress in London in 1955. These decisions helped to maintain British interest in, and influence upon, the Alliance during the succeeding period. Prior to the Cleveland gathering, international commissions had met to discuss religious liberty, evangelism, social justice, world missions, the doctrine of the Church and the doctine of baptism. The need for the formulation of Baptist thought on these matters was increasingly apparent, though the process proved new and somewhat difficult. A manifesto on Religious Freedom was adopted, but of the other commissions that on baptism was alone able to prepare any satisfactory documentary material, and even that consisted only of an address and a questionnaire, which indicated the variety of Baptist thought and practice.[15]

V

Dr. Aubrey's term as secretary of the Union was drawing to a close. His standing in public life led to his appointment in 1947 as a member of the Royal Commission on the Press. During the same year he paid a long-promised visit to America and Canada,

[15] See *The Doctrine of Baptism*, 1951.

receiving the degree of D.C.L. from Acadia University and that of LL.D. from McMaster University.

The Baptist Union Council decided in 1947 that, if all the parties concerned were in agreement, General Superintendents and those serving at the Baptist Church House might postpone retirement from the age of 65 to 68. Mr. W. H. Ball had served the Union for more than fifty years and had been a tower of strength to both Dr. Shakespeare and Dr. Aubrey in the development of the Union's activities. His work for the United Board during the war gained him the M.B.E. On his retirement in 1948, Mr. Ball was made an honorary member of the Council and the Rev. O. D. Wiles was appointed Deputy General Secretary of the Union. A few months later, Dr. Aubrey announced his intention to resign in 1951. The Council at once decided to nominate him as Vice-President of the Union so that his last year of office as General Secretary would be his year as President.

Dr. Aubrey had sensed the changing spiritual climate in Britain. In 1949 he presented, first to the General Purposes Committee of the Union and then to the Council, a call to a concerted effort to promote "Baptist Advance". The resolution approving the call, which was adopted by the Council, acknowledged "many signs of a renewed spirit of eagerness and devotion in the churches". The Kent and Sussex Association was already engaged in a Mid-Century Evangelistic Crusade, the outstanding feature of which was the holding of missions by ministers of the Association, working together usually in pairs. For the ensuing two years, Dr. Aubrey gave much of his time and strength to meetings and conferences of ministers, deacons and church members in all parts of the country. The precise objectives of the new campaign he had deliberately left undefined. Its supreme purpose was a renewed dedication on the part of the churches and their members. There was, unfortunately, little sign of a halt in the declining church statistics, but the effect of the campaign on church officers was considerable.

In an effort to help with the effective Christian training of young people, a Baptist Union Diploma of Christian Knowledge was

instituted, the examinations for which became part of the re-
quirements for the recognition of lay preachers. A Baptist Lectureship was established at the suggestion of the Principals' and
Tutors' Conference and was named after Dr. W. T. Whitley, the
distinguished historian, who had passed away in December 1947.

Broadcasting had become a new and important channel of
communication and the denomination was gratified at the
appointment of the Rev. Edwin H. Robertson to the Religious
Broadcasting Department of the B.B.C. in 1949.[16] When the
Department decided to broadcast Communion Services, guidance
was asked of the Union from a number of quarters. On the advice
of a special committee, the Council agreed that, while it had no
final authority on the matter, its own view was that the broadcasting of such services from Baptist churches was questionable or
even undesirable. At the same time, the Principals' and Tutors'
Conference was asked to draw up a general statement on the
Lord's Supper and its administration, for the guidance of the
churches. The publication of this statement was approved by the
Council in March 1951. Its issue in this manner was evidence of a
deepening theological interest and of a recognition of the Union's
responsibility on such matters.

The financial plight of the ministry caused growing concern.
The decline in the purchasing power of the pound was offset for
most workers by a considerable increase in wages. No such actual
or relative increase was made in the stipends of ministers and
deaconesses. Though the increase in giving to the Home Work
Fund enabled small additions to be made to the standard stipend,
these failed to keep pace with the rising cost of living and the
situation in many manses became increasingly difficult. Nevertheless, small additions were made to the standard stipend in
churches aided from the Home Work Fund:

				Married Ministers	Deaconesses
1948	.	.	.	£300	£208
1949	.	.	.	£312	£221
1950	.	.	.	£325	—

[16] In 1955 Mr. Robertson was succeeded by another Baptist, the Rev. Douglas Stewart.

But in the case of the ministers there was a deduction of £35 if a manse was provided. Many country churches were pastorless. A special committee under the Rev. W. H. Tebbit, General Superintendent of the Eastern Area, though able to describe the unsatisfactory situation, could do little to remedy it. More progress became possible, however, in the establishment of causes in new housing areas, and in 1949 it was agreed that special grants should be made for first pastorates, even where the usual qualifying contribution could not be raised.

At the Assembly in 1950, at which Dr. Aubrey became President of the Union, the Council recommended that on his retirement a year later he should be succeeded by the writer, who after pastoral service in Northamptonshire, had been Young People's Secretary and Editorial Secretary of the Missionary Society and then, for eleven years, Senior Tutor at Regent's Park College, Oxford. At a memorable special session of the Assembly in Westminster Chapel in 1951, grateful tributes were paid to Dr. Aubrey by representative Baptists and by the Archbishop of Canterbury, the Moderator of the Free Church Federal Council and Dr. Sidney Berry. During twenty-six very difficult years, Dr. Aubrey had carried the increasingly heavy burden of the secretaryship of the Union, maintaining and enhancing its position in the life of the nation as well as the denomination. In its own resolution of thanks, the Council spoke fittingly of his "faith, courage and resolution", his "fervent zeal for evangelism" and "deep concern for the spiritual health of the churches", and "his many-sided religious and public services". The tribute was well-deserved.

CHAPTER 13

ON TOWARDS THE TER-JUBILEE

I

In international affairs the nineteen-fifties were years of continued uncertainty, recurrent crises and local hostilities in many parts of the world.

When the decade opened, bitter fighting was going on between North and South Korea, with China supporting the former and a combined force representing the United Nations actively engaged on the side of the latter. There were revolutionary outbreaks of terrorism in Kenya and Malaya, bitter civil war in Indo-China, and later in Indonesia. The Middle East was in a constant state of tension, with Persia, Cyprus and then Suez as the special points of danger. North Africa was the scene of savage outrages. The peoples of Africa as a whole were clearly on the march, with new areas gaining or seeking political independence. In the extreme south of the continent a white minority was endeavouring to safeguard its position by a policy of racial *apartheid*, which caused widespread concern in other parts of the world.

Many of these conflicts were inevitably related to the continuing tension between the two great powers, the Soviet Union and the United States. An unsuccessful revolt in Hungary in 1956 sent a wave of horror and a sense of impotence throughout the "free" world. Germany remained divided and unhappy. As the years passed, scientists and technicians made steady progress with the manufacture and testing of nuclear weapons and space missiles and less obvious progress with plans for the peaceful use of atomic energy. Men and women in all countries felt increasing anxiety lest a third world conflict break out in which civilization would destroy itself and the human race be tainted for generations to come.

In Britain a General Election in 1951 resulted in a Conservative government in place of the Labour administration, which had, during the previous six years, completed the legislative framework of a social welfare state. At another election in 1955, a few months after the retirement of Sir Winston Churchill, the Conservatives increased their majority, but sentiment in Britain remained almost equally divided between the two main parties. The Liberal Party had virtually disappeared and with it the days when Nonconformists were united in their political allegiance. Differences of opinion, whether on Premium Bonds, on British policy in the Suez dispute, or on the manufacture and use of nuclear weapons, cut across ecclesiastical loyalties in a manner unfamiliar and embarrassing. The Festival of Britain, at which the centenary of the Great Exhibition of 1851 was celebrated, followed by the accession of Queen Elizabeth to the throne, raised hopes of a new and glorious Elizabethan Age. But with the constant dangers of inflation, the distractions of foreign affairs and the fears of nuclear warfare, there were few signs of the moral and religious renewal which was clearly needed.

Nevertheless, there were gleams of light in the darkness. So far as the Churches were concerned, the nineteen-fifties brought certain encouragements and some increase of confidence. In these things Baptists shared.

Evangelistic campaigns conducted in Britain by Dr. Billy Graham, of the United States, in 1954 and 1955, recalled in their popular impact those of Moody and Sankey eighty years earlier and showed that the religious climate had changed. Dr. Graham's campaigns were, however, only one illustration of a renewed spiritual interest and wistfulness in many different quarters. Christians were no longer on the defensive, as they had been for at least thirty years. They were eagerly engaged once more in church extension projects, seeking to meet the religious needs of the new towns and housing-estates. Their propaganda was bolder and more successful, particularly among those educated in secondary schools and at the universities. A more dogmatic "Biblical" theology had replaced the "liberal" theology popular a generation or so earlier.[1] Ecclesiastical relations continued to improve. The British Council of Churches was more firmly established as an agency for united action. The Methodist Church and the Church of Scotland each embarked on fresh series of "conversations" with the Church of England, the avowed aim of which was some kind of "inter-communion" along the lines of the Cambridge Sermon (1946) of the Archbishop of Canterbury.

No less significant were the growing activities of the World Council of Churches, the progress made in schemes of Church Union in several parts of the world, and the renewed contacts between Christians on either side of the "iron" and "bamboo" curtains. The World Council held its second Assembly at Evanston, near Chicago, in the summer of 1954. Its Division of Inter-Church Aid and Service to Refugees was extending its work from Europe and the Middle East to Asia and Africa. The World Council and the International Missionary Council, "in association with" one another since 1948, found themselves driven to ever-closer co-operation and began to consider plans for more effective integration. Schemes for Church Union in Ceylon and North India reached their definitive form and were referred to the negotiating churches for decision. Knowledge spread of new patterns of ecumenical relations in communist lands and of the survival there of much effective Christian witness. Within a tense and threatening world situation, the Christian faith was still a vital force, but so also were other religions, which had once seemed dormant or in decay.

II

The activities of the Baptist Union have to be seen against the background of these events and developments.

In the early nineteen-fifties Baptist church statistics continued to show a decline, as did those of most other religious groups in

---

[1] Just as, early in the twentieth century, Baptists were less influenced by Liberal Theology and the Social Gospel than some other denominations, so they were less markedly influenced by the neo-orthodoxy associated with the name of Karl Barth. On the other hand, many Baptists were sympathetic to a revived "fundamentalism".

Britain. A change came in the middle of the decade, and small increases began to be registered. These increases were largely the result of the formation of new churches. More than seventy Baptist churches were formed in the ten years following the close of the Second World War. The immediate post-war increase in the number of Sunday School scholars was not maintained, however. There were fluctuations in the birth-rate and—more important—a sharp decline in the average age of those in the Sunday Schools. This was due to a number of factors, among them Sunday motoring, television and the improvement in the religious instruction given in the day schools. These factors affected, of course, all the Christian Churches and were part of the changing pattern of social life.

Strenuous efforts were made by Baptists to combat the effects of inflation on the grave economic difficulties facing the ministry. Though the increases in the standard stipend often seemed to be too small and to come too late, yet the figure was steadily raised: £325 per annum (1951), £350 (1953), £360 (1954), £370 (1955), £400 (1956), £450 (1957), £480 (1958), with corresponding increases in the stipends of deaconesses. By the close of the decade it was clear that there was a general realization—not only among Baptists—that ministers and clergy had been allowed to sink in the economic scale far below the point at which they could effectively do their work. Under the Home Work Scheme the value of a manse was still reckoned at the nominal figure of £35 per annum. Various devices were adopted in order to allow ministers aided from the central fund to benefit as much as was fairly possible from the chaplaincies with the services and in hospitals, which were available to some of their number. Travelling grants to ministers serving more than one church were increased. But Baptists had reluctantly to accept the fact that many ministers' wives, like other married women, would—in many cases must—undertake independent remunerative employment.

The increase in the scale of grants necessitated a much higher target for the Home Work Fund. In spite of the general increase

in costs, efforts—on the whole successful—were made to check
any substantial rise in the departmental expenditure of the Union,
so that as large a sum as possible was available for ministerial
grants. The number of causes claiming help under the "initial
pastorate" scheme rapidly increased as a result of church extension activities. By 1957 £8,000 was being spent by the Union
under this head. The Home Work Fund total, which had risen
slowly in the five years prior to 1951 to £32,620, jumped in 1952
to £47,064 and six years later reached £68,000. By then the
churches were not only giving their collections on the second
Sunday in March, but their July communion offerings, and were
also engaged throughout the year in regular additional efforts for
the fund.

This represented no mean achievement, particularly when it
was accompanied by the appeal of the Baptist Missionary Society
for an increased income to meet the declining value of the pound
overseas. There were some who wished for a large central Church
Extension Fund. Instead of this, however, the Loan Fund of the
Baptist Union Corporation was greatly augmented by deposits
from churches and individuals. By 1958 over £150,000 was out
on loan. By then the government's War Damage Commission
had paid out almost all the money due to the Churches and the
greater part of it had been spent. Baptists received in all a sum of
at least £1,500,000. Though efforts were made to secure the
"porting" of part of some of the payments, the slow-dying
tradition of independency prevented as wise a strategy in this
matter as might have been hoped for. Churches and Associations
found themselves faced with very costly building schemes. The
Corporation Loan Fund and the Baptist Building Fund enabled
the most urgent projects to be put in hand. The denomination as
a whole was probably no more seriously burdened than it had
been in the eighteen-seventies, and the burden was certainly more
evenly distributed and shared.

The group who suffered most from the financial difficulties of
the time were probably aged and retired ministers. It was possible
in 1951 to raise the statutory benefit from the Superannuation

Fund from £85 per annum to £100, in 1955 to £115, and in 1957 to £125, but so low a figure—even when supplemented by small amounts from other funds—compelled many ministers and their wives to seek National Assistance. A number of generous individual gifts—including three flats for retired ministers at Billericay—failed to meet the great need. The situation was somewhat eased, however, in 1958 when pensions under the National Insurance Scheme became available for all who had been contributing members for ten years.

III

At the beginning of the period under review the denomination suffered heavy personal losses. In 1951 no fewer than four ex-Presidents of the Union passed away: Dr. P. W. Evans, Dr. J. W. Ewing, Mr. H. L. Taylor and Mr. R. Wilson Black.

Dr. Evans had only recently retired from the principalship of Spurgeon's College. His wisdom, graciousness and wit had enabled him to help in the healing of many of the wounds left by the Down Grade controversy, though he did not live to share in the general rejoicing when, in 1955, the Metropolitan Tabernacle rejoined the Union. Dr. Evans had also contributed much to the raising of the standard of ministerial training and the drawing together of the Baptist Colleges. One of Spurgeon's own students, Dr. Ewing had been a well-known figure for over half a century, passing the presidential chair before becoming one of the first group of General Superintendents, and widely respected in evangelical circles outside the denomination. Mr. Taylor and Mr. Black[2] were outstanding and generous lay-leaders, the former for many years the treasurer of the Baptist Missionary Society. In 1952 the Rev. P. T. Thomson died, in 1954 Dr. S. W. Hughes and Mr. C. T. Le Quesne, Q.C., in 1955 Dr. Henry Townsend. Mr. Thomson had brought brilliant intellectual gifts and human understanding to the chairmanship of the Ministerial Recognition Committee. Dr. Hughes, the successor of Dr. Clif-

[2] See H. Townsend, *Robert Wilson Black*, 1954.

ford at Westbourne Park Church and always a popular pulpit and platform figure, was for many years secretary of the National Free Church Council and later of the Free Church Federal Council. Mr. Le Quesne combined legal and theological interests and proved himself a vigilant champion of Baptist convictions, as did Dr. Henry Townsend, for twenty-nine years the principal of Manchester Baptist College and a well-known leader of the Free Churches in the north of England.

By the death in 1956 of Dr. C. E. Wilson, a devoted and trusted missionary statesman passed away. Less than a year later, in October 1957, Dr. M. E. Aubrey died, after a brief illness, at the relatively early age of seventy-two. The event called forth many tributes to his gifts as a preacher, his services to the cause of Christian unity and his ability as an administrator.

These were severe losses. As the nineteen-fifties advanced the gap left by the heavy casualties of the First World War became more apparent. Slowly leadership had to pass to a much younger group of men.

There was a shortage of ministers. Yet another committee on the ministry, appointed in 1951 with the Rev. Henry Bonser as chairman, reported that there were 329 fewer ministers and probationers on the lists of the Baptist Union than in 1910. Many ministers were claimed by administrative posts within or outside the denomination, and new opportunities presented themselves in the teaching profession. In spite of the postponement of retirement and the grouping of churches, many spheres remained without pastoral oversight. Most ministerial candidates married on leaving college and not a few pioneering tasks were committed to deaconesses. There was much discussion—and at times serious difference of opinion—regarding the status of deaconesses and the training that should be given them. The college at Wimbledon had often no more than six or eight students. From 1951–5 the Rev. and Mrs. H. M. Angus struggled gallantly with the educational and domestic difficulties inevitable in so small an establishment. "Struan" was then closed and it was decided that deaconess candidates should be trained side by side with women missionary students and Presbyterian church-sisters at Carey Hall, Selly Oak, of which a Baptist, the Rev. Gwenyth Hubble, was principal. At the same time the normal period of training was lengthened to three years.

The jubilee of the opening of the Baptist Church House was marked by a luncheon in the Connaught Rooms at the Annual Assembly of 1953 and by the restoration and refurnishing of the Shakespeare Room.[3] There were a number of changes in the leadership of the departments of the Union during these years. In 1952 Dr. T. G. Dunning resigned, on becoming secretary of the Temperance Council of the Christian Churches. In his place the Rev. C. H. Cleal, who had been on the staff of the British Council of Churches, was put in charge of a Baptist Union Citizenship Department and this was again brought into close association with the Young People's Department, the Lay Preachers' Federation and the Baptist Diploma Scheme, Mr. Cleal having as his colleagues Mr. John E. T. Hough, a young layman, and first Miss Jean Green, Sunday School Adviser from 1950-5, and then Miss Dorothy Taylor. In 1956 Miss Doris Rose (who had married Dr. T. G. Dunning the previous year) retired from the post of organizing secretary of the deaconess movement and Miss Dorothy Finch, herself at one time a deaconess, was appointed in her place. Also in 1956 Dr. F. Townley Lord resigned the editorship of *The Baptist Times*, his place being taken by the Rev. W. W. Bottoms. A year later Miss Phillis I. Webb intimated her desire to retire after more than thirty-nine years of service at the Church House, during the last ten of which she had been responsible for the minutes of the Council and its more important committees and for much of the detailed work of the Ministerial Recognition Department. This latter work was taken over by Mr. John Hough, the Rev. W. David Jackson, of Histon, joining the Young People's Department and the Rev. R. W. Thomson, of Loughborough, becoming Minute Secretary and at the same

[3] The luncheon was at the invitation of Mrs. Russell James, who continued to be a generous benefactor of Baptist causes until her death in 1957. The restoration of the Shakespeare Room was undertaken by Mr. and Mrs. Edward Vinson and the Baptist Insurance Company.

time secretary of the Psalms and Hymns Trust in succession to Mr. C. H. Parsons.

At the time of the formation of the Carey Kingsgate Press, Mr. H. L. Hemmens had been appointed editor, while remaining also responsible for the periodicals issued by the Baptist Missionary Society. Mr. Hemmens had long been a well-known denominational figure, the right hand man of successive Home Secretaries of the Missionary Society and a leader of the Laymen's Missionary Movement (later known as the Baptist Men's Movement).[4] On his death in 1952, he was succeeded in both his editorial offices by the Rev. A. S. Clement. When two years later Mr. C. H. Parsons retired from the managership of the Carey Kingsgate Press, he was succeeded by Mr. Gordon J. Alden. The time was approaching when a new hymnbook would be needed and it was agreed that the approaching ter-jubilee of the Union would provide a fitting occasion for its publication. Accordingly, the Psalms and Hymns Trustees, to whom Mr. Parsons continued to act as secretary until 1958, appointed an editorial committee with Dr. Hugh Martin, C.H., as chairman. The son of a Baptist minister, Dr. Martin had been for many years manager of the Student Christian Movement Press, an influential figure in all ecumenical developments and the author of many books. In 1953–4 he was Moderator of the Free Church Federal Council. Under his leadership the hymnbook committee rejected the idea of a further revision of the Baptist Church Hymnal and set itself to prepare an entirely new book.

A series of fiftieth anniversaries followed that of the Baptist Church House and recalled the early expansive days of Shakespeare's secretaryship. First came that of the Baptist Insurance Co. Ltd., then those of the London Baptist Property Board, the Baptist Historical Society and the Baptist Women's League. From 1941–57 the Insurance Company had had Mr. Seymour J. Price as General Manager, benefiting greatly from his professional skill and his knowledge of and standing in the denomina-

[4] See H. L. Hemmens, *Such Has Been My Life*, 1953. In 1948, Mr. K. W. Bennett succeeded Mr. Hemmens as secretary of the Baptist Men's Movement.

tion. During his managership nearly £49,000 was paid over to the funds of the Baptist Union. Without the substantial annual sums available from this source, the Union would have been in serious financial difficulties. The special Jubilee offering of £18,000 raised by the Baptist Women's League was also a welcome aid to the funds of the Union.

Unfortunately it proved necessary in 1952 to close the Percy Illingworth Soldiers' Institute at Aldershot. This had been built during the First World War on land which remained the possession of the War Office. The work done by successive Wardens[5] and their helpers—most of them voluntary helpers—was much appreciated by the men who used the Institute, but it became impossible to compete with the canteen directly sponsored by the Army and the property had to be handed over to the authorities.

About the same time, however, the denomination acquired a new asset in a Boys' Home at Stock, Essex, the capital cost of which was made available to the West Ham Central Mission by the Carnegie Trust. Of wider significance was the recognition in 1957 of Regent's Park College as a Permanent Private Hall of Oxford University. The decision to apply for this status, which had been accorded a year or so earlier to Mansfield College, was unanimously approved by the Baptist Union Council. A seal was thus set on the efforts for ministerial education of men like William Newman and F. A. Cox, Joseph Angus, George Gould and Henry Wheeler Robinson. This development, together with the ter-jubilees of Rawdon College and the South Wales Baptist College,[6] and the centenary of Spurgeon's College, helped to focus attention on the needs of the theological colleges and the importance of bringing their policy and equipment into line with the changing situation, educationally and denominationally.

IV

During the Festival of Britain in 1951 the Union shared with

[5] The Rev. Hugh Brock, the Rev. Douglas Hicks, and the Rev. W. A. L. Pearce.
[6] See J. O. Barrett, *A Short History of Rawdon College*, 1954, and D. Mervyn Himbury, *The South Wales Baptist College*, 1957.

THE BAPTIST UNION COUNCIL IN SESSION (1955)

Behind the desk (*left to right*) are: Rev. O. D. Wiles, Deputy General Secretary; Mr. A. S. Clark, Treasurer; Rev. E. A. Payne, General Secretary; Rev. Henry Cook, President; Rev. R. L. Child, Vice-President; Mr. G. G. Fairbairn, Honorary Solicitor

the Missionary Society and the Commonwealth and Colonial Society in holding a Commonwealth and Empire Baptist Congress. There were present representatives from Canada, Australia, New Zealand, South Africa, India, Jamaica, Trinidad, Nigeria, British Cameroons and the Bahamas. It was estimated that there were within the British family of nations about forty Baptist unions, conventions and missionary societies, and over 8,000 churches, with a total membership of approximately 900,000. The Commonwealth Society continued its interest in a number of overseas enterprises and gave assistance to visitors to Britain, as well as to those emigrating from this country. As the result of a visit to Sierra Leone by the secretary, the Rev. F. C. Morton, and the treasurer, Sir Herbert Janes, interest was awakened in the two Baptist churches there and in 1956, with the encouragement of the Baptist Missionary Society and the Union, the Rev. T. Victor Jones undertook a brief period of special service as "superintendent".

The Commonwealth and Empire Congress proved a useful experience in preparation for a much larger undertaking, namely, the holding in London in July 1955 of the Golden Jubilee Congress of the Baptist World Alliance. During his five years as President of the Alliance, Dr. F. Townley Lord travelled more constantly and widely than any of his predecessors. His genial personality helped to strengthen Baptist fellowship in many parts of Europe, North and South America, Australia and New Zealand. At the same time, the General Secretary of the Alliance, Dr. A. T. Ohrn, also travelled extensively, visiting parts of both Asia and Africa. Only a small British delegation could be present at the Baptist Youth Congress held in Rio de Janeiro in 1953, but British Baptists entered enthusiastically into the plans for the World Congress and, in spite of the uncertainties of the time, it was carried through successfully. Of the more than 8,000 delegates, about half came from the United States, some 1,600 from Britain itself, over 400 by specially chartered ship from Australia and New Zealand, a like number from Canada, 300 from Germany and nearly as many from Sweden, with considerable contingents from other European lands. No previous Congress had

had so large a representation from India. Several countries were represented for the first time. A delegation of nine Russians from the Soviet Union was specially warmly greeted, as there had been no similar delegation since the Toronto Congress in 1928. There were, however, no delegates present from Hungary, Rumania, Poland, Czechoslovakia or Bulgaria, nor from China. The climax of the Congress came in a rally in the Arsenal Stadium, attended by the largest Baptist company ever to assemble in Britain and addressed by Dr. Billy Graham.[7]

The presence of the Russians followed a visit to the Soviet Union in 1954 by Dr. Townley Lord and the writer. For a year or so previously the Baptist Union Council had had a desultory and unsatisfactory correspondence with the All-Soviet Council of Evangelical Christian Baptists. The invitation for the British visit came during the easing of tension which followed the death of Stalin. The discovery that there were at least 512,000 Baptist church members scattered throughout the Soviet Union and enjoying freedom of worship, though not of propaganda, came as a surprise and encouragement. The following year the same two visitors received an invitation from the Hungarian Ecumenical Council and were able to make contact with the Baptists of Hungary. These contacts were strengthened in the summer of 1956 when the Central Committee of the World Council of Churches met in Hungary. On his way back from these meetings, the writer was able to spend four days in Czechoslovakia and met representative groups of Baptists in Bratislava and Prague. Baptists from many lands joined in helping the tens of thousands of refugees who entered Austria after the revolt which occurred in Hungary in the following autumn. Early in 1957 two Hungarian Baptist leaders were able to come from Budapest to London, while in the spring the writer accompanied Dr. Henry Cook, the Associate Secretary of the Alliance, on a twelve-day visit to the Baptists of Poland.

[7] See *Golden Jubilee Congress: Official Report*, edited by Arnold T. Ohrn, 1955, and F. Townley Lord, *Baptist World Fellowship, A Short History of the Baptist World Alliance*, 1955.

These renewed contacts were most welcome. The visits made clear that, in spite of many difficulties, Baptist witness had survived in eastern and south-eastern Europe and that in many cases Baptists, though relatively few in number, had an equality of legal status and an evangelistic opportunity not possessed a generation earlier. In the years from 1947 onwards the European Baptist Federation had been slowly growing in effectiveness, though confined in its activities to western Europe. Mrs. F. F. Pepper, of Britain, drew together the women of various lands and the Rev. Joel Sorenson the young people. Generous financial aid was forthcoming from both the American and the Southern Conventions. The European Baptist Seminary, established at Ruschlikon, near Zurich, by the Southern Convention in 1949, proved an admirable centre for training courses and conferences. A European Baptist Congress held in Copenhagen in 1952 was useful, though not fully representative. By 1958 it proved possible to hold in Berlin a further Congress at which delegates were able to be present from almost every land in Europe. The gathering gained in significance from the presence of a considerable number of leaders from other parts of the world, who had come to Europe for the annual meeting of the Executive of the Baptist World Alliance.

V

These assurances of continued and expanding opportunities for Baptist witness in Europe were accompanied by significant developments on the wider stage of the Ecumenical Movement. The fruit of closer contacts between those of different traditions was seen in a new readiness to let aid in emergencies pass beyond confessional boundaries. Through agencies such as Inter-Church Aid hands were stretched out in directions which had formerly been barred by ecclesiastical suspicion and criticism. At the time of the disastrous floods on the east coast of England in the early months of 1953, a substantial gift reached British Baptists from the Lutheran Church of America. Two years later, British Baptists were ready to give help to the Orthodox Christians of Istanbul, when their churches and homes were destroyed by rioters. As Inter-Church Aid extended its operations to Asia, it became apparent that a new pattern of Christian service was slowly developing.

Developments of particular interest to Baptists were taking place in the theological field. In the early years of the Faith and Order Movement the rite of baptism seemed to stand on the periphery of the field of discussion. During the nineteen-forties, however, it moved steadily towards the centre. On the Continent theologians of the eminence of Emil Brunner and Karl Barth began to challenge the contemporary practice of infant baptism on Biblical and theological grounds. Within the Anglican Church there were anxious debates as to the meaning of the rite of Christian initiation and the relation of confirmation to baptism. When the third World Conference on Faith and Order met in Lund in 1952, there was general agreement that baptism and the Lord's Supper are more closely related in the New Testament than had been recognized in the discussions at Lausanne and Edinburgh and that a study of their relationship might provide a new and fruitful line of ecumenical advance.[8] The second Assembly of the World Council of Churches, held in Evanston in 1954, after reviewing the work of the Faith and Order department, declared: "We must learn afresh the implications of the one Baptism for our sharing in the one Eucharist."

The Baptist Union was represented at the Lund Conference by Principal K. C. Dykes, Mr. C. T. Le Quesne, Q.C., and the writer. The Rev. H. Ingli James was present as the representative of the Baptist Union of New Zealand. The Burma Baptist Convention, the Baptist Convention of Ontario and Quebec, the Baptist Union of Denmark and the American Baptist Convention were the other Baptist bodies which sent delegates. Mr. Le Quesne and the writer represented the Baptist Union at the Evanston Assembly, together with Dr. M. E. Aubrey, Principal L. G. Champion and

[8] At the request of the Faith and Order Continuation Committee and in preparation for the Lund Conference, the Baptist Union Council had, in 1948, approved a statement on the Baptist Doctrine of the Church. See Appendix X.

the Rev. Gwenyth Hubble. The National (Negro) Baptist Convention, Inc., sent a strong delegation to Evanston and, two years later, the other Negro Convention and the Baptist Union of Hungary applied for membership of the World Council of Churches. Baptists found themselves with larger opportunities and responsibilities at all levels of the World Council's activities.

Membership of the World Council remained a divisive issue within the world fellowship of Baptists. The Southern Convention continued to be critical of all ecumenical relationships and embarked upon a programme of expansion not only in missionary lands overseas, but in the northern states and in Canada. The Baptist Union of Scotland had never been united in its adherence to the World Council and, in 1955, in view of the strongly critical attitude taken by Charlotte Chapel, Edinburgh, the largest church within its fellowship, decided to withdraw from membership for seven years with the avowed hope that, during this period, the theological basis of the World Council would be elaborated in a manner it would find more acceptable.[9] Sentiment remained divided in Australia and Canada. New issues entered the total situation as plans matured for the closer integration of the International Missionary Council and the World Council, and as the schemes for "united churches" in Ceylon, North India and Pakistan reached their definitive form.

The closer integration of the I.M.C. and the W.C.C. was urged on several grounds and from several quarters, particularly by the leaders of the churches in Asia. From them also came the appeal for Churches transcending the ecclesiastical divisions of post-Reformation Europe. In the negotiations in Ceylon and North India, churches supported by the Baptist Missionary Society were represented. The draft schemes provided for the recognition of alternative forms of baptism—"sponsored baptism in infancy" and "believers' baptism". The question whether to enter the proposed new churches, which were to have an episcopate of the type already familiar in the Church of South

---

[9] In 1957, however, the withdrawal of Charlotte Chapel from the Baptist Union of Scotland was regretfully accepted.

India, involved decisions difficult for Baptists both in Asia and Britain at the very time when they were being called upon to contribute to the general ecumenical discussion on baptism, and when considerable changes were clearly necessary in the familiar pattern of overseas missionary activity.

VI

As the Baptist Union approached its ter-jubilee, therefore, it found itself faced with serious theological as well as practical issues, and these concerned far more than the rite of baptism from which the denomination takes its name.

The increasing practical demands made on the Union by churches and ministers, and the enlarged financial resources entrusted to it, made yet closer links between the Union and the churches inevitable. The implications of this for the doctrine of the Church were only reluctantly faced. Many preferred to continue to pay lip service to a theory of independency that had lost its meaning and relevance. At the same time it was becoming clear that churches cannot live without a coherent and Biblically-grounded theology and that this must include a doctrine of the Church, the ministry and the sacraments. Even for its own internal purposes the Union began to feel the need of a more clearly articulated theology.

Encouraged by the welcome given to the statement on the Lord's Supper issued in 1951, the Union in 1954 set up a committee to prepare a statement on "The Meaning and Practice of Ordination among Baptists". Principal D. S. Russell, of Rawdon College, was appointed chairman and the Rev. J. O. Barrett secretary. The report, published in 1957, contained useful Biblical and historical sections and made a number of wise, practical suggestions. There was general agreement, however, that its chief value lay in the stimulus it provided for further serious theological thinking. At the same time it became necessary for British Baptists to expound and defend their attitude to baptism in the light of contemporary Biblical scholarship and the theological debate in other Christian communions. They could no longer rest content with the exposition of their principles put forward by Dr. Wheeler Robinson in 1911, weighty and effective as that had proved to be for nearly two generations. A new generation of Baptist scholars must be found to share in the ecumenical quest for the truth of God.[10]

The representative functions required of the Union by its membership of the Free Church Federal Council, the British Council of Churches and the World Council of Churches made this the more necessary. Churches cannot escape being social institutions. During recent generations each Christian denomination has tended to develop—has been under pressure to develop—an organization, wherein there are vested interests. These are not necessarily evil, even though they inevitably involve an element of bureaucratic control similar to that exercised in secular organizations. Churches have, however, to be continually alert to the inherent dangers, ever anxious to preserve the freedom of the Spirit and to manifest the divine-human nature of every true form of the Body of Christ.

One of the points where these issues come together most acutely is in the matter of trust deeds. In the previous chapter reference was made to the important developments which took place within the Union at the time of the Forward Movement, when the model trust deed for churches was revised. When, in 1951, Parliament passed the Baptist and Congregational Trusts Act a further significant step was taken. For the first time the Baptist Union and the Congregational Union were officially recognized by Parliament. They received power to approve their own trust corporations for certain purposes; the power to set up model forms of trust deeds and to vary them from time to time; and, even more important, the power to accede to the request of a church to adopt the model form in place of an existing one. The Unions were authorized to require changes as a condition of

[10] The beginnings of this may be seen in Johannes Schneider, *Taufe in der Neuen Testament*, 1952, and *Taufe und Gemeinde im Neuen Testament*, 1956 (English translation by E. A. Payne. *Baptism and Church in the New Testament*, 1957), and in Neville Clark, *An Approach to the Theology of the Sacraments*, 1956.

financial aid. This would seem to be entirely justifiable so long as the basis and organization of the Union maintains its fully representative character and is related to an adequate doctrine of the Church.

The story of the Union is the story of the closer association of gathered churches practising believers' baptism and with a mutually recognized theological tradition and a common ethos and polity. The terms of its association with other groups of Christians it must decide for itself. As they approach the one hundred and fiftieth anniversary of the founding of the Union, those in membership with it have to ask themselves whether its organization is satisfactory; whether the relations to it of the still independent societies can be left as they are;[11] whether the movement of the daughter Unions in Wales and Scotland to a largely separate life should be allowed to continue without an effort at a renewal of closer fellowship; whether, in the same way, the Union should remain content with its present isolation from the Baptist Union of Ireland and the various Strict Baptist Associations in England, or should endeavour once more to secure the adherence of all the churches calling themselves Baptist in Great Britain, and Northern Ireland (if not Eire). These are largely domestic issues and to them must be added the wider ones already mentioned.

The right answers will come only by an understanding of the way by which the Union has come to its present position and by a patient seeking of the will of God for His Church as a whole.

Baptist life in general, and that of the Baptist Union in particular, have been shaped partly by inner conviction and partly by the pressure of outward circumstance. The same is true of other Christian communions. "It is only when we see the Church's life as one great stream of supernatural vitality, flowing down through the centuries and manifesting itself in a bewildering variety of modes and patterns, that we shall be in a position to approach the

[11] In 1953 the Baptist Union Council and the General Committee of the Missionary Society issued a joint statement expressing their conviction that closer relationships were desirable.

Church's history in other than an antiquarian spirit and, in humility and charity, to praise our fathers who begat us, while we try, in fear and trembling, to do for our age what they tried to do for theirs."[12]

●

[12] E. L. Mascall, *The Recovery of Unity*, 1958, p. 66.

APPENDIX I

CHAIRMEN AND PRESIDENTS, SECRETARIES AND TREASURERS OF THE BAPTIST UNION

(i) CHAIRMAN AND PRESIDENTS

1831 UPTON, REV. JAMES, Blackfriars. Died 24th April 1867.

1832 UPTON, REV. JAMES, London. Died 24th April 1867.

1833 RIPPON, REV. JOHN, D.D., London. Died 17th December 1836.

1834 COX, REV. FRANCIS AUGUSTUS, D.D., LL.D., London. Died 5th September 1853.

1835 CLARKE, REV. EDMUND, Truro. Died 8th July 1839.

1836 BIRT, REV. CALEB EVANS, A.M., Portsea. Died 13th December 1854.

1837 HINTON, REV. JOHN HOWARD, A.M., Reading. Died 17th December 1873.

1838 CRAMP, REV. JOHN MOCKETT, A.M., St. Peter's. Died 6th December 1881.

1839 SWAN, REV. THOMAS, Birmingham. Died 9th March 1857.

1840 ACWORTH, REV. JAMES, M.A., LL.D., Bradford. Died 13th October 1883.

1841 SPRIGG, REV. JAMES, A.M., Ipswich. Died 20th March 1868.

1842 PIKE, REV. JOHN GREGORY, Derby. Died 4th September 1854.

1843 GODWIN, REV. BENJAMIN, D.D., Oxford. Died 20th February 1871.

1844 ROFF, REV. ROBERT, Cambridge. Died 29th November 1850.

1845 COX, REV. FRANCIS AUGUSTUS, D.D., LL.D., London (see also 1834).

1846 GILES, REV. JOHN EUSTACE, Leeds. Died 24th June, 1875.

1847 LOW, MR. JAMES, London. Died 7th April 1863.

1848 MURCH, REV. WILLIAM HARRIS, D.D., Rickmansworth. Died
–49   12th July 1859.

1850 BURNS, REV. JABEZ, D.D., London. Died 31st January 1876.

1851 HOBY, REV. JAMES, D.D., London. Died 20th November 1871.

1852 COX, REV. FRANCIS AUGUSTUS, D.D., LL.D. (see also 1834 and 1845).

1853 WEBB, REV. JAMES, Ipswich. Died 23rd January 1881.

1854 HOBY, REV. JAMES, D.D., London (see also 1851).

1855 NOEL, The HON. and REV. BAPTIST WRIOTHESLEY, M.A., London. Died 19th January 1873.

1856 ACWORTH, REV. JAMES, M.A., LL.D., Bradford (see also 1840).

1857 EDWARDS, REV. JAMES, Nottingham. Died 14th August 1887.

1858 EVANS, REV. BENJAMIN, D.D., Scarborough. Died 6th April 1871.

1859 ACWORTH, REV. JAMES, M.A., LL.D., Bradford (see also 1840 and 1856).

1860 STEANE, REV. EDWARD, D.D., London. Died 8th May 1882.

1861 ACWORTH, REV. JAMES, M.A., LL.D., Bradford (see also 1840, 1856 and 1859).

1862 STOVEL, REV. CHARLES, London. Died 22nd October 1883.

1863 HINTON, REV. JOHN HOWARD, A.M., London (see also 1837).

1864 MURSELL, REV. JAMES PHILLIPPO, Leicester. Died 2nd November 1885.

1865 ANGUS, REV. JOSEPH, M.A., D.D., London. Died 28th August 1902.

1866 ALDIS, REV. JOHN, Reading. Died 27th September 1907.

1867 NOEL, HON. and REV. BAPTIST WRIOTHESLEY, M.A., London (see also 1855).

1868 GOTCH, REV. FREDERIC WILLIAM, M.A., LL.D., Bristol. Died 17th May 1890.

1869 BROCK, REV. WILLIAM D.D., London. Died 13th November 1875.

1870 ROBINSON, REV. WILLIAM, Cambridge. Died 25th September 1874.

1871 BIRRELL, REV. CHARLES MITCHELL, Liverpool. Died 16th December 1880.

1872 THOMAS, REV. THOMAS, D.D., Pontypool College. Died 6th December 1881.

1873 UNDERHILL, MR. EDWARD BEAN, LL.D., London. Died 11th May 1901.

1874 STOVEL, REV. CHARLES, London (see also 1862).

1875 M^CLAREN, REV. ALEXANDER, B.A., D.D., Litt.D., Manchester. Died 5th May 1910.

1876 LANDELS, REV. WILLIAM, D.D., London. Died 7th July, 1899.

1877 BROWN, REV. JOHN TURLAND, Northampton. Died 11th June 1899.

1878 BROWN, REV. HUGH STOWELL, Liverpool. Died 24th February, 1886.

1879 GOULD, REV. GEORGE, Norwich. Died 13th February 1882.

1880 TRESTRAIL, REV. FREDERICK, D.D., Newport, I.W. Died 4th November 1890.

1881 DOWSON, REV. HENRY, London. Died 23rd November 1884.

1882 BROWN, REV. JOHN JENKYN, Birmingham. Died 14th March 1907.

1883 CHOWN, REV. JOSEPH PARBERY, London. Died 8th July 1886.

1884 GLOVER, REV. RICHARD, D.D., Bristol. Died 26th March 1919.

1885 GREEN, REV. SAMUEL GOSNELL, B.A., D.D., London. Died 15th September 1905.

1886 WILLIAMS, REV. CHARLES, Accrington. Died 26th March 1907.

1887 CULROSS, REV. JAMES, M.A., D.D., Bristol. Died 29th October 1899.

1888 CLIFFORD, REV. JOHN, M.A., LL.B., B.Sc., F.G.S., D.D., London. Died 20th November, 1923.

1889 WIGNER, REV. JOHN THOMAS, London. Died 22nd October 1902.

1890 OWEN, REV. JAMES, Swansea. Died 14th February 1935.

1891 GRIFFIN, COL. JAMES THEODORE, London. Died 21st January 1902.

1892 ROBERTS, REV. ROBERT HENRY, B.A., London. Died 16th April 1900.

1893 MORRIS, REV. THOMAS MEW, Ipswich. Died 4th June 1904.

1894 SHORT, REV. GEORGE, B.A., Salisbury. Died 3rd December 1910.

1895 GREENHOUGH, REV. JOHN GERSHOM, M.A., Leicester. Died 10th November 1933.

1896 TYMMS, REV. PRINCIPAL THOMAS VINCENT, D.D., Rawdon College. Died 25th May 1921.

1897 GANGE, REV. EDWIN GORSUCH, F.R.A.S., London. Died 13th July 1921.

1898 VINCENT, REV. SAMUEL, Plymouth. Died 3rd April 1910.

1899 CLIFFORD, REV. JOHN, M.A., LL.B., B.Sc., F.G.S., D.D., London. (See also 1888.)

1900 CUFF, REV. WILLIAM, London. Died 21st May, 1926.

1901 MCLAREN, REV. ALEXANDER, B.A., D.D., Litt.D., Manchester (see also 1875).

1902 WOOD, REV. JOHN ROSKRUGE, London. Died 24th March 1917.

1903 WHITE, ALDERMAN GEORGE, M.P., Norwich. Died 11th May 1912.

1904 WILSON, REV. JOHN, M.B.E., D.D., London. Died 7th January 1939.

1905 WILLIS, HIS HONOUR JUDGE WILLIAM, K.C., London. Died 22nd August 1911.

1906 MEYER, REV. FREDERICK BROTHERTON, B.A., D.D., London. Died 28th March 1929.

1907 HENDERSON, REV. PRINCIPAL WILLIAM JOHN, B.A., LL.D., Bristol. Died 1st May 1929.

1908 BROWN, REV. CHARLES, D.D., London. Died 6th June 1947.

1909 MARSHALL, REV. PRINCIPAL JOHN TURNER, M.A., D.D., Manchester. Died 23rd June 1923.

1910 MACALPINE, SIR GEORGE WATSON, LL.D., Accrington. Died 18th April 1920.

1911 EDWARDS, REV. PRINCIPAL WILLIAM, B.A., D.D., LL.D., Cardiff. Died 28th February 1929.

1912 EWING, REV. JOHN WILLIAM, M.A., D.D., London. Died 1st May 1951.

1913 GOULD, REV. PRINCIPAL GEORGE PEARCE, M.A., D.D., London. Died 22nd March 1921.

1914 JOSEPH, REV. CHARLES, Plymouth. Died 14th December 1917.

1915 FORBES, REV. JOHN THOMAS, M.A., D.D., Glasgow. Died 13th February 1936.

1916 PHILLIPS, REV. THOMAS, B.A., London. Died 22nd April 1936.

1917 FULLERTON, REV. WILLIAM YOUNG, London. Died 17th August 1932.

1918 ROBERTS, REV. JOHN EDWARD, M.A., D.D., Manchester. Died 25th January 1929.

1919 MARNHAM, MR. HERBERT, London. Died 8th April 1935.

1920 HILEY, REV. DAVID JOHN, H.C.F., London. Died 30th March 1948.

1921 CARLILE, REV. JOHN CHARLES, C.B.E., D.D., Folkestone. Died 16th August 1941.

1922 ⎰ CHOWN, MR. JOHN, London. Died 11th August 1922.
⎱ CARLILE, REV. JOHN CHARLES, C.H., C.B.E., D.D., Folkestone. (Appointed by the Council.)

1923 BLOMFIELD, REV. PRINCIPAL WILLIAM ERNEST, B.A., D.D., Rawdon. Died 22nd July 1934.

1924 GLOVER, MR. TERROT REAVELEY, M.A., D.D., LL.D., Cambridge. Died 28th May 1943.

1925 PENNY, MR. THOMAS STUBBS, J.P., Taunton. Died 20th July 1944.

1926 RUSHBROOKE, REV. JAMES HENRY, M.A., D.D., London. Died 1st February 1947.

1927 MANDER, REV. HENRY CHARLES, D.D., Bristol. Died 15th November 1934.

1928 DOGGART, MR. ARTHUR ROBERT, J.P., Darlington. Died 16th January 1932.

1929 BROWN, REV. ARTHUR DOUGLAS, D.D., London. Died 27th April 1940.

1930 NEWTON, MR. ARTHUR, London. Died 3rd April 1942.

1931 BONNER, REV. CAREY, London. Died 17th June 1938.

1932 ELLIS, MR. ALFRED, J.P., Amersham. Died 29th August 1936.

1933 CLIFFORD, REV. ROBERT ROWNTREE, A.T.S., London. Died
      18th November 1943.
1934 LAWS, REV. GILBERT, D.D., Norwich.
1935 WOOD, MR. HENRY ERNEST, J.P., C.C., Hutton. Died 2nd
      August 1946.
1936 TOWNSEND, REV. HENRY, M.A., D.D., Manchester. Died 2nd
      July 1955.
1937 TAYLOR, MR. HARRY LANGFORD, Bristol. Died 9th November
      1951.
1938 HUMPHREY, REV. FREDERICK JAMES HARRY, D.S.O., London.
      Died 5th September 1947.
1939 THOMSON, REV. PETER TAYLOR, M.A. Died 28th December
      1952.
1940 EVANS, REV. PERCY WILLIAM, B.A., D.D., London. Died
      23rd March 1951.
1941 BLACK, MR. ROBERT WILSON, J.P., London. Died 22nd Novem-
      ber 1951.
1942 GRIFFITH, REV. BENJAMIN GREY, B.D., London.
1943 MORRIS, REV. SYDNEY GELSON, London.
1944 PRICE, MR. SEYMOUR JAMES, London.
1945 DAKIN, REV. ARTHUR, B.D., D.Th., Bristol.
1946 LEQUESNE, MR. CHARLES THOMAS, Q.C., London. Died 22nd
      November 1954.
1947 LORD, REV. FRED TOWNLEY, B.A., D.D., Litt.D., London.
1948 BROWN, RT. HON. ERNEST, C.H., M.C., London.
1949 HUGHES, REV. SAMUEL WILLIAM, D.D., Walgrave. Died 16th
      September 1954.
1950 AUBREY, REV. MELBOURN EVANS, C.H., M.A., D.C.L., LL.D.,
      London. Died 18th October 1957.
1951 WILLIAMSON, REV. HENRY RAYMOND, M.A., B.D., D.Litt.,
      London.
1952 CLARK, MR. ARNOLD STAFFURTH, J.P., London.
1953 BONSER, REV. HENRY, Worthing.
1954 CHILD, REV. PRINCIPAL ROBERT LEONARD, M.A., B.D., B.Litt.,
      Oxford.
1955 COOK, REV. HENRY, M.A., D.D., London.
1956 JANES, SIR HERBERT, F.R.G.S., Luton.
1957 ROWLEY, REV. HAROLD HENRY, M.A., D.D., F.B.A., Man-
      chester.
1958 DUNNING, REV. THOMAS GEORGE, M.A., PH.D., London.
1959 Middlebrook Rev. J. B.   London.

(ii) SECRETARIES OF THE BAPTIST UNION

1811–1821 *Button, Rev. William, London. Died 2nd August 1821.

1811–1834 *Ivimey, Rev. Joseph, London. Died 8th February 1834.

1813–1819 *Thomas, Rev. Thomas, London. Died 11th October 1819.

1832–1840 *Belcher, Rev. Joseph, D.D., London. Removed to Halifax, Nova Scotia, December 1843. Died 1859.

1834–1846 *Murch, Rev. William Harris, D.D., London. Died 12th July, 1859.

1835–1882 *Steane, Rev. Edward, D.D., London. Died 8th May 1882.

1841–1866 *Hinton, Rev. John Howard, A.M., London. Died 17th December 1873.

1863–1877 *Millard, Rev. James Henry, B.A., Huntingdon. Died 22nd October 1883.

1877–1879 *Booth, Rev. Samuel Harris, London. Died 7th April 1902.

1880–1882 Sampson, Rev. William, London. Died 11th November 1882.

1883–1898 Booth, Rev. Samuel Harris, D.D., London. Died 7th April 1902.

1898–1924 Shakespeare, Rev. John Howard, M.A., D.D., LL.D., London. Died 12th March 1928.

1924–1925 †Carlile, Rev. John Charles, C.H., C.B.E., D.D., D. Litt., Folkestone. Died 4th August 1941.

1925–1951 Aubrey, Rev. Melbourn Evans, C.H., M.A., D.C.L., LL.D., London. Died 18th October, 1957.

1951–   Payne, Rev. Ernest Alexander, M.A., D.D., B.Litt., London.

(iii) TREASURERS OF THE BAPTIST UNION

1834–1847 Low, Mr. James. Died 7th April 1863.

1847–1868 Lowe, Mr. George, F.R.S. Died 25th December, 1868.

1869–1878 Sands, Mr. John. Died 7th November 1878.

1879–1892 Pattison, Mr. Samuel Rowles, F.G.S. Died 27th November 1901.

1892–1899 Baynes, Mr. William Wilberforce. Died June, 1901.

1899–1900 Wood, Mr. Henry, J.P. Died 6th October, 1900.

1900–1935 Marnham, Mr. Herbert. Died 8th April, 1935.

1934–   Clark, Mr. Arnold S., J.P.

* Joint Secretaries.
† Acting Secretary.

APPENDIX II

GENERAL SUPERINTENDENTS

1. North-Western	Hector V. Thomas	1915–24
	J. D. M. Robertson	1924–33
	Herbert Motley	1934–49
	Hubert L. Watson	1949–
2. North-Eastern	J. Gyles Williams	1915–22
	Henry Bonser	1923–49
	J. O. Barrett	1949–
3. East Midland	C. G. Croome	1915–23
	Gummer Butt	1924–29
	J. T. Dawson	1929–32
	C. H. Weaver	1932–43
	H. Ingli James	1943–46
	J. C. Rendall	1947–56
	W. J. Grant	1957–
4. West Midland	R. M. Julian	1915–24
	J. Ivory Cripps	1925–45
	A. J. Klaiber	1945–57
	Charles Hardiman	1957–
5. Western	Frank Durbin	1915–28
	Gummer Butt	1929–37
	A. J. Nixon	1938–51
	H. H. Pewtress	1951–
6. Eastern	N. Hardingham Patrick	1915–24
	R. C. Griffin	1925–34
	W. H. Tebbit	1934–50
	Frank C. Bryan	1950–58
	J. H. G. Adam	1958–
7. Central	C. T. Byford	1915–20
	F. J. Walkey	1920–42

	W. R. Miller	1942–55
	W. W. Bottoms	1955–56
	Douglas H. Hicks	1956–

8. Southern	Thomas Woodhouse	1915–30
	Sydney G. Morris	1931–34
	H. H. Sutton	1934–45
	W. D. Jackson	1946–54
	H. V. Larcombe	1954–

9. Metropolitan	J. W. Ewing	1915–34
	Sydney G. Morris	1934–39
	Henry Cook	1939–54
	W. D. Jackson	1954–

10. South Wales	J. Meredith Jones	1915–34
	Griffith J. Harris	1934–46
	H. Ingli James	1947–56
	William Davies	1956–

11. Scotland (Secretary of the Baptist Union)

	George Yuille	1880–1919
	W. B. Nicolson	1919–20
	Thomas Stewart	1920–30
	James Scott	1930–49
	G. M. Hardie	1949–

APPENDIX III

PRESIDENTS OF THE BAPTIST WOMEN'S LEAGUE

1908–14	MARNHAM, MRS. HERBERT
1915	*BOND, MRS. WINDSOR
1916	*JAMES, MRS. RUSSELL
1917	*EDWARDS, MRS. W., J. P.
1918–19	BROWN, MRS. A. DOUGLAS
1920	*HARDY, MISS MARGARET, M.B.E., J.P.
1921	*MARNHAM, MISS KATE
1922	*FREEMAN, MRS. J.
1923	SPURR, MRS. F. C.
1924	*BONNER, MRS. CAREY
1925	*JAMES, MRS. ENOCH
1926	*ROBERTSON, MRS. J. D. M.
1927	ROWLEY, MRS. F. E.
1928	PARSONS, MRS. F. A.
1929	*WOOD, Mrs. H. Ernest
1930	*BURGESS, Mrs. F. J.
1931	*SCROGGIE, MRS. JOHN
1932	*LORD, MRS. EDMUND
1933	BROWN, MRS. ERNEST
1934	HUGHES, MRS. H. G.
1935	GRIFFITH, MRS. B. GREY
1936	CULE, MRS. EDGAR
1937	*TANNER, Mrs. F. W.
1938	*CLIFFORD, MRS. R. ROWNTREE, O.B.E.
1939	FROGGATT, Mrs. J. A.
1940	ROOKE, MRS. CECIL
1941	*BRITTON, MRS. J. N.
1942–43	BROWN, MRS. ERNEST
1944	SALMON, MRS. DAVID
1945	DAVIES, MRS. D. CHRISTY
1946	LEFEVRE, MRS. F.
1947	WILES, MRS. O. D.
1948	MCMILLAN, MRS. ANGUS, M.A.
1949	PEPPER, MRS. F. F.

* Deceased.

1950	CHANNON, MRS. W. G.
1951	JOHN, MRS. J. HOWARD
1952	PEWTRESS, MRS. H. H.
1953	RUSSELL, MISS MARJORIE
1954	WEBB, MRS. L. G.
1955	BARKER, MISS E.
1956	JONES, MRS. J. ITHEL
1957	BATTEN, MRS. G. CLIFFORD, B.A.
1958	STEWART, MRS. DOUGLAS

APPENDIX IV

STATISTICS

It is impossible to provide complete or completely reliable statistics of the number of Baptist churches and church members during the last one hundred and fifty years. The collection of such figures was one of the aims of John Rippon, and later of Joseph Belcher and J. H. Hinton. From 1866 we have figures in *The Baptist Handbook*, which may be assumed to be reasonably accurate. The earlier estimates given below have to be treated with some reserve. Since membership of Baptist churches is based upon personal profession of faith, community strength may be reckoned at three or four times the membership figure. The peak year for membership and for Sunday School scholars, though not for separate churches, was 1906. Five-year intervals have been taken from 1866–1946. Thereafter the annual statistics have been given.

	CHURCHES	MEMBERS	SCHOLARS
1798	445[1]	c. 30,000[2]	
1812	708[3]		
1832	c. 1,000[4]		
1851	1,929[5]		
1866	2,382	213,767	
1871	2,602	243,395	315,080
1876	2,671	265,797	378,752
1881	2,586	295,035	433,801
1886	2,742	302,615	456,694
1891	2,812	334,163	483,921
1896	2,624	342,112	505,226
1901	2,771	372,998	532,219
1906	2,998	434,741	590,321
1911	3,093	418,608	575,830

[1] Rippon.

[2] For 1789 Angus gives the figure 25,000.

[3] James Bennett, *History of Dissent*, IV., 1812, p. 328. He gives 532 in England and 176 in Wales, and says that nearly 100 belonged to the General Baptists and 20 to the Sandemanians.

[4] Belcher, confirmed by Bennett.

[5] Religious Census.

	CHURCHES	MEMBERS	SCHOLARS
1916	3,158	408,029	531,295
1921	3,068	442,688	517,969
1926	3,124	416,665	525,564
1931	3,186	406,216	479,193
1936	3,202	396,531	418,483
1941	3,267	382,337	377,316
1946	3,283	354,900	302,160
1947	3,277	351,533	297,567
1948	3,269	343,798	310,687
1949	3,287	341,789	318,596
1950	3,348	337,741	323,111
1951	3,351	335,640	320,898
1952	3,291	332,187	326,483
1953	3,285	328,628	328,988
1954	3,273	325,896	327,597
1955	3,256	326,633	325,786
1956	3,273	327,806	319,338
1957	3,272	327,048	310,696

At the present time the aggregate membership of churches directly affiliated to the Baptist Union of Great Britain and Ireland is about 250,000. The Baptist Union of Wales and Monmouthshire has a membership of 98,500, the Baptist Union of Scotland a membership of 20,000, and the Baptist Union of Ireland a membership of just over 5,000. A number of churches in these other Unions are also directly affiliated to the Baptist Union of Great Britain and Ireland.

In the churches in India, Pakistan, Ceylon, Belgian Congo, Angola, Jamaica and Trinidad, with which the Baptist Missionary Society is now connected, there are in all over 2,500 congregations, with nearly 110,000 members and 50,000 scholars.

At the second Baptist World Congress, held in Philadelphia in 1911, a world total of 6,715,111 Baptists was claimed. By 1923 this had risen to 9,401,522. The figure issued by the Baptist World Alliance headquarters in 1938 was 12,028,163. The world total is now estimated to be over 22,000,000.

APPENDIX V

A NOTE ON FUNDS

1. The *Fixed Assets* of the Baptist Union include the Baptist Church House, the Girls' Hostel, the Haven, three houses—one in Leicester, one at Tottenham, and one at Little Kingshill—three flats for retired ministers at Billericay and two in Herne Bay.

2. The *Investments* include the trust capital account of the Sustentation Fund (costing £370,000 and producing an income of about £13,750), the Original Home Work Fund (costing £32,000 and producing an income of about £1,250) and general investments (including those earmarked for Deaconess training and work on the continent of Europe) costing about £67,000.

3. *Associated Organizations.* The Baptist Union receives annual grants, which may vary from year to year, from the Psalms and Hymns Trust and the Baptist Insurance Co. Ltd. Companies have been formed to administer the affairs of Arundel House and *The Baptist Times*; both companies have been lent capital by the Baptist Union. Funds of the Union are also invested in the Carey Kingsgate Press Ltd., a company jointly controlled by the Union and the Missionary Society.

4. *Income.* To the above sources of income there are added the annual subscriptions of the churches, Associations and Colleges (amounting to some £3,000); the subscriptions of the Personal Members (amounting to about £3,500); and the contributions to the Home Work Fund. Legacies are placed in a Legacy Equalization Account and spread over five years. For services rendered, the various departments of the Union receive certain payments and contributions, but these fall short of the cost of the departments to the Union by some £9,000 to £10,000 a year.

5. The *Superannuation Fund* consists of the trust capital raised in 1927 and the assets of certain amalgamated societies. Its invested funds cost over £1,000,000 and yield an income of about £41,500. Premiums produce about £20,000 per annum and the annuities being paid amount to nearly £60,000. The Superannuation Fund for Deaconesses possesses no substantial capital.

6. The *Victory Thanksgiving Fund*, raised in 1945–6, is a wasting fund from which capital grants are made to work in this country and on the continent of Europe.

7. The *Baptist Union Scholarship Fund* has investments costing £13,000, which produce an annual income of £500.

8. The *Church Extension Fund*, built up at the time of the Forward Movement, has now come to an end, though small token gifts of £100 continue to be made by the Baptist Union at the opening of a first building and a similar amount is at present available for sites and first buildings from the Wilson Black Trust, at the discretion of the trustees.

9. The *Baptist Union Corporation Loan Fund* is made up almost entirely of deposits by churches and individuals and is lent out to help with building schemes and the purchase of manses.

10. The *Baptist Building Fund* is controlled by its own Managers. It consists of a circulating fund of some £220,000 available to the churches in interest-free loans repayable in ten years by half-yearly instalments.

11. The *Particular Baptist Fund*, established in 1717, provides grants in aid to ministers and students approved by the Managers, who are the ministers and messengers of certain churches in London and its vicinity.

12. *Smaller Trust Funds*. There are a number of smaller Baptist trust funds for the benefit of ministers and churches, such as the Joseph Davis Trust, the Abraham Atkins Trust, the Honiton Trust and the Seward Trust, all of which are administered by their own trustees in accordance with the original terms of the trusts. The Dr. John Ward Trust, established 1754, and the Havelock Trust, established 1862, are for the benefit of students.

DECLARATORY STATEMENT, ADOPTED BY THE BAPTIST UNION ASSEMBLY, 23rd April 1888

"Whilst expressly disavowing and disallowing any power to control belief or restrict inquiry, yet in view of the uneasiness produced in the churches by recent discussions, and to show our agreement with one another, and with our fellow Christians on the great truths of the Gospel, the Council deem it right to say that:

(*a*) Baptized in the name of the Father, and of the Son, and of the Holy Ghost, we have avowed repentance towards God and faith in the Lord Jesus Christ—the very elements of a new life; as in the Lord's Supper we avow our union with one another, while partaking of the symbol of the Body of our Lord, broken for us, and of the Blood shed for the remission of sins. The Union, therefore, is an association of churches and ministers, professing not only to believe the facts and doctrines of the Gospel, but to have undergone the spiritual change expressed or implied in them. This change is the fundamental principle of our church life.

(*b*) The following facts and doctrines are commonly believed by the Churches of the Union:

1. The Divine Inspiration and Authority of the Holy Scriptures as the supreme and sufficient rule of our faith and practice: and the right and duty of individual judgment in the interpretation of it.

2. The fallen and sinful state of man.

3. The Deity, the Incarnation, the Resurrection of the Lord Jesus Christ, and His Sacrificial and Mediatorial Work.

4. Justification by Faith—a faith that works by love and produces holiness.

5. The Work of the Holy Spirit in the conversion of sinners, and in the sanctification of all who believe.

6. The Resurrection; the Judgment at the Last Day, according to the words of our Lord in Matthew xxv, 46.[1]

---

[1] It should be stated, as an historical fact, that there have been brethren in the Union, working cordially with it, who, whilst reverently bowing to the authority of Holy Scripture, and rejecting dogmas of Purgatory and Universalism, have not held the common interpretation of these words of our Lord."

APPENDIX VII

LETTER ON REUNION, accepted at the Autumn Session of the Baptist Union, 1889, as a reply to a letter from the Archbishop of Canterbury.

To the Most Reverend His Grace the Lord Archbishop of Canterbury.
May it please Your Grace,

We, the pastors and delegates of the Baptist Union of Great Britain and Ireland, assembled in Birmingham, desire respectfully to reply to the letter, dated 10th April 1889, which Your Grace addressed to the Rev. Dr. Clifford, M.A., who was then our president, and the receipt of which was acknowledged by him.

We regard, with sincere gratitude to the Divine Head of the Church, the manifestation of a growing desire for union amongst the various bodies of professed believers in the Lord Jesus Christ in this land. We rejoice in the increasingly frank and cordial recognition of the graces and gifts bestowed on communities of Christ's disciples, differing in ecclesiastical organization, and we are, therefore, glad to recognize as one of the signs of the outpouring of the Spirit of Christian brotherhood the resolution passed at the Lambeth Conference.

Mindful of the prayer of our Lord for the unity of His people, we are, we trust, as deeply concerned as Your Grace to promote fraternal intercourse, practical co-operation and also organic union amongst societies of Christians, whenever such fellowship can be secured without impairing the sole and absolute authority of the Lord Jesus Christ over His people, and without a departure from His teaching concerning the doctrine, worship, and government of His Church, as contained in the New Testament Scriptures.

We have carefully examined the Articles on which we are invited to consider the readiness of the Anglican Episcopate to confer with us as to "what steps can be taken, either towards corporate reunion, or towards such relations as may prepare the way for fuller organic unity hereafter", which are:

"(a) The Holy Scriptures of the Old and New Testaments as 'containing all things necessary to salvation', and as being the rule and ultimate standard of faith.

"(b) The Apostles' Creed, as the Baptismal Symbol; and the Nicene Creed, as the sufficient statement of the Christian faith.

"(c) The two Sacraments ordained by Christ Himself—Baptism and the Supper of the Lord—ministered with unfailing use of Christ's words of Institution, and of the elements ordained by Him.

"(*d*) The Historic Episcopate, locally adapted in the methods of its administration to the varying needs of the nations and peoples called of God into the Unity of His Church." (See *Encycl. Letter*, pp. 88, 24, 25).

As to the first of these Articles (*a*), we are in full accord with Your Grace. The supreme authority of Holy Scripture in matters of religious faith and duty is a cardinal principle underlying our Church organization and individual life.

The other three Articles (*b*, *c* and *d*) laid down in the *Encyclical Letter* contain terms so obviously susceptible of two or more interpretations that they do not seem to us to promise a profitable issue to any deliberations founded upon them. For instance: Our churches hold that they have "the Historic Episcopate" as it is laid down in the New Testament, and they do not consider the Diocesan Episcopate of the Anglican Communion to be in accordance with the New Testament law of Church government.

But our chief difficulty as Baptists in approaching the suggested conference arises from the fact that our churches hold and teach:

(1) That the Christianity of the New Testament was essentially the introduction of a spiritual, personal, and non-sacerdotal religion.

(2) That the New Testament law of Baptism requires a profession of faith in the Lord Jesus Christ as a prerequisite to the administration of the rite; or, as it is well expressed in the Catechism of the Church of England, in answer to the question, "What is required of persons to be baptized?"—"Repentance, whereby they forsake sin, and Faith, whereby they steadfastly believe the promises of God"; and that the administration of baptism to infants, "when by reason of their tender age" they cannot satisfy these conditions, is contrary to the teaching of Holy Scripture, and to the practice of the Primitive and Apostolic Church.

(3) That, in subjection to the teaching of the Word of God, the internal government of each Christian church should be conducted by the professed servants of the Saviour, and should be in no way controlled by the Sovereign powers of the State.

These principles—excepting our views on Christian baptism—we hold, as your Grace is fully aware, in common with other Free Churches in this country, with whom we are not only united by the ties of brotherhood but also by a common concern for the salvation and well-being of all men.

Having laid before Your Grace this frank statement of our position, we are the more anxious to acknowledge the spirit of devotedness to the welfare of our fellow-countrymen which we witness in many of the members of the Established Church. With all that tends to promote spiritual religion and social reformation we earnestly sympathize, and while we do not think the suggested conference would advance the special object of "Home Reunion" which your Grace has in view, we do regard the mere suggestion of such a conference as tending to bring about a more direct and closely-knit federation in those consecrated labours in which all sections of Christ's Church are engaged. In our judgment, such co-operation would be a truer index of the growth and power of the spirit of Christian brotherhood than a comprehensive organization and a mere outward conformity.

Signed on behalf of the Baptist Union of Great Britain and Ireland.

APPENDIX VIII

DECLARATORY STATEMENT OF COMMON FAITH AND PRACTICE, adopted
on 26th March 1917 as the Doctrinal basis of the projected Federal
Council of the Evangelical Free Churches of England; approved by the
Baptist Union Assembly, April 1918; accepted as the Doctrinal basis
of the Free Church Federal Council, September 1940.

(1) The Evangelical Free Churches of England claim and cherish
their place as inheritors, along with others, of the historic faith of
Christendom, which found expression in the ecumenical creeds of
the early and undivided Church; and this Declaratory Statement
does not profess to be a comprehensive creed, but is a declaration of
such truths as, in the circumstances, it seems proper to rehearse and
emphasize.

(2) It is an essential element in the proposals for federation that
each of the federating Churches should preserve its own autonomy
as regards faith and practice; this Statement, therefore, is not to be
imposed as a disciplinary standard on any of these Churches, nor, on
the other hand, does it supersede or in any way alter the place of
whatever doctrinal standards any of these Churches may maintain
in their constitution.

I

There is One Living and True God, Who is revealed to us as Father,
Son, and Holy Spirit; Him alone we worship and adore.

II

We believe that God so loved the world as to give His Son to be the
Revealer of the Father and the Redeemer of mankind; that the Son of
God, for us men and for our salvation, became man in Jesus Christ,
Who, having lived on earth the perfect human life, died for our sins,
rose again from the dead, and now is exalted Lord over all; and that
the Holy Spirit, Who witnesses to us of Christ, makes the salvation
which is in Him to be effective in our hearts and lives.

III

We acknowledge that all men are sinful, and unable to deliver themselves from either the guilt or power of their sin; but we have received

and rejoice in the Gospel of the grace of the Holy God, wherein all who truly turn from sin are freely forgiven through faith in our Lord Jesus Christ, and are called and enabled, through the Spirit dwelling and working within them to live in fellowship with God and for His service; and in this new life, which is to be nurtured by the right use of the means of grace, we are to grow, daily dying unto sin and living unto Him Who in His mercy has redeemed us.

IV

We believe that the Catholic or Universal Church is the whole company of the redeemed in heaven and on earth, and we recognize as belonging to this holy fellowship all who are united to God through faith in Christ.

The Church on earth—which is One through the Apostolic Gospel and through the living union of all its true members with its one Head, even Christ and which is Holy through the indwelling Holy Spirit Who sanctifies the Body and its members—is ordained to be the visible Body of Christ, to worship God through Him, to promote the fellowship of His people and the ends of His Kingdom, and to go into all the world and proclaim His Gospel for the salvation of men and the brotherhood of all mankind. Of this visible Church, and every branch thereof, the only Head is the Lord Jesus Christ; and in its faith, order, discipline and duty, it must be free to obey Him alone as it interprets His holy will.

V

We receive, as given by the Lord to His Church on earth, the Holy Scriptures, the Sacraments of the Gospel, and the Christian Ministry.

The Scriptures, delivered through men moved by the Holy Ghost, record and interpret the revelation of redemption, and contain the sure Word of God concerning our salvation and all things necessary thereto. Of this we are convinced by the witness of the Holy Spirit in the hearts of men to and with the Word; and this Spirit, thus speaking from the Scriptures to believers and to the Church, is the supreme Authority by which all opinions in religion are finally to be judged.

The Sacraments—Baptism and the Lord's Supper—are instituted by Christ, Who is Himself certainly and really present in His own ordinances (though not bodily in the elements thereof), and are signs and seals of His Gospel not to be separated therefrom. They confirm the promises and gifts of salvation, and, when rightly used by believers with faith and prayer, are, through the operation of the Holy Spirit, true means of grace.

The Ministry is an office within the Church—not a sacerdotal order —instituted for the preaching of the Word, the ministration of the Sacraments and the care of souls. It is a vocation from God, upon which therefore no one is qualified to enter save through the call of the Holy Spirit in the heart; and this inward call is to be authenticated by the call of the Church, which is followed by ordination to the work of the Ministry in the name of the Church. While thus maintaining the Ministry as an office, we do not limit the ministries of the New Testament to those who are thus ordained, but affirm the priesthood of all believers and the obligation resting upon them to fulfil their vocation according to the gift bestowed upon them by the Holy Spirit.

VI

We affirm the sovereign authority of our Lord Jesus Christ over every department of human life, and we hold that individuals and peoples are responsible to Him in their several spheres and are bound to render Him obedience and seek always the furtherance of His Kingdom upon earth, not, however, in any way constraining belief, imposing religious disabilities, or denying the rights of conscience.

VII

In the assurance, given us in the Gospel, of the love of God our Father, to each of us and to all men, and in the faith that Jesus Christ, Who died, overcame death and has passed into the heavens, the first-fruits of them that slept, we are made confident of the hope of Immortality, and trust to God our souls and the souls of the departed. We believe that the whole world must stand before the final Judgment of the Lord Jesus Christ. And, with glad and solemn hearts, we look for the consummation and bliss of the life everlasting, wherein the people of God, freed for ever from sorrow and from sin, shall serve Him and see His face in the perfected communion of all saints in the Church triumphant.

These things, as all else in our Christian faith, we hold in reverent submission to the guidance and teaching of the Holy Spirit Who is Truth, and we shall ever seek of Him enlightenment and grace both to unlearn our errors and also more fully to learn the mind and will of God, Whom to know is life eternal, and to serve, is perfect freedom.

And, being thus called of God unto the purpose of His redeeming love wherein He is delivering the world from sin and misery and is reconciling all things to Himself in Christ Jesus, and being animated with faith in the final triumph of our Lord, we set before us as our end and aim, to carry the Gospel to every creature and to serve and stablish, in our land and throughout the earth, His reign of righteousness, joy and peace.

Grace be with all those that love our Lord Jesus Christ in sincerity. And to God be glory in the Church by Christ Jesus, throughout all ages, world without end.

Amen.

APPENDIX IX

Reply of the Churches in Membership with the Baptist Union to the "Appeal to all Christian People" issued by the Lambeth Conference of 1920.
Adopted unanimously by THE ASSEMBLY of the BAPTIST UNION at Leeds on Tuesday, 4th May 1926

We, the representatives of Churches in membership with the Baptist Union of Great Britain and Ireland, gathered in Annual Assembly, greet in the name of our Lord Jesus Christ all Christian people, and at this time especially those within the Anglican Church.

The "Appeal to all Christian People", issued by the Lambeth Conference of 1920, and transmitted to us by the Archbishop of Canterbury, has stirred deeply our minds and hearts. We received it with the respect and sympathy due to a message from brethren in Christ representing a great historic communion and moved by a spirit of brotherly love toward their fellow-Christians; and we have sought to give it the prayerful consideration which it manifestly deserves.

Our reply has been postponed in order that the Federal Council of the Free Churches of England might report upon conversations held with representative Anglican Bishops for the purpose of elucidating the Appeal and the Resolutions that, in the Report of the Lambeth Conference, accompanied it. These conversations having been suspended, and certain documents having been issued by the Joint Conference of Bishops and members of the Federal Council, we are now able to present our reply.

We recognize fully and gladly the courtesy and lofty purpose of those who made the Appeal. These qualities are manifest not only in the document itself but also in the attitude of their representatives throughout the discussion of the high matters which they brought before us. We associate ourselves with our Anglican brethren in longing and prayer for a larger unity among all who follow and serve our Lord and Saviour Jesus Christ. While we cannot recall without thankfulness and pride the loyalty to truth which constrained our spiritual ancestors to form the Churches of our faith and order, we sorrow sincerely for whatever has been unworthy in the relations of Christian communities to one another; and we express our repentance for any bitter or unjust word or deed through which we may have obscured the testimony of the Gospel or hindered the advance of the Kingdom of God.

We believe in the Catholic Church as the holy Society of believers in our Lord Jesus Christ, which He founded, of which He is the only Head, and in which He dwells by His Spirit, so that though made up of many communions, organized in various modes, and scattered throughout the world, it is yet one in Him.

We believe that this holy society is truly to be found wherever companies of believers unite as Churches on the ground of a confession of personal faith. Every local community thus constituted is regarded by us as both enabled and responsible for self-government through His indwelling Spirit Who supplies wisdom, love, and power, and Who, as we believe, leads these communities to associate freely in wider organizations for fellowship and the propagation of the Gospel.

We reverence and obey the Lord Jesus Christ, our God and Saviour, as the sole and absolute authority in all matters pertaining to faith and practice, as revealed in the Scriptures, and we hold that each Church has liberty to interpret and administer His laws. We do not judge the conscience of those who take another view, but we believe that this principle of the freedom of the individual Church under Christ has the sanction of Scripture and the justification of history, and therefore we cannot abandon it without being false to our trust. Moreover, it is plain to us that the headship and sole authority of our Lord in His Church excludes any such relations with the State as may impair its liberty.

This view of the Church determines our attitude towards the special issues raised by the Lambeth Appeal.

The Scriptures, in and through which the Spirit of God speaks, possess for us supreme and unique authority. While we recognize the historic value of ancient creeds, we cannot give them a place of authority comparable with that of the Scriptures.

Christian Baptism and the Communion of the Lord's Supper are duly received by us not only as rites instituted and hallowed by our Lord Himself, but as means of grace to all who receive them in faith.

Because we hold the Church to be a community of Christian believers, the ordinance of baptism is administered among us to those only who make a personal confession of repentance and faith. We baptize by immersion in water in accordance with the mode of baptism received by our Lord and practised by His earliest followers as recorded in the New Testament, and because this symbolic representation guards the thought of that inner baptism of the Holy Spirit which is central in Christian experience. In our judgment the baptism of infants incapable of offering a personal confession of faith subverts the conception of the Church as the fellowship of believers. We recognize that those concerning whom Jesus said, "Of such is the Kingdom of Heaven" belong to God, and believe that no rite is needed to bring them into relation with Him. But many of our Churches hold services at which infants are presented, the duties, privileges, and responsibilities of parents emphasized, and the prayers of the Church offered for children and parents.

The Lord's Supper is observed regularly and devoutly by our Churches. Its value for us depends upon both the presence of our Lord and the faith with which we receive the bread and wine that show forth His redemptive sacrifice; but not upon the official position of a celebrant or upon any change in the elements due to words of consecration. It seems to us contrary to the simplicity that is in Christ that the full effect of the Lord's Supper as a means of grace should be held to depend on episcopal ordination.

In general, the place given to Sacraments by the Lambeth Appeal would, it appears, exclude from the universal Church of our Lord bodies of devoted Christians with whom we enjoy fellowship, and to this exclusion we cannot assent.

Our doctrine of the Church determines our conception of the ministry. We hold firmly the priesthood of all believers, and therefore have no separated order of priests. The ministry is for us a gift of the Spirit to the Church, and is an office involving both the inward call of God and the commission of the Church. We can discover no ground for believing that such commission can be given only through an episcopate, and we hold that the individual Church is competent to confer it. For us there is no more exalted office than a ministry charged with preaching the Word of God and with the care of souls. Those called to devote their whole lives to such tasks are held in special honour. Yet any full description of the ministerial functions exercised among us must also take account of other believers who, at the call of the Church, may preside at the observance of the Lord's Supper or fulfil any other duties which the Church assigns to them.

Our ministry is one of those which our brethren of the Anglican Church cordially recognize in their Appeal as having been "manifestly blessed and owned by the Holy Spirit as effective means of grace". Since God has used it in building up Baptist Churches throughout the world which now comprise more than eleven million communicants, we cannot in any way deny its validity and sufficiency.

The deepening sense of friendship and unity between the various parts of the one Church of Christ gladdens us. We thank God that many ancient misunderstandings are passing away, that in our own country hostility and bitterness are giving place to charity and co-operation, and that the Lambeth Appeal by its language and spirit has drawn the Churches nearer to one another.

It will be gathered from this reply that union of such a kind as the Bishops have contemplated is not possible for us. We would say this not only with that frankness which we believe is the highest courtesy among Christian brethren, but with the assurance of our regret that the way in which they would have us to go with them is not open.

Further progress in the direction of Christian unity can be secured, we are convinced, only by unreserved mutual recognition. We gladly acknowledge the reality of the ministry of our Anglican brethren, whose representative Bishops have similarly acknowledged the reality of our ministry. This mutual recognition is significant and full of hope.

We believe that the time has come when the Churches of Christ should unite their forces to meet the need of the world. We therefore are prepared to join the Church of England in exploring the possibility of a federation of equal and autonomous Churches in which the several parts of the Church of Christ would co-operate in bringing before men the will and claims of our Lord.

We assure our brethren of our earnest prayer that the blessing of God may rest upon the Churches of the Anglican Communion, and that He may continue to impart abundantly to its members the riches of His grace.

Finally, we would reaffirm our belief in the real spiritual unity of all who are loyal to Christ and His truth and our eagerness to welcome every means by which, in common action for the spread of His message and the helping and healing of men, that unity may be displayed to the world.

Grace be with all them that love our Lord Jesus Christ in sincerity.

APPENDIX X

THE BAPTIST DOCTRINE OF THE CHURCH

A Statement approved by the Council of the Baptist Union of Great
Britain and Ireland, March 1948

1. The Baptist Union of Great Britain and Ireland represents more
than three thousand churches and about three hundred thousand members. Through its membership in the Baptist World Alliance it is in
fellowship with other Baptist communities through the world num-
bering about thirteen million, who have accepted the responsibilities
of full communicant membership.

Baptists have a continuous history in Great Britain since the beginning of the seventeenth century. Many of their principles, however,
were explicitly proclaimed in the second half of the sixteenth century
by the radical wing of the Reformation movement. They claim as
their heritage also the great central stream of Christian doctrine and
piety through the centuries, and have continuity with the New Testament Church in that they rejoice to believe and seek faithfully to proclaim the Apostolic Gospel and endeavour to build up the life of their
churches after what seems to them the New Testament pattern.

THE ONE HOLY CATHOLIC CHURCH

2. Although Baptists have for so long held a position separate from
that of other communions, they have always claimed to be part of the
one holy catholic Church of our Lord Jesus Christ. They believe in
the catholic Church as the holy society of believers in our Lord Jesus
Christ, which He founded, of which He is the only Head, and in
which He dwells by His Spirit, so that though manifested in many
communions, organized in various modes, and scattered throughout
the world, it is yet one in Him.[1] The Church is the Body of Christ and
a chosen instrument of the divine purpose in history.

In the worship, fellowship and witness of the one Church we know
ourselves to be united in the communion of saints, not only with all
believers upon earth, but also with those who have entered into life
everlasting.

[1] See Reply of the Baptist Union Annual Assembly to the Lambeth Conference
Appeal to all Christian People, 4th May 1926.

The origin of the Church is in the Gospel—in the mighty acts of God, the Incarnation, Ministry, Death, Resurrection and Ascension of our Lord and the Descent of the Holy Spirit. Thus it is the power of God in Christ which created the Church and which sustains it through the centuries. It is historically significant that Christ, at the outset of His ministry, "chose twelve to be with Him" and gathered His people into a new community. In our judgment there is no evidence in the New Testament to show that He formally organized the Church, but He did create it. This "New Israel", the expansion of which is recorded in the Acts of the Apostles and the Epistles, is the heir to the "Old Israel", yet it is marked by vital and significant differences. It is based upon the New Covenant; membership is not constituted by racial origins but by a personal allegiance; the ritual of temple and synagogue has given place to the ordinances of the Gospel and the national consciousness has widened to world horizons. The Messianic community was reborn by the events of the Gospel and is "a new creation". Therefore, whilst there is an historical continuity with the Old Israel, Old Testament analogies do not determine the character and structure of the New Testament Church.

The structure of local Baptist churches

3. (a) It is in membership of a local church in one place that the fellowship of the one holy catholic Church becomes significant. Indeed, such gathered companies of believers are the local manifestation of the one Church of God on earth and in heaven. Thus the church at Ephesus is described, in words which strictly belong to the whole catholic Church, as "the church of God, which He hath purchased with His own blood" (Acts xx. 28). The vital relationship to Christ which is implied in full communicant membership in a local church carries with it membership in the Church which is both in time and in eternity, both militant and triumphant. To worship and serve in such a local Christian community is, for Baptists, of the essence of Churchmanship.

Such churches are gathered by the will of Christ and live by the indwelling of His Spirit. They do not have their origin, primarily, in human resolution. Thus the Baptist Confession of 1677,[2] which deals at length with doctrine and church order, uses phrases which indicate that local churches are formed by the response of believing men to the Lord's command. Out of many such phrases we may quote the following: "Therefore they do willingly consent to walk together according to the appointment of Christ." Churches are gathered "according to

[2] W. J. McGlothlin, *Baptist Confessions of Faith*, p. 265.

His mind, declared in His word". Membership was not regarded as a private option, for the *Confession* continues: "All believers are bound to join themselves to particular churches when and where they have opportunity so to do." In our tradition discipleship involves both church membership and a full acceptance of the idea of churchmanship.

(*b*) The basis of our membership in the church is a conscious and deliberate acceptance of Christ as Saviour and Lord by each individual. There is, we hold, a personal crisis in the soul's life when a man stands alone in God's presence, responds to God's gracious activity, accepts His forgiveness and commits himself to the Christian way of life. Such a crisis may be swift and emotional or slow-developing and undramatic, and is normally experienced within and because of our life in the Christian community, but it is always a personal experience wherein God offers His salvation in Christ, and the individual, responding by faith, receives the assurance of the Spirit that by grace he is the child of God. It is this vital evangelical experience which underlies the Baptist conception of the Church and is both expressed and safeguarded by the sacrament of Believers' Baptism.

(*c*) The life of a gathered Baptist church centres in worship, in the preaching of the Word, in the observance of the two sacraments of Believers' Baptism and the Lord's Supper, in growth in fellowship and in witness and service to the world outside. Our forms of worship are in the Reformed tradition and are not generally regulated by liturgical forms. Our tradition is one of spontaneity and freedom, but we hold that there should be disciplined preparation of every part of the service. The sermon, as an exposition of the Word of God and a means of building up the faith and life of the congregation, has a central place in public worship. The scriptures are held by us to be the primary authority both for the individual in his belief and way of life and for the Church in its teaching and modes of government. It is the objective revelation given in scripture which is the safeguard against a purely subjective authority in religion. We firmly hold that each man must search the scriptures for himself and seek the illumination of the Holy Spirit to interpret them. We know also that Church history and Christian experience through the centuries are a guide to the meaning of scripture. Above all, we hold that the eternal Gospel—the life, death and resurrection of our Lord—is the fixed point from which our interpretation, both of the Old and New Testaments, and of later developments in the Church, must proceed.

The worship, preaching, sacramental observances, fellowship and witness are all congregational acts of the whole church in which each member shares responsibility, for all are held to be of equal standing in Christ, though there is a diversity of gifts and a difference of functions. This responsibility and this equality are focused in the church meeting which, under Christ, cares for the well-being of the believing community and appoints its officers. It is the responsibility of each member, according to his gifts, to build up the life of his brother and to maintain the spiritual health of the church (Rom. xv. 14). It is the church meeting which takes the responsibility of exercising that discipline whereby the church withdraws from members who are unruly and have ceased to share in her convictions and life.

The church meeting, though outwardly a democratic way of ordering the affairs of the church, has deeper significance. It is the occasion when, as individuals and as a community, we submit ourselves to the guidance of the Holy Spirit and stand under the judgments of God that we may know what is the mind of Christ. We believe that the structure of local churches just described springs from the Gospel and best preserves its essential features.

(d) The Christian doctrine of the Trinity asserts a relationship of Persons within the Godhead, and God has revealed Himself in the Person of His Son, our Saviour Jesus Christ. Thus the Gospel is the basis of the Christian evaluation of men and women as persons. Behind the idea of the gathered church lies the profound conviction of the importance of each man's growth to spiritual maturity and of the responsibility which, as a member of the divine family, he should constantly exercise.

(e) Although each local church is held to be competent, under Christ, to rule its own life, Baptists, throughout their history, have been aware of the perils of isolation and have sought safeguards against exaggerated individualism. From the seventeenth century there have been "Associations" of Baptist churches which sometimes appointed Messengers; more recently, their fellowship with one another has been greatly strengthened by the Baptist Union, the Baptist Missionary Society and the Baptist World Alliance. In recent years, General Superintendents have been appointed by the Baptist Union to have the care of churches in different areas. Indeed, we believe that a local church lacks one of the marks of a truly Christian community if it does not seek the fellowship of other Baptist churches, does not seek a true relationship with Christians and churches of other communions and is not conscious of its place in the one catholic Church. To quote again from the Confession of 1677:

"As each church and all the members of it are bound to pray continually for the good and prosperity of all the churches of Christ in all places; and upon occasions to further it . . . so the churches

. . . ought to hold communion amongst themselves for their peace, increase of love and mutual edification."

The Ministry

4. A properly ordered Baptist church will have its duly appointed officers. These will include the minister (or pastor), elders, deacons, Sunday school teachers and other church workers. The Baptist conception of the ministry is governed by the principle that it is a ministry of a church and not only a ministry of an individual. It is the church which preaches the Word and celebrates the sacraments, and it is the church which, through pastoral oversight, feeds the flock and ministers to the world. It normally does these things through the person of its minister, but not solely through him. Any member of the church may be authorized by it, on occasion, to exercise the functions of the ministry, in accordance with the principle of the priesthood of all believers, to preach the Word, to administer baptism, to preside at the Lord's table, to visit, and comfort or rebuke members of the fellowship.

Baptists, however, have had from the beginning an exalted conception of the office of the Christian minister and have taken care to call men to serve as pastors. The minister's authority to exercise his office comes from the call of God in his personal experience, but this call is tested and approved by the church of which he is a member and (as is increasingly the rule) by the representatives of a large group of churches. He receives intellectual and spiritual training and is then invited to exercise his gift in a particular sphere. His authority, therefore, is from Christ through the believing community. It is not derived from a chain of bishops held to be lineally descended from the Apostles, and we gratefully affirm that to our non-episcopal communities, as to those episcopally governed, the gifts of the Spirit and the power of God are freely given.

Many among us hold that since the ministry is the gift of God to the Church and the call to exercise the functions of a minister comes from Him, a man who is so called is not only the minister of a local Baptist church but also a minister of the whole Church of Jesus Christ.

Ordination takes place when a man has satisfactorily completed his college training and has been called to the pastorate of a local church, appointed to chaplaincy service or accepted for service abroad by the Committee of the Baptist Missionary Society. The ordination service is presided over by either the Principal of his college, a General Superintendent or a senior minister and is shared in by other ministers and lay representatives of the church. Though there is no prescribed or set form of service, it invariably includes either a personal statement of

10*

faith or answers to a series of questions regarding the faith. From the seventeenth century onwards, ordination took place with the laying on of hands: in the nineteenth century this custom fell into disuse, but is now again increasingly practised.

THE SACRAMENTS

5. In the preceding sections we have sought to describe the life and ministry of Baptist churches. It is in their total activity of worship and prayer, sacrament and service that the grace of God is continuously given to believing men and women.

We recognize the two sacraments of Believers' Baptism and the Lord's Supper as being of the Lord's ordaining. We hold that both are "means of grace" to those who receive them in faith, and that Christ is really and truly present, not in the material elements, but in the heart and mind and soul of the believer and in the Christian community which observes the sacrament. Our confidence in this rests upon the promises of Christ and not upon any power bestowed on the celebrant in virtue of ordination or succession in ministry. We believe it is important not to isolate the sacraments from the whole action of divine grace, but to see them always in the context of the total activity of the worshipping, believing and serving fellowship of the church.

Following the guidance of the New Testament we administer Baptism only to those who have made a responsible and credible profession of "repentance towards God and faith in the Lord Jesus Christ". Such persons are then immersed in the name of the Father, the Son and the Holy Spirit. Salvation is the work of God in Christ, which becomes operative when it is accepted in faith. Thus we do not baptize infants. There is, however, a practice in our churches of presenting young children at a service of public worship where the responsibilities of the parents and the church are recognized and prayers are offered for the parents and the child. Baptists believe that from birth all children are within the love and care of the heavenly Father and therefore within the operation of the saving grace of Christ; hence they have never been troubled by the distinction between baptized and unbaptized children. They have had a notable share with other groups of Christian people in service to children in Sunday schools, orphanages, education and child welfare.

We would claim that the baptism of believers by immersion is in accordance with and sets forth the central facts of the Gospel. It is an "acted creed". We value the symbolism of immersion following the Pauline teaching of the believer's participation in the death, burial and resurrection of our Lord (Romans vi. 3). As a matter of history, however, the recovery of the truth that baptism is only for believers preceded by some years the return by Baptists to the primitive mode of baptizing by immersion, and it is a credible and responsible profession of faith on the part of the candidate for baptism which we hold to be essential to the rite. As a means of grace to the believer and to the church and as an act of obedience to our Lord's command, we treasure this sacrament. The New Testament clearly indicates a connection of the gift of the Holy Spirit with the experience of baptism which, without making the rite the necessary or inevitable channel of that gift, yet makes it the appropriate occasion of a new and deeper reception of it.

The Lord's Supper is celebrated regularly in our churches. The form of service, which is "congregational" and in which laymen have a part, preserves the New Testament conception of the Supper as an act of fellowship, a community meal. Yet as baptism is more than a dramatic representation of the facts of our redemption, so the Communion Service is more than a commemoration of the Last Supper and a showing forth "of the Lord's death until He come". Here the grace of God is offered and is received in faith; here the real presence of Christ is manifest in the joy and peace both of the believing soul and of the community; here we are in communion, not only with our fellow-members in the church, not only with the Church militant on earth and triumphant in heaven, but also with our risen and glorified Lord.

Membership of our local churches is normally consequent on Believers' Baptism, but differences of outlook and practice exist amongst us. "Close Membership" Baptist churches receive into their membership only those who have professed their faith in Christ by passing through the waters of baptism: "Open Membership" churches, though they consist, in the main, of baptized believers, receive also those Christians who profess such faith otherwise than in Believers' Baptism.

Similar differences are to be found amongst us on the question of those who may partake of the Lord's Supper. "Close Communion" churches invite to the Lord's table only those baptized on profession of faith. "Open Communion" churches welcome to the service all "who love the Lord Jesus Christ in sincerity". These differences do not prevent churches of different types from being in fellowship one with another nor from co-operating in the work of the Baptist Union, the Baptist Missionary Society and the Baptist World Alliance. They are united in the conviction that, in New Testament teaching, personal faith in Christ is essential to the sacraments of the Gospel and the membership of the Church.

CHURCH AND STATE

6. Our conviction of Christ's Lordship over His Church leads us to insist that churches formed by His will must be free from all other rule in matters relating to their spiritual life. Any form of control by the State in these matters appears to us to challenge the "Crown Rights of the Redeemer". We also hold that this freedom in Christ implies the right of the church to exercise responsible self-government. This has been the Baptist position since the seventeenth century, and it appears to us that the growth of the omnicompetent state and the threat to liberty which has appeared in many parts of the world today make more than ever necessary this witness to spiritual freedom and responsibility which has always been characteristic of the Baptist movement.

This freedom, however, has not led to irresponsibility in our duties as citizens. We believe it is a Christian obligation to honour and serve the State and to labour for the well-being of all men and women. Baptists have shared in many working-class movements, have a not undistinguished record in social service, and were pioneers in the modern missionary movement. They hold that there is a responsibility laid upon each member of the church and upon the churches themselves to apply their faith to all the perplexities of contemporary life.

It will be seen that in this statement of the doctrine of the Church the emphasis falls time and again upon the central fact of evangelical experience, that when God offers His forgiveness, love and power the gift must be personally accepted in faith by each individual. From this follows the believer's endeavour to walk in the way of the Lord and to be obedient to His commandments. From this follows, also, our traditional defence of civil and religious liberty. It governs our conception of the Church and our teaching on Believers' Baptism. Gratefully recognizing the gifts bestowed by God upon other communions, we offer these insights which He has entrusted to us for the service of His whole Church.

BIBLIOGRAPHY

W. J. McGlothlin, *Baptist Confessions of Faith*, Baptist Historical Soc., 1911.

The Baptist Reply to the Lambeth Appeal, adopted by the Baptist Union Assembly, 4th May 1926 (reprinted in G. K. A. Bell, *Documents on Christian Unity*, second series, pp. 102 ff).

Report of a Special Committee set up by the Baptist Union on the question of Union between Baptists, Congregationalists and Presbyterians, 1937.

Arthur Dakin, *The Baptist View of the Church and Ministry*, Kingsgate Press, 1944.

E. A. Payne, *The Fellowship of Believers: Baptist Thought and Practice Yesterday and Today*, Kingsgate Press, 1944. (Reprints part of the 1677 Confession of the Particular Baptists and the Reply to the Lambeth Appeal.)

E. A. Payne, *The Baptist Movement in the Reformation and Onwards*, Kingsgate Press, 1947.

Henry Cook, *What Baptists Stand For*, Kingsgate Press, 1947.

Robert C. Walton, *The Gathered Community*, Carey Press, 1946.

W. T. Whitley, *History of British Baptists*, Kingsgate Press, second edition, 1932.

H. Wheeler Robinson, *Baptist Principles*, Kingsgate Press, third edition, 1938.

H. Wheeler Robinson, *The Life and Faith of the Baptists*, revised edition, Kingsgate Press, 1946.

A. C. Underwood, *A History of English Baptists*, Kingsgate Press, 1947.

P. W. Evans, *Sacraments in the New Testament*, Tyndale Press, 1947.

The Baptist Position. A Statement Prepared by the Commission on Baptist Principles and Policy for Study and Discussion within the Baptist Convention of Ontario and Quebec, 1947.

W. O. Carver, "Baptist Churches" in *The Nature of the Church*. A Report of the American Theological Committee (1945), of the Continuation Committee, World Conference on Faith and Order.

APPENDIX XI

CHURCH RELATIONS IN ENGLAND

Report approved by the Council of the Baptist Union, March 1953

In March 1951 the Baptist Union Council set up a special Committee to consider the report *Church Relations in England* prepared by representatives appointed by the Archbishop of Canterbury and representatives appointed by the various Free Churches, including the Baptist Union. The Committee consisted of the following:

Rev. Arthur Dakin, B.D., D.Th. (Chairman)
Rt. Hon. Ernest Brown, C.H., M.C.
Rev. F. C. Bryan, M.A.
Rev. R. L. Child, M.A., B.D.
Rev. P. Rowntree Clifford, M.A.
Rev. K. C. Dykes, M.A., B.D.
Rev. Graham W. Hughes, B.A., B.D.
Mr. C. T. Le Quesne, Q.C.
Mrs. Angus McMillan, M.A.

with the Rev. H. Ingli James, B.A., B.D., B.Litt., and the Rev. E. A. Payne, M.A., D.D., serving in a consultative capacity. The Committee has met on a number of occasions and presents the following report to the Council:

1. The document before us, bearing the title *Church Relations in England*, is the report of conversations between representatives of the Archbishop of Canterbury and representatives appointed by the Evangelical Free Churches of England. These conversations took place as a result of the sermon preached by the Archbishop in Cambridge in November 1946. We desire to place on record our appreciation of the words and spirit of the Archbishop, and our appreciation also of the friendly spirit which clearly characterized the conversations and which finds expression in the report. We rejoice to read of "the deep spiritual unity in Christ of which the members of the Conference were increasingly conscious". (p. 46.)

2. In his Cambridge sermon the Archbishop made suggestions on the subject of intercommunion between the Church of England and the Free Churches of this country. It is with the matter of intercommunion

that the report specifically deals. The Conference met for the sole purpose of examining the implications of the Archbishop's suggestions and what would be involved were they to be implemented. The report is in no sense a document offering terms. It consists of the Archbishop's suggestions together with the Conference's unanimous statement as to what their adoption would involve. The main chapters of the report summarize discussions of general theological issues regarding church, ministry and sacraments. Obviously individual statements are made therein which invite further explication and to which Baptists should not be held to have given formal approval. We have felt it right however to confine our report to the main question, namely, the steps suggested for the achievement of intercommunion. Whether the authorities of the Church of England will go further and make an approach to the individual Free Churches along the lines suggested in the concluding chapter no doubt depends to a considerable extent upon the kind of assurances or indications given by the various Free Church authorities, as well as upon the discussions proceeding in the Church of England itself.

3. The Archbishop expressed his main purpose in the sentence: "My longing is, not yet that we should be *united* with other Churches in this country, but that we should grow to *full* communion with them" (p. 10). He then went on to suggest that since the non-episcopal Churches have accepted the principle that episcopacy must exist along with other elements in a re-united Church,[1] a beginning might be made by the Free Churches taking episcopacy into their own systems (pp. 10, 11). Let them, said the Archbishop, take it and try it out on their own ground. The Archbishop expressed the opinion that there are no insuperable barriers to full communion between the Churches save those connected with the ministry and government of the Church. This is confirmed by the declaration made in the Interim Report (March 1949) and repeated in the document before us that:

"On the doctrines of God the Father, the Person and Work of Christ, the Person and mission of the Holy Spirit, the Trinity, and the Life Everlasting we have found nothing which separates any one of these Communions from one another. All acknowledge the apostolic faith as contained in the Scriptures and expressed in the Apostles' and Nicene Creeds" (p. 26).[2]

[1] See Appendix below.
[2] Baptists are among those who object to formal subscription to creeds on the grounds set out in the Report (pp. 27–8). We note with satisfaction that those engaged in the Conversations were agreed that "the Holy Scriptures contain sufficiently all doctrine required of necessity for eternal salvation through faith in Jesus Christ" (p. 44).

The Archbishop's hope is that the taking of episcopacy into their own systems by the Free Churches might lead to "a free and unfettered exchange of life in worship and sacrament" (p. 9).

4. What exactly the taking of episcopacy into our system would mean, the Conference states quite clearly in the concluding section of its report. "The Free Church would take episcopacy into its system by the acceptance of an episcopate consecrated in the first instance through Bishops of one or more of the historic Episcopal Churches, and thus linked with the episcopate of the past, and would adopt episcopal ordination as its rule for the future. The Church of England would acknowledge that the Bishops and episcopally ordained Presbyters were from the outset duly commissioned and authorized for the same offices in the Church of God as its own Bishops and Priests" (p. 44). Thereafter, "the Church of England would agree to admit to communion baptized and duly commended communicant members of the Free Church in good standing, and would officially authorize duly commended communicant members of the Church of England in good standing to receive the sacrament of Holy Communion at the hands of such Ministers of the Free Church as had been either consecrated to the episcopate or episcopally ordained or further commissioned to the Presbyterate" (p. 45). The three functions of a Bishop which are specially emphasized are (1) ordination, (2) decision, in concurrence with Presbyters and laity, on any changes in matters of doctrine and policy, and (3) the pastoral oversight of Ministers and churches. The Bishop's traditional prerogative of confirmation is not put forward in this document as a necessary condition of intercommunion, though it is stated that "the Church of England, without making it a condition of intercommunion, would express the hope that the rite of Confirmation, episcopally ministered, would in due course come to be widely, and in the end, generally, used in the Free Church" (p. 45) which adopted episcopacy. It is explicitly recognized that a Free Church, adopting these proposals, would be free to maintain the relations of fellowship and intercommunion with other Churches which it at present enjoys, even though these Churches remain non-episcopal.

5. These, then, are the implications of the Archbishop's suggestions as understood by the joint Conference and presented in the report. For those Baptists who issue an "open invitation" to the Lord's Table (see paragraph 9), there is of course from their side no obstacle to fellowship in the service with members of other Christian traditions. We are, however, here dealing with the fact that an episcopally ordained minis-

try is, in the view of most, if not all, Anglicans, a necessary pre-condition for intercommunion. The question before us is whether there could be Baptist Bishops, linked in the manner suggested with the episcopal successions of the past and exercising the functions mentioned above.

6. Any such step would undoubtedly be a departure from the traditional emphasis expressed in our church order and found at present in all the Baptist communions throughout the world. That such a departure would be involved might not in itself justify our rejection of the proposals. But since, in our opinion, acceptance would jeopardize some of the cherished convictions on which we build and which we believe we hold in trust for the whole Church, it is necessary for us frankly to state the difficulties and objections as we see them. While we do this, however, we would, at the same time, insist that with others we also are alive to the need for all Christians to draw together, and, if possible in intercommunion. Such an intimacy of fellowship is necessary that all Christians may realize our Lord's own thought and prayer as given in the New Testament, and that Christians may make a more effective witness against the secularity of the world. The Church, as described in the New Testament, is one and indivisible. Its oneness, we agree, ought to be more clearly expressed in unity of worship and service, till the conditions of earth are more fully a reflection of conditions in heaven. This is our view, as indeed it is bound to be the view of all earnest disciples of our Lord—ours and theirs.

7. The difficulties in the way of Baptists moving in the direction indicated are, in our opinion, the following:

(i) Our main difficulty with the proposals before us comes from the fact that they bind intercommunion with episcopacy. The claims commonly made for episcopacy are, in our judgment, not proven.[3] They cannot be substantiated from the New Testament; nor, as we think, are they borne out by Church history. The episcopate has not preserved either the unity or the continuity of the Church. The continuity of the Church, as it seems to us, is a continuity of life in Christ brought into being by the proclamation of the Word and by steadfast continuance "in the Apostles' doctrine and fellowship and in the breaking of bread, and in prayers" (Acts ii. 41–2). It does not depend on the doubtful continuity of a ministerial succession supposed to reach back to the Apostles. Rather than stress exclusively some one form of

[3] See E. A. Payne, *The Free Churches and Episcopacy*, Carey Kingsgate Press, 1952. We are in general agreement with the views there set forth.

church order, we feel bound to put the emphasis on the continuing activity of the Holy Spirit manifested throughout the Body of Christ, on the spiritual life and service shown by Christians in all ages and in all sections of the Church. The report assumes that, if one of the Free Churches decided to introduce episcopacy into its system, "the Free Church and the Church of England would accord to each other the same liberty of interpretation of the nature of episcopacy and of priesthood as obtains in the Church of England" (p. 44). But this does not remove our hesitations. We are aware that in the Church of South India communions formerly episcopal and non-episcopal have found it possible to unite. But both in the report and in South India the link with one or more of "the historic episcopal churches" is insisted upon. Such an insistence on one particular historic link is however for us in itself a stumbling block. Further, we cannot but note with concern that, even though the Church of South India has secured this link, the Church of England has not at present felt able to enter into full communion with it.

We cannot believe that intercommunion between Christian Churches should be made dependent upon episcopacy. A properly authenticated and recognized ministry there should be, but this does not in our view depend upon having a special order of bishops. We believe that before there can be satisfactory progress towards intercommunion in this country the claims made on behalf of the present Free Church ministries must be more properly recognized. It is admitted in the report that if the proposals before us were adopted, in the early stages at least, "grave difficulties would be involved in the existence of two types of Minister within a single Church," those who had received episcopal ordination and those who had not (p. 44) and that the Church of England would allow its members to receive the sacrament of Holy Communion at the hands only of such ministers of the Free Church as had been consecrated to the episcopate or episcopally ordained (p. 45). This would result in a situation which would be, in our opinion, quite unacceptable, indeed intolerable.

(ii) Though further words are perhaps unnecessary, we think it may be well, in view of the prominence given to this matter in the report, that we comment on the linking of episcopacy and ordination. Baptists regard ordination as a function of the whole Church acting through the fellowship of the local church. The local company of believers after seeking the guidance of the Holy Spirit chooses those who have received gifts for special office. The actual ordaining is in our view of God, even as the ministry is a ministry under God for the edification of the Church, i.e. the Church as a whole. The service is the public acknowledgment in the Church that a candidate has been called of God to the work of the ministry. To say that someone must of necessity by virtue of his office take part in such a service because, if he does not, there will be no regular or proper ordination would be to introduce a new and alien element, a legalistic and coercive element, into our church life. We believe that an ordination cannot take place except in and through the fellowship of Christian people; but that fellowship is more important than the presence and act of any individual, whatever his status or title.

(iii) Similar considerations would arise were there any suggestion that by right of office a bishop, or indeed anyone else, must share in the rite of confirmation, or any similar service. Baptists believe that the admission of new members is a function of the local church, and they would be unwilling to delegate it exclusively to a particular officer.

(iv) Further, Baptists would have difficulty in binding the sacraments as closely to the official ministry as the report seems to suggest would have to be the case. Following the Reformers, we regard the sacraments of baptism and the Lord's Supper as closely related to the preaching of the Word. Both the preaching of the Word and the administration of the Sacraments are committed to those called out by the local church for such service. But they are not committed exclusively to the ordained ministry. We find no difficulty in allowing any church member—man or woman—to preach and administer the sacraments on occasion, provided such person is duly authorized by the local church in which these acts take place. In Baptist churches where and when there is a pastor, it is he who administers the sacraments. But many of our churches have to depend on the services of "Lay preachers", who may be invited to administer the sacraments as well as to conduct public worship.[4] Moreover, both in the Baptist Union and in the Baptist Associations, "laymen" are from time to time invited to preside at united Communion Services.

8. In stressing these matters, we would not wish to give the impression that we are merely standing on tradition or for a church order that is rigid and unalterable. There has been not a little modification of our church order in the immediate past. The appointment of General Superintendents charged with spiritual and administrative responsibilities toward churches and ministers, the grouping of churches

[4] It is hardly correct to suggest, as the report seems to do, that what is called "lay celebration" is among Baptists "infrequent" (p. 42).

under the pastoral oversight of either a single minister or a group of ministers, the much larger role now played by the Baptist Union in the name and on behalf of all the churches affiliated to it—all these represent changes arising from new needs. We believe they have been dictated by new insights into the mind of Christ for our churches and that in adopting them we have followed the guidance of the Holy Spirit. We may well be led to introduce other changes; but we must be careful that they are in line with our true development, that they do not disrupt the fellowship of our churches and that they are in accord with the New Testament.

9. One further matter calls for comment. Complete intercommunion—or, better, "mutual open communion"—does not as yet exist even for all members of Baptist churches. There are various types of Baptist church: (*a*) Those which admit to the Lord's Table only their own members, all of whom must have been baptized as believers, (*b*) Those which admit to the Lord's Table only those Christians who have been baptized as believers, (*c*) Those which give an "open invitation" to all Christians to sit down with them at the Lord's Table, though admitting to membership only those who have been baptized as believers, and (*d*) Those which not only give an "open invitation" but have "open membership" based upon "repentance toward God and faith in our Lord Jesus Christ"; only believer's baptism by immersion is practised, but it is not insisted on as a condition of membership. There are few Baptist churches of the first type in this country and probably none in membership with the Baptist Union of Great Britain and Ireland. The great majority belong to either the third or fourth categories. An increasing number of churches have "open membership", but we do not feel that we could at the present time advocate proposals which would inevitably be rejected by certain of our number on grounds of deep Christian conviction. The Baptist Union Council has recently authorized the issue of a statement on "The Lord's Supper"[5] drawn up for it by the Principals of the eight Baptist Theological Colleges in the United Kingdom. In that statement an appeal is made to churches which practise "closed communion" prayerfully to review their position. So long however as these ambiguities remain and Baptists are divided amongst themselves, they must be slow to criticize other denominations who do not feel able to authorize immediate intercommunion among all Christians.

[5] *The Lord's Supper: A Baptist Statement*, Carey Kingsgate Press, 1951. On the issues referred to in this paragraph see also the "Report of the special Committee appointed by the Baptist Union on the question of reunion between Baptists, Congregationalists and Presbyterians", 1937.

10. We have therefore to conclude that the report *Church Relations in England* does not, as it stands, offer a plan of development which Baptists would consider it either right or practicable to try to implement. Nevertheless, we are glad that the conversations took place. The report does good service in that it indicates with valuable clarity where the points at issue really lie. We are well aware that certain of the suggestions made would be as difficult for many in the Church of England to accept as it would be for us to receive episcopacy. This fact confirms us in our view that the report does not really indicate the right step forward. We hope that conversations between the Churches will continue. In particular, we believe that both within our own denomination and in company with those of other communions, there is need for further examination of (1) the place of the local church in the Body of Christ, (2) the nature and authority of the ministry of the Church, (3) the manner of the calling out and ordaining of ministers, and (4) the nature of *episcope* as exercised in New Testament times, and its relation both to the present forms of episcopacy and to other methods of oversight. As Baptists we need to give further thought to the functions of the General Superintendents and the representative nature of the office to which we have called them. We have to re-examine our view of the ministry, both as an office and as a function of the whole church. We have to try to resolve the differences among us regarding access to the Lord's Table. In the discussion of these and other matters, both among ourselves and in the wider fellowship of the Ecumenical Movement, we are convinced that we must constantly test our thought and practice by New Testament standards.

11. Finally, even if intercommunion between Anglicans and Baptists be not yet possible, this should not hinder us from seeking other means whereby we may demonstrate our unity in Christ and may worship and work together. Baptists greatly value their membership of the British Council of Churches and the World Council of Churches, and rejoice that those of so many Christian traditions are now able to talk and act together. Baptists welcome every opportunity of united witness. We are not satisfied with church relations in England as they are at present. Though the form in which Christ would have the unity of His Church manifest is not yet fully apparent to us Baptists will continue to pray that the Holy Spirit will lead us into all truth and that we may "grow up into Him in all things, which is the head, even Christ". (Eph. iv. 15.)

Appendix

1. In his Cambridge sermon the Archbishop of Canterbury stated

that "the non-episcopal Churches have accepted the principle that episcopacy must exist along with other elements in a reunited Church" (p. 10). The question has been raised whether, and, if so, in what manner Baptists may be said to have committed themselves to episcopacy. The following appear to be the facts:

2. The last article of the Lambeth Quadrilateral, adopted by the Anglican bishops in 1888 as providing a basis for reunion discussions, referred to "The Historic Episcopate, locally adapted in the methods of its administration to the varying needs of the nations and peoples called of God into the Unity of His Church". In the Lambeth Appeal of 1920 this was amended to: "A ministry acknowledged by every part of the Church as possessing not only the inward call of the Spirit, but also the commission of Christ and the authority of the whole body."

3. The Federal Council of the Evangelical Free Churches and The National Free Church Council set up a Joint Committee to consider the Lambeth Appeal. The Report of this Joint Committee, which contained Baptist representatives, was sent to each of the federated Churches, and on 27th April 1921 the Baptist Union Assembly passed a resolution in the course of which it was said: "The Assembly generally endorses the Report of the Federal Council as expressing the common view and attitude of the Evangelical Free Churches of England" (Bell, *Documents*, I, p. 104). In the course of the Report the sentences occurred: "We . . . have an open mind towards episcopal order as towards any other. To this, however, we must add that we cannot be expected to consider any form of polity which claims to be an exclusive channel of grace or which fails to recognize the place and the rights of the Christian people in the affairs of the Church" (ibid., p. 133).

4. In September 1921 (Bell I, pp. 141–2) the Federal Council of the Evangelical Free Churches appointed representatives of the Free Churches for the purpose of a Joint Conference with Anglican representatives. The Baptist representatives were Dr. Charles Brown, Dr. W. Y. Fullerton, Sir Alfred Pearce Gould and Dr. J. H. Shakespeare. A committee of thirteen was set up by the Joint Conference to prepare a report and to submit it to the Joint Conference. A Report was issued in May 1922. It dealt fully with matters which were said to have been "accepted by the Conference". Section II, paragraphs 8–10 read:

"8. In view of the fact that the Episcopate was from early times and for many centuries accepted, and by the greater part of

Christendom is still accepted, as the means whereby (the) authority of the whole body is given, we agree that it ought to be accepted as such for the United Church of the future.

9. Similarly, in view of the place which the Council of Presbyters and the Congregations of the faithful had in the constitution of the early Church, and the preservation of these elements of presbyteral and congregational order in large sections of Christendom, we agree that they should be maintained with a representative and constitutional Episcopate as permanent elements in the order and life of the United Church.

10. The acceptance of Episcopal Ordination for the future would not imply the acceptance of any particular theory as to its origin or character . . ." (Ibid., pp. 149–50.)

5. The Federal Council at its Annual Assembly in September 1922, in receiving this report, welcomed "the association of presbyteral and congregational order along with episcopal", but noted that further discussion would be needed as to what was meant by "a representative and constitutional episcopate" (ibid., pp. 152, 153). Free Church representatives were appointed for further conversations. The Baptists so appointed were Dr. Brown, Dr. J. C. Carlile, Dr. Fullerton, Mr. Herbert Marnham and Dr. Shakespeare. These same representatives were reappointed in September 1923.

6. In July 1924 the Joint Conference of Anglicans and Free Churchmen adopted and issued "A Memorandum on a Constitutional Episcopate" (ibid., II, 68 f.). At the next Annual Assembly of the Federal Council, held in September 1924, it was suggested that judgment on this and other interim reports should be suspended until some general statement on the results of the Conversations was available. The following year the Conversations were suspended by mutual agreement. The Federal Council at its Annual Assembly in September 1925, in a series of resolutions reviewing the Conversations, drew attention to the agreements on Episcopacy cited above, but emphasized the fact that neither the Joint Committee nor the Council was committed to the details set out in the Memorandum on a Constitutional Episcopate (ibid., pp. 99–100).

7. At a meeting of the Baptist Union Council on 9th–10th February 1926 the Council had before them (*inter alia*) the report issued in May 1922. They appointed a committee to draw up a Reply to the Lambeth

appeal of 1920. They did not adopt the Report of May 1922 either in February 1926 or subsequently. In May 1926 the Baptist Union Assembly adopted a Reply to the Lambeth appeal. In this reply the only reference to episcopacy is in the following sentences: "The ministry is for us a gift of the Spirit to the Church, and is an office involving both the inward call of God and the commission of the Church. We can discover no ground for believing that such commission can be given only through an Episcopate, and we hold that the individual Church is competent to confer it" (ibid., pp. 105–6).

8. A further series of Conversations between Anglican and Free Church representatives took place in the 1930s. The Baptist representatives were the Rev. M. E. Aubrey, Dr. Charles Brown, Dr. Gilbert Laws and the Rev. Hugh Martin. At the close of these Conversations an "Outline of a Reunion Scheme for the Church of England and the Free Churches in England" was issued. This scheme based itself on the agreement of 1922, cited above, and provided for a constitutional Episcopate (ibid., III, p. 79, 85 f.).

9. The "Outline of a Reunion Scheme" was considered by the Baptist Union Council in November, 1938. In the course of a series of comments which were sent to the Federal Council it was stated:

(The Members of the Council) "do not regard the congregational form of Church government, practised by themselves, as essential to the constitution of the Church, though they believe that it does, in many respects, express important elements in the life of the truly Christian society. They are prepared to consider any change of order in Baptist Church polity which would increase the efficiency of the Church by helping to make it a truer fellowship of the Holy Spirit. But they are unable to take for granted an episcopal form of government, simply on the ground of its large place in the history of the Church, nor do they think that an acknowledged ambiguity in the meaning of 'episcopal ordination' would provide a sure foundation for organic union."

10. In September 1941 the Free Church Federal Council issued a reply to the documents which had come from the second series of Conversations, together with comments on all the discussions which had taken place since 1920. In the course of this reply it was stated: "From the outset of the Conversations it was recognized that the insurmountable obstacle was not the acceptance of the Episcopate as one element in the organization, a matter on which our Churches have not com-

mitted themselves, but have been willing to confer, but the requirement of Episcopal ordination for non-episcopal ordained ministers" (ibid., p. 106). "We cannot accept the theory of Apostolical Succession" (p. 112). "Should the Free Churches accept an Episcopate, it would not be on account of this theory, but on the grounds stated in mutual agreement in the Report as accepted by the Conference in May 1922" (p. 113).

11. In August 1927, the first World Conference on Faith and Order met at Lausanne. The Baptist Union was not represented at this Conference. The Report stated that the Conference recognized that episcopal, presbyteral and congregational elements must each have an appropriate place in the order of life of a reunited Church (ibid., II, p. 11). The second World Conference on Faith and Order met in Edinburgh in 1937. The Baptist Union was represented by the Rev. M. E. Aubrey, Dr. J. H. Rushbrooke, Dr. Gilbert Laws, Mr. C. T. Le Quesne and the Rev. Hugh Martin. In its report the Conference stated that it started its consideration of the ministry from the formula accepted at Lausanne. It was agreed that the Episcopate envisaged must be both constitutional and representative of the whole Church. "It should, however, be recognized that there are members of the Conference who are not persuaded that it is God's will that the one spiritual life of the undivided Church would be expressed through any one form of government, but would find place side by side for Churches of differing form of government" (ibid., III, pp. 269–70).

12. This survey indicates that while there are grounds for the statement made by the Archbishop of Canterbury in his sermon, it is clear that the Free Church representatives in the various conversations and conferences, while recognizing the position taken by the Anglicans on this matter and expressing themselves as willing to discuss the acceptance of an episcopate as one element in a United Church, have not committed themselves to any particular form of episcopacy or to any definition of its functions. Matters have never reached the stage at which the individual Free Churches have had before them definite proposals for either acceptance or rejection.

INDICES

I. PERSONS

2. SUBJECTS